P9-CFP-108

Praise for *The Growing Seasons*

"Hynes has a great gift for making an ordinary life seem worth the telling. It is extremely pleasant to spend time in someone else's past, when it is called up as honestly and meaningfully as this."
—*St. Louis Post-Dispatch*

"Remember corduroy knickers? Remember listening to *Little Orphan Annie* on the radio? Well, forget it. Samuel Hynes' *Growing Seasons* isn't that kind of memoir at all. Hynes takes us back to the past so convincingly that it doesn't feel like the past—simply a place where people do things differently. Life unfolds from day to day, from season to season . . . it ought to make for boring reading, but it doesn't. It helps that we like Sam. For the hero of a memoir, he's remarkably unstuck on himself, uncommonly alert to the reality of the people around him. His portrait of his father hits home. . . . It's hard to bring alive a character who puts out so few signals, but Hynes reads them beautifully. He's also a deceptively plain writer. Without raising his voice, he commands your attention. Now and then, though, you do put down the book for a moment of thought. The best memoirs lead the reader into his own past; *Growing Seasons* fits that category."
—Dan Sullivan, *Minneapolis Star-Tribune*

"A recollection of the people, the sights, sounds, smells—the feel— of a boyhood in a harsh and splendid time in America . . . told with uncommon narrative skill. It's a work evocative for those who remember just which war was The War and instructive to everyone else. Comfortable as an old cardigan and more than simple nostalgia: a memoir in turns sagacious and poignant, the way it ought to be."
—*Kirkus Reviews* (starred)

"This honest, scrupulously organized study of Hynes' Depression-era boyhood has the simple effectiveness of a family photograph. Like a stunningly precise diary, Hynes dwells on nothing, nor does he artificially heighten events, not even two local murders. What Hynes achieves with journalistic eloquence is showing a way of life and presenting an affectionate portrait of people who rarely verbalize their feelings but show love in subtle, unexpected ways."
—*Publishers Weekly*

ABOUT THE AUTHOR

Samuel Hynes is Woodrow Wilson Professor of Literature
Emeritus at Princeton University and the author of several
major works of literary criticism, including *The Auden Generation*, *The Edwardian Turn of Mind*, and *A War Imagined*. Hynes's
wartime experiences as a Marine corps pilot were the basis
for his highly praised memoir *Flights of Passage*. *The Soldier's
Tale*, his book about soldiers' narratives of the two world wars
and Vietnam, won a Robert F. Kennedy Award. A fellow of
the Royal Society of Literature, Hynes lives in Princeton,
New Jersey.

THE
GROWING
SEASONS

An American Boyhood

Before the War

Samuel Hynes

PENGUIN BOOKS

PENGUIN BOOKS

Published by the Penguin Group

Penguin Group (USA) Inc., 375 Hudson Street, New York, New York 10014, U.S.A.

Penguin Books Ltd, 80 Strand, London WC2R 0RL, England

Penguin Books Australia Ltd, 250 Camberwell Road,
  Camberwell, Victoria 3124, Australia

Penguin Books Canada Ltd, 10 Alcorn Avenue, Toronto, Ontario, Canada M4V 3B2

Penguin Books India (P) Ltd, 11 Community Centre,
  Panchsheel Park, New Delhi – 110 017, India

Penguin Books (N.Z.) Ltd, Cnr Rosedale and Airborne Roads,
  Albany, Auckland, New Zealand

Penguin Books (South Africa) (Pty) Ltd, 24 Sturdee Avenue,
  Rosebank, Johannesburg 2196, South Africa

Penguin Books Ltd, Registered Offices:
80 Strand, London WC2R 0RL, England

First published in the United States of America by Viking Penguin,
  a member of Penguin Putnam Inc. 2003
Published in Penguin Books 2004

10 9 8 7 6 5 4 3 2 1

Copyright © Samuel Hynes, 2003
All rights reserved

Photograph of Bernice Rosen on page 174 courtesy of the *Star Tribune*.

CIP data available
ISBN 0–670–03193–3 (hc.)
ISBN 0 14 20.0396 4 (pbk.)

Printed in the United States of America
Set in Bembo
Designed by Nancy Resnick

Except in the United States of America, this book is sold subject to the condition that it
shall not, by way of trade or otherwise, be lent, resold, hired out, or otherwise circulated
without the publisher's prior consent in any form of binding or cover other than that in
which it is published and without a similar condition including this condition being
imposed on the subsequent purchaser.

The scanning, uploading and distribution of this book via the Internet or via any
other means without the permission of the publisher is illegal and punishable by law.
Please purchase only authorized electronic editions, and do not participate in or
encourage electronic piracy of copyrighted materials. Your support of the
author's rights is appreciated.

This book is dedicated to
Jim Blake
Pat Champion Edwards
Otto Leonardson
Craig McCarthy
Bob Michaud

When men and women of my generation speak of "before the war," they aren't simply talking about a date in the past; they're looking back across the great chasm of the Second World War to a time that seems as distant and as different from our present lives as some foreign place.

That time was the years of the Great Depression, when nobody had any money and folks lived confined and frugal lives. Or so we say. Yet when I call up memories of those days, the life I recover doesn't seem hard or narrow, but generous and free and full of opportunities. An ordinary curious boy in an ordinary small-town sort of American city could find plenty of things to engage his curiosity then: there were all the world's temptations around him—the risks to be taken, the rules to be broken, the girls, the cars, the drinking, the sex, all the excitements that animate the growing years. He could learn how to be free and get away with it. He could discover himself.

As my generation grew toward adulthood the war came and swept us into it; we were the privates and the junior officers who did the fighting. And were changed by it, as everything in our world was changed—our lives and our nation's life, our expectations, our hopes, our connections with the past. When that change came, the country of our childhood before the war became another country, lost and gone, except in the shards and fragments that memory preserves.

In writing this account of my growing seasons I have tried

to be faithful to the boy I was then, to look with his eyes and speak with his voice. Old friends who were with me then may remember some of those days differently; to them I can only say that the past is many stories, all of them different, all of them true. My stories are put down as I remember them; only here and there I have changed a name or altered a detail to avoid embarrassing an old acquaintance.

THE
GROWING
SEASONS

CHAPTER ONE

The summer my father got married I lived on a farm. It wasn't his first marriage, of course, there was my mother, before. I was five when she died, but I remembered her, not as an everyday presence but in fragments of memory, in pictures and sounds and smells and touches. I remembered how she looked, not from a distance but up close, as a child in its mother's arms might see her: a small, soft body, a strong face with dark, sad eyes (on the right eyelid a small growth, a mole perhaps), thick chestnut hair coiled in a knot behind. I remembered her in the dining room of our house, ironing and singing a little song to herself while my brother and I lay on the carpet coloring in books, how she dipped her fingers in a shallow bowl of water to sprinkle a shirt, how the drops danced from her hand like blessings, catching the light from the window, and the warm smell of the iron and the steaming cloth. And I remembered lying warm against her in the back seat of our Ford as we drove home late at night—returning to Chicago from Rolling Prairie, perhaps—and how she sang to soothe me on the journey, songs from an old war, "Tenting Tonight" and "Just Before the Battle, Mother," melancholy songs, but comforting to a small boy because she sang them so quietly in the darkness and I, close to her, didn't hear her voice but felt it, a warm vibration through her breast as she held me.

One other memory. I enter a white room where she lies

motionless on a white bed. Her face is pale under the bright hair, the eyes are circled by deep shadows. I approach the bed, but only the eyes turn toward me.

My father didn't talk much about my mother after she died, that wasn't his way, but occasionally a memory would escape his reticence. He told me once about a Christmas before the first war when she gave him a silver watch chain. He pulled the watch from his pocket and showed me the chain and the penknife at the end with his initials on it. "She saved up for it," he said with a kind of wonderment, "for a whole year." He carried that watch and chain until he was an old man, long after other men were wearing wristwatches, long after the silver initials had worn away. So I knew he loved her, though he never said so, not out loud.

There was also the photograph album, covered in dark green leatherette with black pages held in place by a cord. In it someone—my mother, I suppose—had mounted family photographs

and written beneath them in white ink the names of the people and the places and dates. In one picture my mother stands by the front porch of a white frame house. Victorian gingerbread carving decorates the roofline, and roses climb on a trellis. She faces my father, who has his back to the camera. Her hands are on her hips, and her head is cocked quizzically, as though he has just asked her something— perhaps to marry him—and she hasn't decided what her answer will be, or has decided but won't tell him yet. In another picture they sit together in a field of tall grass. They are looking into each other's face, and smiling. That's what happiness looks like. Beneath the photograph the white ink inscription reads: "Just married. 1915."

A few remembered images and a couple of photographs don't amount to much, they don't compose a portrait or a life. But they were enough to leave a residue of tenderness in a child. It wasn't like not having had a mother at all.

My mother died in the first April of the Great Depression, in St. Paul, where Standard Oil had sent my father to work. A month later they fired him. Forty-two years old, grieving for his dead wife, out of work and out of money, and with two small boys to care for: what could a man do? What he did was go west, to Colorado, where he had heard there was work for him. He settled us first with a family in Julesberg, a little town in the sugar-beet fields near the Nebraska line, and then in a Ft. Collins boardinghouse, while he drove around the state trying to sell something on commission (oil, I suppose, that was what he knew). He must have failed as a salesman there; before the end of the next year we were traveling again, to Philadelphia, where his brother had a business, and had offered him a job. It must have been hard for my father to turn back east; generation after generation our family had always moved westward. That was what Americans did: west was opportunity, west was a new start. If you had gumption you went west.

The job in Philadelphia wasn't a real job; it was only my uncle being charitable. My father couldn't accept charity, not even from his own brother; he packed us up and drove again, south this time, to Fairhope, Alabama, a town on Mobile Bay where his sister, Elva, lived. He'd leave my brother and me with her while he looked for a real job.

My father didn't like to talk about himself much, but he told the story of his arrival in Fairhope many times: how he drove up the sandy street to Aunt Elva's house, how she was watching for him on the screen porch and ran out to the car, waving a yellow telegram and shouting "A job! A job! You've got a job in Moline, Illinois! You only have to get there!"

"I had five dollars in my pocket," my father said. "All the money I had in the world. I figured it would just buy enough gas to get to Moline. And it did. Now isn't that something?" And he'd fall silent, astonished at the one piece of real good luck he'd had in his whole life. Or maybe the one case of divine intervention. I don't think he distinguished between the two.

He left the next morning, and in the fall my brother and I joined him in Moline. It was our first journey on a train, and our first without our father. I wrote about it in a letter to my grandmother. And, I suppose because it was the first letter I ever wrote to her, she saved it. I was two weeks short of my eighth birthday.

Aug 14 1932
1913 15th St E

Dear grandma
I had a fine time on the train and made many friends. The first man we met was a man by the name of Mr Ingram who was very nice to us he bought us each a bottle of pop and some candy. We met an other man who told us many fish storys and said they were true. I think Daddy picked a pretty good place to to vc. Chuck and I went to Christian Sunday school today and liked it very much. There is nothing more to say so I will say goodby love Sam

The pretty-good place to live was another boardinghouse. We weren't there long; a few months later we moved to Minneapolis. Had he been fired again? Or offered a better job? Or simply transferred? I don't know. Adults know those things; but they don't tell children.

Later, when I traced our travels in those hard years on a map, I saw the pattern of my father's desperation: west and then all the way back east, south and then the whole way north, he had drawn his cross on the country. Seven moves in three years. No stop longer than a year. No steady, lasting job. Living in boardinghouses. Taking his family's charity. And always the two small boys.

But for me those were happy days. *Julesberg:* the plains lie flat and empty all around; the horizon is an exact and distant line. I sneak into a sugar-beet field with a gang of boys and steal sugar beets, and sit in the grass at the edge of the field and eat them with salt. One boy has a .22 rifle; we take turns shooting—at insulators on the telephone lines, at magpies. I aim at a cow far off in a field. The other boys say I'll never hit her that far away; she's probably in Nebraska. I fire and the cow jumps and lumbers off with her tail in the air. *Ft. Collins:* I ride a pinto pony up a mountain canyon, and drink clear water from a mountain stream, and wear a big hat and a bandanna around my neck. *Philadelphia:* in the bank above a stream in a vacant lot, neighborhood kids dig a cave, and we play robbers there, and hunt rats. *Fairhope:* the beach along the bay is endless, white, shadowed by pines; back in the bayous behind the town a rope hangs from a high branch of a water oak; I swing from it, out over the still black water, and drop into its coolness. Sometimes a cottonmouth swims past, ignoring me, minding his own business. *Moline:* in my school the fire escape is a hollow tube that you slide down when the fire bell rings; my father takes us across the river to Davenport to see a Fu Manchu movie in which Chinamen throw little hatchets at one another, and I am pleasurably frightened.

Even the hardships were lit with happiness. On the journey east from Ft. Collins a Great Plains blizzard swept down on us out of the north. Snow and sleet erased the world, day turned to night, and my father could keep driving only by following the taillight of a snowplow. My brother and I hugged together in the back seat of the Ford, wrapped in an Indian blanket, and sang songs—"Old MacDonald Had a Farm" and "Row Row Row Your Boat"—and my father made a joke. That was memorable because he never made jokes and couldn't remember the ones that other people told him. "We're the Rice Krispies boys," he said. "Chuck is Snap, Sam is Crackle, and I'm Pop!" It wasn't much of a joke—he'd made it up from the writing on a cereal box—but we laughed because it made us feel connected to his strength, and though the sleet rattled against the windows and the headlights showed only two cones of streaming snow, we knew we were all right. After a while we reached a town and spent the night. In the morning the sky was clear and the road was plowed.

My first remembered image of my father is from that journey. I see him from behind, from the backseat; he looms up in the darkness, tall, broad-shouldered, and steady, silhouetted against the light of the headlights reflected back from the falling snow, his big hands gripping the steering wheel, willing the car on through the drifts.

Other images come from the photograph album: my father in his first grown-up job, a seventeen-year-old powerhouse worker in overalls, standing before a panel of dials and fuses, with one hand on a brass switch handle, controlling power; and from his cowboy days in Wyoming, maybe twenty-one by then, standing

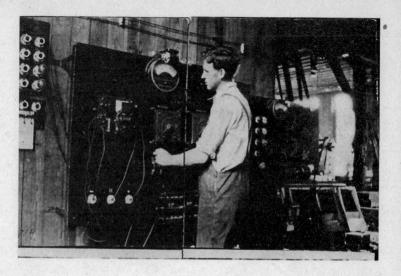

beside his horse; and from his war, a brown studio portrait in a private's uniform, standing tall and straight and self-conscious. Images of strength, and of the kinds of work a strong man might be proud to do.

Still, strong though he was, my father must have felt considerable relief on his second wedding day, whatever else he felt; after those hard years he would have a home (in Minneapolis—we had moved again), and a wife to share his burdens, and his sons would have a woman to share in caring for them, someone they would call "mother." The woman he chose was an odd one, for him—an Irish-Catholic widow with three children. My father despised the Irish: there were only two kinds, he said, lace-curtain Irish and pig-in-the-parlor Irish, and both kinds were awful. And he hated Catholics. He was a Mason and a Protestant Republican; he had voted against Al Smith in 1928 because he believed that if Smith won he'd dig a tunnel from the White House to the Vatican. What was he doing marrying a woman who was both Irish and Catholic? He might get a home, but there would be crucifixes and bleeding hearts of Jesus hanging on the bedroom walls. He might shift the weight of his two children onto her shoulders, but he'd take on the heavier weight of her three. And worst of all, he'd have to submit to being married by a Catholic priest. Not in the church, he wasn't Catholic enough for that, but in some outbuilding of the church, furtively, in a corner.

It's not surprising that the photograph in the family album of the wedding party is not very cheerful. The new-made fam-

ily huddles together on some Minneapolis street corner, perhaps outside the restaurant where we've just eaten the wedding breakfast. The bride stands at the center of the group, holding a bouquet of flowers. Sunlight is bright on her face; she squints at the camera through her thick glasses, not quite smiling—this is a solemn occasion—but looking as though she will, once the picture is taken. Her children stand protectively around her: her son, Bill, behind, her daughters, Rose Marie and Eileen, on either side. The girls wear steeply tilted white hats. One of them smiles.

My father, at the back, towers over the rest of us. His eyes are deeply shadowed and his mouth is set in a stern line. Chuck is on the right, wearing long pants (he's two years older than I am) and grinning optimistically. I'm on the other side, thumbs stuck in the pockets of my knickers. The look on my face says, "You'll never get me to smile, I've read 'Snow White' and 'Cinderella,' I know about stepmothers and stepsisters." Around us the life of the street goes indifferently on; a woman passes carrying a cake in a box, a man in a white cap ambles along the curb. They don't know that the group they are passing is not a family but two very different families gathered on a street corner almost, it seems, accidentally. Below the photograph my new stepmother has written the date: June 18, 1934.

Because my parents—no, that isn't right, my stepmother wasn't my parent; better call them, as we usually did, the folks. Because the folks were country people, it must have seemed right as well as convenient to send my brother and me to live on a farm while they went on their honeymoon and got used to being a middle-aged couple with five kids. My father knew of a farm out in the middle of the state, near Litchfield, that was worked by a childless couple; they would take us on for the summer if he promised that we'd do the kinds of work that farm boys our age did. My father must have thought that though one summer wouldn't make us country boys, it would give us something of what he felt when he remembered his own boyhood; and of course it would seem right to him that we should work for our keep.

All our journeys began in the morning dark, whatever the destination: "We'll make a good start," my father would say. In the kitchen in the half-light of dawn we whisper over a hasty breakfast (the rest of the family is asleep), while my father says impatiently, "Shake a leg! Shake a leg!" opening the back door quietly ("Don't let the screen door slam"), and the garage doors, and backing (quietly, the car's engine whispering, too) into the empty street. The houses along the block are dark, except here and there a kitchen window lit—a wife whose husband is on the early shift is making breakfast, or an upstairs window, the bathroom probably—some working man shaving.

Our route is west along West Thirty-fifth Street into the night's last darkness, and north on Lyndale. At that time of earliest morning the traffic lights are still switched to amber, and make patches of yellow light on the shadowy street. There are no other cars moving, and no walkers on the sidewalks. The air is still cool, but as the sun rises and the eastern sky turns gold and then flame-colored, my father says, as he always does on hot summer mornings, "It's going to be a scorcher!"

U.S. Highway 12 runs due west from Minneapolis to Litchfield. But it doesn't stop there, my father says; it goes straight on to South Dakota, up into North Dakota, through Montana and Idaho, and clear across Washington State to the Pacific Ocean. Right across the whole Northwest Territory—that's what they called it before there were states. Folks still call these parts the Northwest; you see it in the papers.

I imagine that line on the globe at school, running on and on through the Northwest Territory, right over the horizon, over the curve of the world to the blue end of the land, and dropping into the ocean with a plop.

Beyond the city suburbs and the cottages around Lake Minnetonka the farms begin, and my father becomes a country man. The corn looks good, he says. Knee-high by the Fourth, folks say; a good crop should be knee-high by the Fourth. He means the Fourth of July. Birds circle above a wood and he says: Hawks. Must be a dead animal in there. He holds the steering wheel as though the car were a plow and drives it on into the summer morning.

Out here the sky seems wider, but not higher; in Minnesota a summer sky is like a blue enormous plate, and the clouds that float on it ("fair-weather cumulus," my father calls them) seem close to the earth and friendly, like sheep drifting in a flock. As the sun rises in the sky heat waves begin to shimmer on the road ahead, blurring the outlines of things, and mirage pools lie like water on the blacktop. My father breathes deeply of the country air and rolls up his shirtsleeves.

Along the roadside the usual furniture of country highways: solitary mailboxes on posts at the ends of rutted roads; telegraph poles marking the line of railroad tracks; crisscross warning signs where the tracks cross a road. Little signboards set on posts recite Burma-Shave rhymes, one line to a sign. My brother and I chant them as we pass: PITY ALL / THE MIGHTY CAESARS / HAD TO PULL THEM / OUT WITH TWEEZERS, and HE'S UNHAPPY / IN THE GRAVE / HE CANNOT GET / HIS BURMA-SHAVE. On the ends of barns advertisements covering the entire wall urge us to Chew Bull Durham and Visit Rock City. A sign at the edge of a town announces TOURIST CABINS and we can see them, back from the road in a grove of trees, a row of little sheds no bigger than a double bed ("like privies," my father says), lonely, shabby, and unwelcoming. A big house on the main street has a shy, embarrassed notice on its broad lawn: TOURIST ROOMS—some widow trying to get through age and hard times by renting her spare rooms. But there are no tourists.

Halfway along our journey we approach Waverly. Long before the town itself comes in sight I can see the twin spires of its church rising tall above the level farmland. "Catholics," my father says. "They always build their church on the highest hill in town." Certainly they have done that in Waverly: the vast church sits stranded on its height, like Noah's Ark on Ararat, looking down on the nothing much that is the town—a few houses, a store with a gas pump. My father seems pleased that the town has not grown and prospered around the church; this time the Catholics got it wrong.

As he drove through the country, my father told us country stories, some from his childhood, others he'd heard from the old folks back in Indiana. He told us about the Pig Woman of La Porte, who had a farm near his home when he was a boy. The Pig Woman was a big, strong Norwegian, my father said, weighed two hundred pounds and built like a man; she could carry a hundred-pound shoat under her arm. A woman like that could work a farm herself; but from time to time she would advertise in some farmer's newspaper for a companion, a husband or a partner, to share her life. A few weeks later a stranger would get off the train from Chicago and ask directions to the Pig Woman's farm.

Did you ever see one?

Oh yes, I'd see them working around her place, slopping the hogs or mending a sty. And then they'd be dead. A cleaver fell off a shelf and hit one man in the head; split it right open.

Or they'd be gone: "Just walked off," the Pig Woman would say, though nobody had seen him go. "Went to Oregon." Or California. Somewhere.

After a while another ad would be in the paper, and another stranger would climb down from the train at the La Porte depot.

Well, folks began to wonder, and relatives of the missing men began to turn up in town asking questions. They got the sheriff interested, and he started poking around.

And right then, when folks were after her, the Pig Woman's house burned down. Right to the ground. And when they sifted the ashes they found the bones of a woman. *But she didn't have a head!* The coroner said it was the Pig Woman, but folks who saw the remains said those bones weren't near big enough, that the Pig Woman had killed some other poor soul and cut her head off and left her body in the burning house.

So maybe the Pig Woman is still alive, my father said. She might be anywhere—she might be living in that farmhouse up there on the hill, or in the next town!

And what about all the bodies? What did she do with the bodies? (We knew, we'd heard the story before, but we wanted him to tell us.)

Well, some folks said she buried them under the hogpen. Others said she fed them to the pigs, and then slaughtered the pigs and made sausage, and sold it in La Porte. Some folks couldn't eat pork sausages ever again.

What he didn't tell us, because he couldn't bear to, was that there were other bones in the ashes of the Pig Woman's house. She had murdered her three children.

My father knew older stories that had been preserved and repeated in the family memory, stories of our pioneer ancestors going back to William Hynes, who left Northern Ireland in the early eighteenth century and came to Philadelphia, and later moved west into Maryland and died there; and of his son Thomas, who married and bought land there in Maryland, and his wife must have liked the place because he called it "Abigail's Delight" after her, but moved on anyway, down the Ohio River on a flatboat into Kentucky and died at Lick Creek; and of Thomas's son, another William, who went on a little way farther west and died at Bardstown; and William's son, another Thomas, who took the family up into Illinois and died at Greenville. To my father those ancestors were chosen, like Moses and Aaron in the Bible; they led the way into the wilderness, filling it and taming it and then moving on—and always west. Their lives gave him the right to be proud of the family, and a little condescending (but always politely) toward more recent, and so less fortunate immigrants. He was American in a way the new ones couldn't be, because his ancestors had been here when the nation was being made.

He wasn't much interested in the families those old Hyneses married into; he thought of them as foreigners with funny names. There were two Massachusetts brothers somewhere way back called Love and Wrestling, and a Marylander named Polycarpus Rose, and a Frenchwoman from New Orleans whose name was Barbara Chenault (my father was suspicious of her; being French, she might have been Catholic).

I liked those funny names: What would it be like to be called Polycarpus? *Hi, what's your name? Polycarpus, what's yours?* And I liked having the blood of Englishmen and Frenchmen in my veins along with all the Irish. But to my father none of those collateral connections existed; he was a Scotch-Irish-Presbyterian named Hynes, exactly like the first of the American line, old William, and that's all there was to it.

Of the family stories my father told, the best one was about his great-grandfather, the second William, when he was a boy in Kentucky in the Revolutionary War times. Kentucky was frontier country then; there were no roads where Will lived by the Salt River, and no towns, only trails and farms and here and there a mill or a store. Indians lived in the woods—wild Indians, who raided and robbed the settlers, and sometimes killed them.

Did they cut off their scalps?

I don't know, I expect they did.

Will and his family had to live in a fort with other farming families, and only left it in the daytime to work their fields.

Well, one day Will's father sent him on horseback to a mill miles away with a sack of corn to be ground. It was past noon when he got there, and he had to wait a long time for his grist, so it was near sundown before the miller hoisted the big sack onto the horse's back and Will began the long ride home. He'd ridden some miles through the woods, and the sun had gone down, when he felt the sack slipping slowly (here the telling slowed, this was the beginning of the scary part), sliding from under him, till it fell to the ground. He tried to lift it back up, but it was too heavy. And it was too precious to leave behind. What should he do? He couldn't yell for help; what if an Indian heard him? He'd have to stay right there in the woods all night, alone in the dark, and look for help in the morning.

He tied his horse to a tree and settled down to wait. By then the night was growing cold, and he didn't have a warm coat to cover him. Do you know what he did? We didn't. Well, he'd noticed that the corn had been heated by the grinding, and it was still warm; so he just snuggled up against the sack and went to sleep.

He woke up at first light, chilly and stiff and hungry, and saw smoke rising in the air a little way off. It might be a friendly farmer's cabin—a long pause here in the telling—or it might be an Indian campfire! He crept toward it through the bushes, quiet as an Indian, careful not to step on a twig or a dry leaf. It was a cabin. The farmer's wife fed him and warmed him at the fire, and the farmer lifted the sack of meal onto the horse again, and Will rode home. And weren't his folks glad to see him! They thought the Indians had got him.

I could see my father wished he had been that boy, in that frontier time when kids had adventures and folks were kind. So did I. I could imagine myself in Will's place, alone in the woods at dusk surrounded by Indians. A kid could do what Will did, if he was brave, and had good sense.

But if our folks got that far into Indian country, how come they didn't keep going? Why didn't they go all the way to the

real West and become cowboys and shoot buffaloes and fight Indians on horseback?

It was my grandmother, my father said. Elvira Powers. She was a Yankee from Vermont. An educated woman, went to a ladies' academy up there and became a teacher. Then she saw a letter in the paper from a Presbyterian minister in Illinois asking for someone to come and teach in his school, and she went. Not because she wanted to—she liked it fine in the East—but because if she didn't go the kids out there wouldn't have anyone to teach them.

Elvira was a great letter writer. She wrote long letters home (I suppose she was homesick) and the family kept them all. Your Uncle Lee has them, you can read them. There's one that goes on for pages and pages about how she got from Vermont to Illinois. What a trip! First a train (she called it "the cars") from Morrisville to Albany, then another train to Buffalo, a steamer across Lake Erie to Sandusky, another train down the whole length of Ohio from Cleveland to Cincinnati, then a riverboat down the Ohio River to St. Louis, another boat up the Mississippi to Alton, and a carriage (because there wasn't even a stagecoach there) to Hillsboro, where the school was. It took her three weeks.

Elvira didn't much like the West, on first sight. The "Beautiful Ohio" was a muddy stream, and Cincinnati didn't have the neat appearance that Eastern cities had, and besides it was smoky, and Western riverboats didn't run as regularly as Eastern boats did.

It wasn't a boring trip, though; the Lake Erie steamer got stuck on a sandbar, and so did the paddle-wheel riverboat on the Ohio. And when they were on the Mississippi somebody yelled: "Stop the boat! Child overboard!" and she saw a little boy, smaller than you, floating away behind them, and the ship's crew had to launch a boat and row back and get him.

Was he drowned?

No, he floated on top of the water without sinking at all. When they brought him back Elvira said he looked as bright as if nothing had happened.

At the end of her letter Elvira tells how she arrived in Hillsboro, Illinois, and was taken to the house of the Reverend Mr. Hynes, the man who had written the letter for a teacher, and how kind he was. That was your great-grandfather, Thomas Woodruff Hynes. He was pastor of the Greenville Presbyterian Church. He'd had two wives already, by then, both dead—the second had died only a few months before—and five children (two had died). He waited a decent year and then married Elvira.

Did she love him? Did he love her?

Hard to say. When she wrote home about being married there wasn't much love talk in her letters: a household with three small children in it was a responsibility; she hoped strength would be given her according to her day; she thought her preacher husband's company would be improving to her—things like that. It all sounds more like a job than a marriage. Or like going to school, or church. I guess they both got what they wanted: he got a mother for his children, she got obligations.

But maybe she was happy. She liked the farm: she called it "Looking-Glass Prairie" at the top of her letters. She went on teaching some, and she liked that; and she wrote poems that were printed in the *Greenville Advocate*. And she had her own children—four of them. The last-born only lived nine months. A few months after it died Elvira died, too—worn out, I guess, by the childbearing and the farm and the preacher husband. Poor thing, my father said. So young. (He must have been thinking of my mother.) The next year Thomas Woodruff married again, and had two more children.

How many was that altogether?

Four wives. Eleven children. But four of them died young.

What of?

Smallpox. Diphtheria. Croup. Scarlet fever. Pneumonia. Falling down the well. I don't know. Country graveyards are full of little headstones from those days.

Thomas Woodruff lived to be eighty. He's in the family album, an old man in a black preacher's suit, holding a great-grandson and leaning on a thick cane. His full beard is snowy white (his wife—the last one—washed it in lemon juice every morning), his face is seamed and weathered. He isn't looking at the child in his arms; his tired eyes look out from their deep dark sockets past the camera toward something less tangible: time, or death. Or maybe eternity, for he was a believing man.

Was he the one who cut his own ear off?

That was him.

How?

Well, the way he told the story was like this. On the farm where he lived when he was a little boy there was an old log corncrib that was used for storing farm implements. The other children were playing in it and had left him outside. So he thought he would sneak in through a crack at the back and surprise them. But when he pushed his head through the crack, he knocked against a sharp scythe that was hanging on the wall inside, and it swung back and cut his ear right off.

What did he do?

Nothing, I guess, except holler. The other kids picked him up and took him into the house. Somebody brought the ear along, and his aunt Kate, who was visiting at the time, just took it and sewed it back on. He'd show you the scar, if you asked nicely.

But why did your grandmother keep your grandfather from going west?

Well, they had their farm near Greenville, and one day Grandfather came home from town all stirred up (he was an excitable man) and told my grandmother he'd met a man who was taking a wagon train west in a few days, and there was room for one more family. All the way to Oregon! Grandfather said. There's free land out there, good farming land. And they need preachers. Let's go!

But my grandmother said no. "I came all the way out here from Vermont," she said. "Greenville's far enough west for me."

Grandfather was very disappointed. "Well," he said, "I guess I'll just have to go back and tell that nice Mr. Donner we can't go with him."

That wasn't the end of the story. The wagon train got stuck in the snow up in the mountains, for a whole winter. *And they ate each other!* What if they'd eaten Grandfather? my father asked. Who would *I* be? He looked back over his shoulder at Chuck and me in the backseat: Who would *you* be?

When my father wasn't telling stories there was nothing much to do. The two-lane highway ran on westward through the same fields, and my father would get behind a truck and have to slow down, and get mad, or go around him and speed up, and that was all the variety there was. At times like that my brother and I played White Horse. In this game you each took a side of the road, and got one point for every white horse you passed on your side, but your score was erased if you passed a graveyard. There were lots of white horses on the road to Litchfield, grazing in pastures or pulling farm machines, but lots of graveyards, too. If I was erased too often I quit the game and read the map instead.

Gas stations gave maps away free; every kid had a collection. You could ride your bike into any station and the man who ran it would give you one—Minnesota, of course (but you already had that one), or a neighboring state, South Dakota or Iowa, or, if you were lucky, someplace farther off—New England, or the Gulf Coast. I loved my maps, I read them like storybooks. So I was happy, sitting in the backseat with Minnesota spread across my knees, looking at the different colors—green for state forests (they were mostly in the north, where the Indian reservations were), blue for the lakes (which were everywhere, but were bigger in the north), red for the main roads, and black for the little ones.

And reading the place-names. There's a whole history of the Northwest in those names, I found it on the map before I read history books. The state's first people—the Chippewa (who lived in the woods) and the Sioux (who lived on the plains)—were mostly gone, but they had left their words on the land: Esquagamah, Kebekona, Kandiyohi, Mahtowa, Nay-Tah-Waush, and in translation Medicine Lake and Bad Medicine Lake, Good Thunder, Grey Eagle. And then the first white men, the French, who named Belle Plaine, Lac Qui Parle, Frontenac, Pomme de Terre, Mille Lacs, and Lake Pepin—more often the names of rivers and lakes than of towns, the French were trappers, they didn't settle. After them the Northern Europeans—Germans, Scandinavians, Bohemians—who named their prairie towns for the cities they had left: Heidelberg, Cologne, New Munich, Oslo, Upsala, New Prague. And the Irish: Coleraine, Kilkenny. Many of the settlers were Roman Catholics, they spread their saints across the state: Bonifacius, Clair, Francis, Hilaire, Nicholas, Rosa, Wendel. And their feasts: Assumption, Sacred Heart.

Some towns spoke the dreams of the folks who settled there: Freeborn, Hope, Independence, Welcome, and Young America. Others took their names from what they saw: there must be apples growing in Apple Valley, and lots of lakes in Fifty Lakes. And the dirt must really be blue in Blue Earth, and white in White Earth. And somebody was robbed at Thief River Falls, and somebody went blind at Blind Lake. But most of all I liked the inexplicable names: Why Sleepy Eye? Yellow Medicine? Artichoke? Climax? And why, far up in the northeast corner of the state, nearly in Canada, a town called Embarrass?

The fields we drove through had been Sioux country before the white man came and fenced and farmed it. My father knew stories about the Indians, too. How they fought back against the settlers, attacked farms, and killed whole families, how the farmers built stockades to withdraw into when the Indians came (there was one at Crow River, just beyond the farm we were going to). How the Sioux chief Little Crow led his braves in a war to clear the whole Minnesota River Valley of white people and killed four hundred of them before he lost a last hopeless battle at Wood Lake, down by Granite Falls, against soldiers from Ft. Snelling. And how after the Indians had lost they still fought on in a kind of violent despair, killing and scalping and burning. And how their leaders were hanged at Mankato, thirty-eight of them on one scaffold. It wasn't so long ago, my father said. There are old folks in Litchfield who remember the Indian war.

I wanted to know what had happened to the rest of the Sioux. Most of them moved west, or north into Canada; some were rounded up and put on reservations in South Dakota. Were they still there? My father said most of them died. It was a sad story. I knew that the white men had to win; otherwise there would be no America, no Minnesota, no Highway 12. But the Sioux, with their warbonnets and their bareback horses and their lances, they were brave and free. I'd rather have been a Sioux than a settler.

As we approached Litchfield the railroad came closer to the road and ran companionably beside it into town. Ahead I could see the town's tall grain elevators beside the tracks, thrusting into the sky like cathedral towers out of the perfect flatness of the plains. The redbrick heart of the town was at the foot of the elevators, where Main Street crossed the tracks: the depot, the hotel, the feed store, and the German butcher ("best baloney in the whole state," my father said). And the opera house, for there was an opera house; someone in the town's past had wanted Litchfield to be not only a prosperous town but a civilized one. It was closed now.

We drove up Main Street past the stores, past a shady park with a bandstand, past a white-painted church. In a block or two we were among fields again, and then for a moment in an even smaller town, a village—two white churches, a creamery, a beer parlor, a couple of houses. "Manannah," my father said. "Where the Heggs bring their milk."

Beyond the village we turned off the highway onto a dirt road, dusty and washboarded. Pebbles rattled up against the fenders. At the side of the road, lonely among cornfields, a country cemetery, weed-grown, its iron fence leaning. "Four people in there the Indians killed," my father said, and turned again by a mailbox on a post onto a track that was only wheel marks through the weeds, and I could see the farm ahead on a low green knoll: a white house, blue in the shadows of a stand of pines, beyond it a barn, painted red once but weathered back to the color of old wood, a tall silo, a windmill, all lifted on their little hill above the level of the fields, peering out over the crops, watching them grow.

CHAPTER TWO

My father drove into the farmyard and stopped by the house. "Well," he said, "here we are." He always said that at the end of a journey. It wasn't an exclamation, and it wasn't a statement—we didn't need to be told where we were; it was more a mark of punctuation, the period at the end of a long task that he'd managed to complete without disaster.

The yard held summer like a bowl. June sun poured down on the baked dirt, and the air was filled with a sort of hum, as though growing was a sound. We got out of the car and stood there, hens pecking and clucking at our feet, dogs barking, sun hot on our heads, and waited for the farm to acknowledge us.

A tall woman appeared at the door of the house and stood looking out at us through the screen, shading her eyes with her hand. She called toward the barn, "Lloyd! Company!" and a man in bib overalls came out of the barn and hurried across the yard. Mr. Hegg seemed small compared to his wife. His sun-burned face and arms were the color of the barn, and his wild curly hair was the same color only brighter, like a barn on fire. As he came toward us he mopped his face with a bandanna handkerchief; he didn't want to meet strangers sweating.

Mrs. Hegg led us into the house, where lunch was spread on the dining-room table. While we ate, my father talked with Mr. Hegg about the crops, and told Mrs. Hegg to make farmers of us. Then, after the pie and coffee, he got back in the car and drove away. Chuck and I stood in the shade of the pine trees in the front yard watching him go—down the track and along the washboard road, raising a tail of dust behind him, and onto the highway and out of sight. We were alone with strangers in a place we knew nothing about, where everything would have to be learned—places, people, animals, work, words, everything.

Mrs. Hegg showed us her house. First the kitchen: a cast-iron wood-burning stove (she called it "the range") twice as big as our stove back home, with round holes on the top with iron lids on them, and an iron handle for picking the lids up when they got hot, and a tank on the end of the range full of water that heated when a fire was burning. A wooden table, scrubbed to a soft whiteness; above it a hanging lamp and a twisted strip of paper with dead flies sticking to it. A sink, white enamel like our kitchen sink at home, but with no water faucets, only a bucket on a shelf with a blue enamel dipper in it. Under the sink a drain-pipe that ran out through the wall and emptied on the ground outside. A blue-and-white towel on a roller beside the sink. Against the wall on the other side of the range a cupboard painted green, with boxes of salt and sugar and stuff in it, and everyday dishes and cooking pots. On the wall by the range a calendar from the Manannah Cooperative Creamery and a tin box with a little trough at the bottom full of wooden matches.

We'd seen the dining room; it was just a dining room. The parlor, beyond it, was better: a square box like a little piano that Mrs. Hegg said was a harmonium; we could play it if we wanted to, but we'd have to pump hard on the pedals because it was old, and an accordion, and a bookcase with *The Complete Works of O. Henry* (Mrs. Hegg said she'd bought them off the wagon of a traveling salesman) and a copy of Chic Sale's *The Specialist* (a whole book about country toilets!), and a sofa and chair covered in black horsehair that prickled your legs when you sat on them, and a kerosene lamp with a tall glass chimney and a green shade. The parlor smelled of dust and closed-in air; you could tell nobody went in there to play the harmonium or read O. Henry, ever.

Our bedroom was above the parlor, up a flight of stairs steep as a ladder. A small room under leaning eaves, with one window facing a woodpile and the grove. Two small beds covered with patchwork quilts, a chest of drawers, a rag rug. Nothing else. No lamp: "You go to bed to sleep," Mrs. Hegg said.

"Go look around the yard," she said. We went out into the sunlight. Nothing grew in the yard. Around the edges buildings stood in a wide circle, facing inward. The barn was the most important, you could see that. We looked in the wide door on the left; two horses stood in stalls with their behinds toward us. The room smelled of horse sweat and manure and hay: good smells. Tangles of leather straps and strings and brass buckles hung on the wall; that was harness, I knew that, but I didn't know the names of the pieces or what they were for. The horses snuffled at their hay and stamped their hairy hooves.

In the next room metal racks like picture frames hung in two long rows, and the floor was littered with straw. Manure smell, again, but different. The room at the end was full of silver cans and smelled of milk. That was the cleanest smell.

A ladder led up to a square hole in the ceiling. The room up there was as big as the barn, a high emptiness smelling of dry, dusty hay. The hayloft. The air was warm and unmoving there, dust motes floated in the sunbeams that slanted through the open door at the end. High up in the rafters swallows swooped and twittered; yet the loft seemed very quiet. We dared each other to stand at the very edge of the loft door and look down at the yard below, at the pigpen and the sty and the grunting pigs. From the door you could look straight into the tops of the trees in the grove, and beyond to the green and gold fields patched with the shadows of floating clouds, and beyond the greenness blue, the color of distance, lighter and lighter on each farther line of hills, all the way to the faded hazy horizon.

A rope hung from the peak of the barn roof by the hayloft door. Like the rope over the Fairhope bayou; you could grab it and swing out through the door, way out, and back again. Chuck wasn't sure, he dared me to do it first. And I did, swinging up and away from solid things into emptiness, not seeing the space below me but feeling it, and hung poised for an instant at the top of the swing, motionless and weightless in air, and then swooped back to the solid world before fear overcame my excitement. Then Chuck did it. Like flying, he said.

At the other end of the barn was a fenced-in square of mud and manure, with a watering trough and a hard white block by the trough that was salt, and the windmill for pumping water to the trough, and a hand pump for drinking water with a tank of cold water that had milk and butter in it—Mrs. Hegg's icebox. The low shed beyond the pump was dark inside. I could see poles running lengthwise up under the roof. The floor was spattered with white stuff like dirty whitewash, and strewn with chicken feathers. The smell in the shed was sharp, and got up my nose. Next to that shed another shed with rows of boxes in it, and hens sitting in them. When I looked in, the hens turned their little red eyes toward me angrily.

Across the yard from the chicken-feathers house, at the edge of the grove, two rough unpainted buildings weathered the color of dirt, or chewing tobacco. One was made of slats set apart; you could see right through it to the other side. It was partly full of dry ears of corn. In the other shed a Model T truck, old and rusty and with its paint worn off, as weathered as the shed it stood in. In a lean-to stuck to the side of the shed another Model T sunk on the dirt floor, its rear end toward the door. It had no wheels, and without them it looked like a car that had been crippled and died. Beside the dead Ford a stone wheel in a wooden frame, with a little iron seat, and pedals for turning it; it looked like a kid's tricycle turned upside down. On the wall above the grindstone tricycle a slender strip of steel longer than my two arms stretched way out hung on wooden pegs. It had teeth along one edge and wooden handles at the ends. When I lifted it from its pegs it whipped and whanged. Beside it a curved blade on the end of a long handle; I knew what that was, it was a scythe, like the one that cut off my great-grandfather's ear. Dangling from a nail next to the scythe a cluster of steel mouths toothed like small fierce animals; they looked as though they might snap at you if you came too close.

Around the edges of the yard between the buildings machines crouched in the weeds: two big wheels set far apart with curved steel claws hung between them; a long wooden box with wheels at the ends; another pair of wheels with steel disks big as dinner plates between.

All these things—the wheelless truck, the whipping saw, the steel mouths, the dinner plates and claws on wheels—must be parts of the farm's workings; I'd have to learn what they were and what they did. Maybe I'd even have to work them.

One other building stood apart, outside the circle of the yard, beyond the sheds and the woodpile: a narrow unpainted box like a coffin on end. Inside, a seat like a bench, with two holes cut in it. An old Sears Roebuck catalog. Nothing else. It was warm in there, and full of the sleepy buzzing of flies. I looked down through the holes at the piles of human waste below. So much shit on a farm! In the pigsty, the stable, the cow room, the barnyard, the chicken house, here: every living creature dumped its load somewhere, manuring the earth.

We hadn't come to the farm just to look at things; my father had promised we'd work for our keep. The next day we began to learn our chores. When the water bucket in the kitchen was empty, one of us took it across the yard to the pump and filled it. Full, it was heavy; I had to carry it with both hands and walk straddling it. The water splashed and blinked in the sun. When I had put the bucket up on the sink, I drank a dipperful; the water was cold and tasted of stones. Every day we took a basket to the henhouse and gathered eggs from the nests. If a hen was on her nest you had to approach cautiously, slide your hand under her into the feathery warmth, feel for an egg, and draw it slowly out. The hen might try to peck you—after all, it was her egg—but it didn't really hurt. Hens who didn't want their eggs taken made nests under a shed or in the bushes, and we had to look for them; that was a game, like hide-and-seek. Sometimes a hen laid her eggs in an odd, remote place and then forgot about them, and when we found them they were old and rotten. Then we could throw them against a rock. They made a fine stink.

The vegetable garden was down past the privy, behind the grove: beans on poles, potatoes, cabbages, turnips, rutabagas in rows—all the root vegetables that would go into the root cellar to feed the Heggs through the long country winter. We chopped at weeds with hoes, and the sun beat down on our straw hats, and the rows stretched on. The humming heat was full of country sounds—bobwhites whistling, the buzzing of insects, a mower far off. The hoe blades, polished by the earth they dug in, flashed in the sun, and the weeds fell and withered, and new weeds grew. This was work, we had to do it, my father had promised. Everybody has to work.

In the evening one of us brought the cows home. The lane that led down from the cow yard to the pasture was full of cow pies, flat round disks like the bases on a baseball field. On the long walk down I played a solitary country kid's game, jumping from one pie to the next as though they were stepping-stones. If a pie was old and dried out it was no fun, no better than first base; but if it was just the right age the top would be dried and firm, but the inside would still be liquid, and if I tromped hard on it, it would shoot wet manure out the sides. If it was too new and soft, my foot would sink into the squishy center and my shoe would be covered in cow shit, and I'd have to wash it off in the creek.

The creek that ran through the pasture at the end of the lane was the north branch of the Crow River, but folks didn't call it that, it was just "the creek," the way Manannah was just "town" and the Manannah Cooperative Creamery was just "the creamery" and the Union Protestant Church was just "church"—as though no other creek or town or creamery or church existed anywhere else. Country places had no proper names, because they didn't need any.

The pasture along the banks of the creek was a bog; round-topped hummocks stood up out of the black standing water there, you could run across the bog on the hummock tops if you were quick and agile and didn't care. If you slipped, you went into the water over the tops of your Keds; but they smelled of cow manure and hot dirty feet anyway. And you had to try; it was another country game, another test.

When Mr. Hegg told me I could try milking, he said it as though he was conferring a favor, or an honor. I felt that way, too; milking was a grown-up farmer's job, not something only kids did, like weeding and bringing the cows home. It looked simple enough: you put your pail under the cow's udder and your three-legged milking stool close under her right flank, and leaned your head against her hairy side. Then you gripped two catty-cornered teats and began to squeeze them alternately. The teats felt funny at first, rough and scaly, yet yielding and elastic. No milk came. Squeeze harder, Mr. Hegg said, they don't mind. And pull down. I did, and thin streams of milk spurted into the pail, making first a drumming noise on the pail's bottom and then, as the pail filled, a muted, bubbling, contented sound.

The barn cat slunk in along the wall and sat watching me with her yellow eyes. She had no name, she was just the Barn Cat. I squirted a stream of milk at her and hit her on the nose; she jumped and snarled, but then settled to licking her face. What was it like, that milk straight from the udder? I bent over and squirted some into my own mouth: warm, blood heat, the temperature of the cow's insides, and rich as butter. Nothing like milk from the icebox back home.

When my hands grew tired Mr. Hegg took over to strip the udder of its last milk; if you didn't do that, he said, the cow would dry up. I stepped back to admire my first milked cow—and sank into an oozy pit. "You're standing in the gutter," Mr. Hegg said. It was like the gutter of a city street; it ran along be-hind the cows to collect the piss and cow manure they dropped—not to keep the barn clean, but to save the manure so it could be spread on the fields. It was full now. Covered with scattered straw, it looked like the rest of the barn floor; but it was liquid, and I was standing up to my knee in it. "Go out to the pump and wash yourself off," Mr. Hegg said. He was laughing at me, and my shit-covered leg. It was the only time I heard him laugh that whole summer.

The farm days passed, and the strange farmyard things became familiar and took on names. The bending length of steel on the shed wall was a two-man crosscut saw; Chuck and I used it to cut firewood for the kitchen range, each of us hanging on to a handle and dragging the teeth across a log balanced in the saw-buck. The trick was to pull but never push; draw the long blade toward you, then let the person on the other end draw it back. If you forgot and pushed, the blade buckled and stuck in the log.

The grounded truck body in the lean-to was there for its engine. It wasn't dead, trucks don't die in the country, they take root and become power plants. Mr. Hegg ran a belt around the truck's rear axle and connected it to a circular saw. Then he cranked the engine. When it coughed he ran 'round to the steering wheel and pushed levers up and down until the engine was running. When he put the truck in gear, the saw whirled and its teeth ate through the planks that Mr. Hegg fed it. We had to stand well back while he worked, the belt might fly off and whip across the yard and kill us dead!

The machines that stood in the weeds around the yard were put to work, and by working named themselves. The one with the curved claws was a cultivator; it dragged weeds out from between the corn rows. The long-box one was a drill; it planted seeds. The one with the steel dinner plates was a disk harrow, for loosening the soil. Duke and Molly dragged the machines across the tilled fields. Mr. Hegg sat in the steel saddle, looking back over his shoulder at the furrows he was making, tense as he drove: Were the disks biting at the right depth? Were the marks of the cultivator running straight?

I learned to speak the language of farms: the words for the parts of wagons and machines and harness: whippletree, tongue, bit, blinder, trace chain, hame, belly band; and the names of the fields: the East Forty, the Bottom, the Creek Patch; and the family names of the creatures: pigs were Poland Chinas or Belted Hampshires, cows were Jerseys (honey-colored), or Guernseys (darker, like molasses), or Holsteins (black and white), chickens were Rhode Island Reds or Plymouth Rocks or Wyandottes.

All the creatures had their languages—not words they could speak, but sounds and words you used when you addressed them, that they understood. I wanted to speak in those tongues. The language of pigs was "Soooo-EEEEE! Pigpigpigpig"; cows came to you (if they felt like it) if you called "COM-M-M-M-ME Bossy"; chickens scurried up to "HERE chick-chick-chick-chick."

Mr. Hegg took the steel mouths down from the lean-to

wall. Gopher traps, he said. He showed us how to set one; open the jaws wide, and lock them open with a sort of trigger. Then put the trap down gently in the opening of a gopher's hole. The gopher will trip the trigger when he goes in or out, and the fierce jaws will seize him. But watch out for your fingers. Mr. Hegg picked up a stick and thrust it into the set trap; the jaws snapped shut and bit the stick in two.

If we trapped gophers we could cut off their tails and sell them to the county agent who came to the creamery in Manannah every Thursday. Chuck wouldn't do it; he didn't want to kill things, not even gophers. I took the traps and walked off into the fields with the dogs, along the fence lines, watching for patches of fresh-dug earth and the little tunnels that were gopher holes, and set my traps. Every day I returned and found the sprung traps and small dead creatures caught in them, brown with black stripes along their backs, and cut off their tails and threw the little bodies into the weeds. I didn't mind their deadness; gophers ate the crops, killing them was a necessary farm job, like chopping weeds. I had begun to think like a farmer.

And to earn like one—in small amounts, a penny a tail. Money wasn't a part of farm life; Mr. Hegg didn't jingle coins in his pocket the way my father did, he and Mrs. Hegg didn't talk about buying things, or what things cost in stores. They only bought what the farm couldn't produce: salt, sugar, overalls, coffee, kerosene, flour, machine parts. Everything else they grew, or made, or did without. All that summer I never bought anything.

There are other necessary killings, on a farm. On a Sunday morning after church Mrs. Hegg tells me to go out and kill the Rhode Island Red for dinner. I know which hen she means; I have become an intimate of hens. I know how to call them, feed them, steal their eggs. I have even learned how to put one to sleep: you pick a bird up, put its head under its wing, and rock it gently to and fro like a baby. When you put it back on the ground, if you do it gently, it will go on sleeping for a minute; then it will wake up with a flurry of feathers and stalk off clucking crossly because you have played it a low, mean trick.

I know how to kill a chicken. You grab one in the yard and carry it to the chopping block by the woodpile. A hatchet is stuck in the block. You put the chicken's head on the block and chop it off with the hatchet. Easy enough. But the Rhode Island Red won't cooperate; she moves her head about, turning to look up at me with a red accusing eye. I chop and miss, and the hen flusters and squawks, I chop again and take off the head and most of the neck. The headless corpse leaps from my hand onto the grass and flops around with its wings spread, dead but still moving, and then is still. Mrs. Hegg scalds it and plucks it and puts it in the oven, and we eat it for Sunday dinner. I don't regret its dying.

Country summer wasn't all work; there were patches of perfect idleness, like sun-filled clearings in the woods, time enough for me to read straight through *The Complete Works of O. Henry* and for Chuck to learn to play "My Country 'Tis of Thee" on the accordion. In a snapshot taken on the shady front lawn that summer,

Chuck kneels on one knee, playing the accordion, while Lady, the black-and-white collie bitch, looks up at him as if astonished by the noises he is making; I lie on my stomach in the grass reading O. Henry; in the foreground Lady's son, Jack, looks away from us at something more interesting than having his picture taken. It's an image of that summer life as true as the weeds and the cows.

Beyond the East Forty the creek turned and ran south along the foot of a low wooded hill. The pastures and woods there were unworked country spaces; they seemed unaware of the farming life around, as though it was all still wilderness, as though no time at all had passed since the last of the Sioux folded their tepees and vanished westward. I went there alone sometimes, to wander and just look at things: how the birch trees grew on the hillside, the shapes of the rocky outcrops, the rabbit burrows under the tree roots, the broad furry leaves of the mulleins in the pastures. Or with Chuck and the Nelson boys from the next farm to play cowboys and Indians, creeping through underbrush (Indians) and galloping down hills (cowboys), or just running and shouting about nothing at all, because there was no one to see or hear us there, and because it was summer.

We swam in the creek at the bend where the cows crossed. The water was deep there, and so clear you could see the sandy bottom. Frogs croaked on the banks, and garter snakes slid into the water and swam wiggling off. Above the surface of the stream dragonflies hovered; the Nelson boys called them darning needles ("if they land on your face they'll sew your eyes shut!"). Sometimes deep under water a dark shadow swam slowly past ("ol' snapping turtle, bite your pecker clean off!").

Beyond the sandy patch, upstream and down, the creek bottom was mud, deep and soft and squishy. If you strayed from the sand into the mud, you'd come out of the water with fat worm-like things clinging to your legs. When I first saw them my guts turned at their dark sliminess, but Olaf Nelson said calmly,

"Leeches," and pulled one off and threw it against a rock. It burst in a splatter of blood. My blood. I took a leech between my fingers and threw it, and then another, and the splotches of red on the rocks made me feel better. It was just another kind of country killing.

Sometimes we played in the grove that stood in the middle of Mr. Nelson's cornfield, below our place. There in the cool shade we were settlers surrounded by Little Crow's warriors, or the U.S. Cavalry planning a raid on an Indian camp. Mrs. Hegg said that long ago the town of Manannah had stood where the grove was, before it moved east half a mile or so to where it is now. I imagined the town's migration: in the nighttime, under a pale moon, the houses and the sheds and the church silently rise from their foundations and move silently across the dark fields, all together like cows going home to be milked, to their new ground, and sink down there with one low tired sigh.

When I explored the grove I found signs of that once-upon-a-time town: rusting lengths of iron, bricks with mortar on them, a wheel, broken crockery, a green-glass bottle. And the rusted blade and haft of a knife, hammered out of one piece of iron—an Indian's scalping knife, I was sure. Once people had built and furnished their homes with these shards, or used them to work the land; now, broken and useless, they were returning to the earth, like everything else. I didn't know what they were called, or what work they had done; they were pieces of the history of this country place that I couldn't read.

In high summer full dark came late. Long past my bedtime light still lay along the western horizon. There were no lights lit on the farm then; the Heggs went to bed when we did, when the daylight faded. If I stayed awake, or woke later and crept into the farmyard to go to the privy, I could stand there in perfect darkness unmarred by any earthly light—no car on the distant highway, no other farm light anywhere. Only the stars were not-darkness. If I looked up at the night sky and spread my arms wide and turned slowly around and around and around, I could make them wheel in the blackness, and feel the whole earth rolling.

At first the night seemed as silent as it was dark. Then my ear would begin to mark small solitary noises: a cow shifting in the yard; a dog barking far off no louder than a cricket; a night bird calling—pinpricks of sound in the silence.

But the darkness wasn't absolute, either. I learned there what you can't learn in cities—that you can see the world by the light of the stars alone: the barn hunched over the yard, the silo, the pines tall around the house all leaned over me, blacker than the night sky, visible, protective presences.

Mr. Hegg's parents' farm was just down the gravel road. Their place was bigger and more prosperous looking than the Heggs', the buildings broader, the silo taller, the house whiter, the porch wider and cooler, the outbuildings redder, the barn so vast that I felt overwhelmed and shy in it.

A boy who belonged to the farm—a grandson, or the son of a farmworker—took me into the great barn to see a stallion service a mare. I didn't know what that meant, but I wanted to learn. The mare, broad as a haystack, moved restlessly in her stall. Two men led the stallion in and placed him behind her. He snorted and stamped, and from between his hind legs a great red something grew. He reared, and the men shouted and shoved until his forefeet were on her back, and then the red thing disappeared. "Now she'll have a colt," the farm boy said with satisfaction. The show was over. Something heroic had just happened there in the barn, something like a parade or a brass band playing. I was glad I had seen it. I knew it had been an act of sex; that was how new life got made. But on such a scale! With such rearing and whinnying! That couldn't be what ordinary creatures like people did. Only stallions, and maybe gods, would do it that way.

Other new lives got made that summer. Lady, the old black-and-white collie, had a litter of puppies in the hay in the corner of the stables. Chuck saw them being born. Some came out dead, he said, and one that was alive was a runt, and she *killed* that one! I told Mrs. Hegg and she said angrily: "She's too old to have puppies." I asked her who the puppies' father was. She didn't answer. Jack was the only male dog around, but I knew it couldn't be him, because he was her son. Two of the puppies survived, and lived in the stable for a while, and Mrs. Hegg took my picture holding them. Then they disappeared—given away, maybe.

In the pigsty the sow, pink and fat with teats that bulged down to the ground, also had a litter, and before Mr. Hegg could carry the farrow away she ate one. Pigs did that, it was part of the country story, too: birth and death, breeding and killing.

The barn cat had kittens under the barn. If I got down on my hands and knees and peered into the shadows there, I could see them, blind-eyed and mewing, and then, older, playing in the straw. They were fierce as foxes; if I approached them they hissed and bared their little teeth. Don't touch them, Mrs. Hegg said, they're not pets, they're wild animals. Then they, too, disappeared; too many cats for one barn.

They drowned them, Chuck said. From the drowned lost kittens a memory rose from earliest childhood, from the time when my mother was alive and we lived in Chicago. My brother has pushed me in my wicker carriage to the pond in the park. I sit contentedly looking at the water while he throws stones into it. A man comes up to him with a sack in his hand. He tells my brother that he will give him a quarter if he throws the sack into the pond. The sack is alive; it wiggles and bulges and utters small noises. Chuck looks up in the man's face and says "NO!" very loudly and firmly. The man throws the sack into the pond himself and hurries away. As it sinks the sack opens and a kitten swims up to the surface and tries to swim to shore; but it sinks like the sack. Chuck stands watching the kitten drown, and I sit in my wicker carriage, watching him watch.

So Chuck knows what happens to kittens. And so do I.

Summer in the country has only one holiday, one day in the growing season when farmwork stops and farmers squander daylight and working time. No work today, Mr. Hegg said, it's the Fourth of July. He didn't really mean that, quite: the cows still had to be milked and the milk run through the separator, the animals still had to be fed. But then we all washed at the kitchen sink and put on clean overalls, and Mr. Hegg went to back the truck out of the shed.

But I hadn't walked my trapline. I would do that while Mrs. Hegg packed the picnic lunch. I set off down past the grove and the garden and along the fence by the cornfield, checking my traps—one sprung but empty, another with a dead gopher in it, another empty—until I saw through the weeds a different creature caught, first patches of white, then as I came closer black stripes, and I was caught, too, in a pungent cloud that soaked me like a sudden shower of rain. I knew what it was; I had smelled it before, driving along country roads after dark, a penetrating musky odor in the night air and my father would say, "Somebody hit a skunk." I could see the animal crouched by the fence post, facing me, one foreleg held in the trap's teeth. I couldn't kill it, and I couldn't release it. I turned and ran, and the smell ran with me, so strong that before I had burst through the kitchen door Mrs. Hegg knew just what had happened. "Take those clothes off," she said, "every stitch." She filled the washbasin with hot water from the reservoir, and threw a piece of yellow soap into it. "Now scrub yourself all over."

The scrubbing didn't do much good. You can wear your skin off with yellow soap and you still won't get rid of skunk smell. When I dried myself and dressed again I looked clean enough, but I still moved in that fierce aroma, more skunk than boy.

Lake Koronis—but we didn't call it that, it was just "the lake"—wasn't a vacation resort. There were no little summer cabins along the shore, no docks, no boats. It was just a lake in the middle of woods and fields, a part of the country landscape. In a pasture by the water's edge a scatter of trucks and wagons and people in their clean farm clothes, the men in little circles, talking, while the women spread blankets and tablecloths on the ground and lay out their picnic lunches, and children run in and out among the wagons, or splash in the lake.

The picnic food is familiar, just what my stepmother would have fixed: cold fried chicken and potato salad, and maybe a yellow layer cake with soft white frosting for dessert. And after? No speeches, certainly. Maybe picnic games: sack races and egg-and-spoon races and three-legged races, two kids with one leg each stuck in the same gunnysack. Horseshoes, for sure: I can hear the ring of the shoes against lengths of pipe driven in the ground for stakes, and the soft comments of the players.

Wandering the picnic camp after lunch, I come around a parked truck. A young woman sits on the truck's running board nursing a baby. I have never seen a baby being nursed before, nor a woman's naked breast. I stop still. I know this is not an indecent or an improper scene, but something tender as life, and none of my business. The mother looks up, but she doesn't see me, she's like someone in a trance, and the baby goes on sucking.

The farmers have undressed behind their trucks and wagons and put on woolen bathing suits that cover their chests and thighs like BVDs. They step out shyly, picking their barefoot way through the weeds and sandburs to the shore. Their faces and necks and forearms are burned the color of new bricks by the sun; the other parts of their exposed bodies are white as milk. Marked so distinctly and so strangely, they seem a different variety of our common species, like Belted Hampshires among Poland Chinas. They walk slowly a little way into the water and crouch and splash themselves, and shout how fine the water is; but they don't swim. Most of them don't know how.

Their wives don't join them in their splashing; they sit in little groups on the blankets under the trees, talking quietly, or take their shoes and stockings off and paddle in the shallows of the lake. It is all done very solemnly, the splashing and the paddling, as though these acts are rituals, like the baptisms in the Bible, that will make them better people, and maybe make our nation better, too, since it's the Fourth of July. Then we all gather our possessions, the blankets and the plates and the wet bathing suits, and pack them in the trucks and wagons and drive off, and the picnic ground becomes a pasture again.

Haying and threshing aren't holidays, but they feel like holidays, summer days when the lonely farm becomes full of teams and wagons and people shouting.

Haying: it's high summer. The air smells of heat and growing things. Mr. Hegg walks into the fields to test the ripeness of the grass, and looks up at the sky, watching the weather, because it will have to be right—hot and dry—for the haying. He hitches Molly and Duke to the mower and drives it 'round and 'round the hay fields, starting at the outside edge and then in smaller and smaller circles until he reaches the center, and all the grass lies flat on the earth, and it isn't grass but hay.

Neighbors bring their wagons into the yard, and stop and talk for a while, and then drive off into the fields and take their pitchforks down from the wagons and begin to toss the grass fork load by fork load onto the wagon beds. I'm too small to throw grass that high, so I'm put on a wagon to stomp the hay down as the load rises, to make room for more, and more. High above the sweating haymakers I jump and jump, as though jumping were a game, or a dance. When the wagon can hold no more the horses pull it to the barn and up a ramp at the loft-door end. A hay sling hangs from the rope we swung on; it clutches the hay in enormous handfuls and lifts it into the loft. I run into the barn and up the ladder into the loft to watch the hills of hay building against the eaves and to smell the sweet smell. When the hills are tall I jump from a rafter into the soft sweetness.

Threshing time is summer's crown. Like haying it's full of people and bustle, but now there are monster machines that clatter and roar, and more people, and more excitement. The days before, Mr. Hegg has been in the fields with the binder, an awkward, unlikely-looking machine that has sat unnoticed all summer long behind the barn. A low-slung blade at the front cuts the grain, and then a reel made of slats ties the fallen stalks into sheaves and throws them back onto the stubby field to be stacked together in shocks.

Now the shocks stand in rows across the fields. The yard begins to fill early with neighbors in their work clothes, with their teams and wagons. They stand around smoking and talking, waiting for the threshing machine to arrive. It will come from another farm to work for us for a day and then move on. I can see it, far off across the fields, a creaking dragon drawn slowly along the road by a steam engine that puffs smoke rings into the hot still air, and I can hear the *thump-thump-thump* of the dragon's beating heart.

The engine puffs up the knoll into the yard and pulls the threshing machine into position in a field near the house. It sits there all day, ruling the harvest. Cut sheaves are brought to it like tributes and tossed onto a belt that feeds them into the dragon's open mouth. That part is scary—the bundles moving steadily up the belt to be swallowed, and more coming, and the dragon always wanting more. It could eat *you* as easy as not. From a spout at the side grain sprays down into a waiting wagon; straw piles up at the other end. The field is full of rackety commotion—steam engine thumping, men shouting, threshing machine clattering— and of dust so thick the sun shines redly through it. I stand by the grove and watch, or climb the straw pile and slide down.

When the threshing is over, and the steam engine has pulled the threshing machine back down the hill and along the road to some other farm, Mrs. Hegg and the other farmers' wives spread out the threshers' dinner on tables in the yard: platters and plates and bowls of roasted chickens, boiled potatoes, mashed potatoes, sweet potatoes, peas and beans and tomatoes fresh from the garden, salads, new-baked bread and rolls cover the tabletops; dishes of watermelon pickles, tomato relish, corn relish, pickled peaches, and homemade jams and jellies are squeezed into the spaces between the platters and plates, as though if the table wasn't covered completely, if you could see even one little spot of empty tabletop, Mrs. Hegg would be disgraced among her neighbors. This is more than a meal; it is a celebration of the year's growing. The fields around us—the South Forty and the Bottom and the Creek Patch—have provided all this nourishment; the Heggs have made it through another country year.

In the country, summer ends slowly and at different times: when the harvest is in and the hayloft and the silo are full, when the sun's heat cools, when the sound of cicadas comes from the grove, when the farm wife begins her canning and the farmer's work becomes preparations for winter. My country summer didn't end like that; it just stopped, suddenly and unexpectedly, one still-hot day when my father drove into the yard. He climbed slowly out of the car, stretching and unfolding his big body the way he did, and stood for a moment looking down at his two sons. "Well," he said. "Well, well."

I ran upstairs and packed what I owned, which wasn't much: a spare pair of overalls, some sun-faded shirts, and my private treasures—a stone that was possibly an arrowhead, the bleached jawbone of some small animal, my scalping knife. We said good-bye to Mr. and Mrs. Hegg and the dogs and got into the car, and my father drove us down the farm track and onto the washboard road, and left onto the highway, toward Manannah. Looking back across the fields, I could see the white house solitary on its piney knoll, and behind it the barn and the silo and the windmill. Then Nelson's grove hid it all. Good-bye to country summer; I wasn't a country kid anymore.

But for one season I had been one, like my father, and his father, and all those other country people in our family before him: the one who couldn't go to Oregon, the one who dropped the grist in the forest, the one who left Abigail's Delight to try life in Kentucky. I had been my ancestors.

CHAPTER THREE

T he house I came back to was new to me, but it was familiar, too; I had lived in houses like it before—big houses
with a lot of small rooms, and a lot of people in them. Straight
ahead as I went upstairs was the bedroom I would share with my
brother. We'd always shared a room in the boardinghouses we
lived in, that part was the same. And my father's room was next
door to ours, as it had always been. Sure, there were strangers in
the house—my new stepmother slept in my father's bed, and
two girls who were now my stepsisters shared a room, and in a
little room at the back my new stepbrother lived. But strangers
were familiar, too; there had always been strangers in the boardinghouses, I was used to eating meals with folks I didn't know,
and meeting them on the stairs.

Yet there was a difference. In this house I could go wherever
I wanted—up to the attic, with its sloping roof and splintery
plank floor, down to the cellar where the coal bin was, and the
furnace with its iron shaker, and the fruit cellar under the stairs
that my stepmother had already begun to fill with her canning.
I could go into the backyard and tightrope-walk along the back
fence and no one would stop me, and into the garage where
someone had fastened old license plates on the wall, all different
colors, like medals on an old soldier's chest. And tomorrow I
could do the same things, if I wanted to. I lived here.

It was a square, useful-looking house. Built from a Sears and
Roebuck kit, my father said. You just choose a model from the

catalog (this one's called the Langston) and they send it out on the back of a truck, every board you need cut to fit, every nail and screw and shingle, every windowpane. All you have to do is put it together. Lasts forever. He slammed his hand against the

THE LANGSTON $2,964⁰⁰

doorjamb. Nothing shook. Three thousand dollars, that's what a new one costs. F.O.B.

I sat on our front porch swing and looked at the block I lived on now. Two rows of plain frame houses faced each other across the narrow, elm-shaded street, each house separate on its own lot, but so close to its neighbors they almost touched. Close to the street, too, only a few feet of grass between the houses and the curb. Lawns didn't count for much on West Thirty-fifth Street.

The houses looked pretty much the same to me—brown or gray or in-between-colored with white trim, low-roofed, each with a screen porch across the front, shadowy now in the summer morning light. Some had dormer windows (they must have attic rooms like ours); some had bushes along the front, lilacs or bridal wreath. Down at the far end of the block a bright orange car was parked in a driveway. A company car, my father said, the man who lives there works for the Northfield and Southern. That's why it's orange. The car cast an orange reflection on the white house next door.

Dark-looking people came out of the house on the corner opposite: Greeks, my stepmother said, there's another family of them at the other end of the block. I bet there isn't another block in the whole town with Greeks at both ends. Some houses had kids; a black-haired girl jumped rope on the sidewalk by the orange car, and I could hear distant shouts of other kids playing. An old man came out of a house down the block and walked toward the streetcar stop at the next corner; he was wearing spats, even though it was summer. That's Mr. Andrews, my stepmother said; he's a floorwalker down at the New England Furniture Company.

The iceman's truck came around the corner and stopped by the curb. The ice was stacked in the back under a tarpaulin; it would be cool under there, and damp from the melting ice. The iceman threw a gunnysack over his shoulder, picked up a block of ice with his tongs, swung it onto the sack, and disappeared around a house to put the ice in the icebox on the back porch. While he was out of sight kids I didn't know sneaked from between two houses and climbed into the truck and stole slivers of ice and ran away. The iceman would probably give them pieces of ice if they asked; but what would be the fun of that?

Two men came to fix a broken place in our front sidewalk. They mixed cement and sand and water in a flat tub and spread the mixture where the broken sidewalk had been and smoothed it with trowels. When they had finished and left I wrote my initials in the wet cement: s.h. 1934. *My* initials in *my* sidewalk in front of *my* house. They'd be there for a long time, I thought, as permanent as the cement.

————

Neighborhood kids gathered in the alley that ran through the middle of my block. Unpaved, cindery, and rutted, it ran among garages and garbage cans, between backyards so full of apple trees that kids called it Apple Alley. I met kids my age there, the ice stealers and the distant shouters, and learned their names—Buck and Cliff and Wilbur (called Birdy) and Dickie D., and Donna, who lived in the house beyond my backyard fence, and Denise the black-haired girl—and there we played the endless games of summer, Annie Annie Over, and Kick the Can, games that have no shape and need no equipment bought from a store. You can play Annie Annie Over with just an old tennis ball, and all you need for Kick the Can is an empty tin can. There were plenty of cans in the garbage in Apple Alley, cans that had held pork and beans, and Vienna sausages, and tuna fish. The best were the red-and-white Campbell's soup cans, everybody agreed on that.

Because August was still summer, we went out to play after supper, as though day would go on forever. From the screen porches on the block parents could hear their children's voices floating from the alley, thin with distance: "Annie Annie Over!" And then, when the last sloping light had turned the elms to black silhouettes, the cry that ended all hide-and-seek games: "Olie Olie Olson, all in free-e-e-e," fading at the end like a sad bugle call.

As twilight gathered, and the familiar objects of the street blurred into shadows, we left the alley and came nearer home, to the corner, where the streetlamp cast a bright puddle of light on the pavement below, and played a kind of baseball there with lengths of broomstick for both bat and ball and the four street corners for bases, until mothers began to call from the porches, two notes, first falling, then rising: "WILL-L-L-bur! Wil-BUR!

Bedtime!" The game broke up then, and the players scurried through the darkness—it was night now—to the security of their lighted doors.

While I was away that summer when I was ten, a war was fought in Minneapolis. Men armed with guns and clubs patrolled the streets, and met in battles in the Market. Men died. None of that turmoil had reached the Heggs' farm; it sat apart on its low hill like an island in a green sea, and no messages in bottles washed ashore. Conversation, when the Heggs spoke, was of crops and relatives and neighbors: island news. The things that happened beyond the horizon and became history were no concerns of theirs.

In the city it was different. Public events drop into city life like stones into a pond; ripples spread, and eventually reach even the little houses in the neighborhoods, and touch the people in them. The Teamsters' strike touched even us, in our new house on West Thirty-fifth Street.

The strike was over by the time I came back from the farm, but it was still news at our dinner table. The members of my new family talked about it with high-pitched remembered excitement, like veterans of some fierce campaign. The strikers had stopped all truck traffic in the city, and wouldn't let farmers bring their produce in from the country. Downtown, in the market district, gangs of pickets—

What's a picket?

A man with a club

—held up the delivery of food to the city's grocery stores. My new stepmother talked about the shortages in the corner store; you couldn't buy bread, or fresh vegetables, or meat. Or gas, my father added angrily; you couldn't buy a gallon of gas. Kravitz the dry cleaner over on Nicollet couldn't deliver the clothes he cleaned; you had to carry them home yourself. My new stepsisters were afraid to go shopping in the Loop: there were gangs of rough-looking men on the street corners. My new stepbrother had seen soldiers in tin helmets with rifles marching along Hennepin Avenue and driving around in trucks. Once he saw a tank.

They all had stories to tell. My father knew a man who owned a gas station. He stayed open (a man's got to make a living, my father said) and strikers came with a rope and tied one end around the pump and the other end to a truck and pulled the pump right off its base and dragged it down the street. An ice-cream-truck driver was making a delivery and strikers jumped into his truck and threw all his ice cream out onto the pavement. When the driver saw what they'd done he grabbed a shotgun from his truck, climbed onto the roof, and began shooting. He hit two strikers; but the ice cream was all melted by then— the temperature was 105 that day, and every day of the strike.

The fiercest battle of the war was fought in the Market. I knew where that was, downtown the other side of Hennepin Avenue. The streets there were paved with cobblestones, and the buildings were soot-stained warehouses with loading docks, and the air was full of the smell of rotting vegetables and the sound of truck engines. The two armies faced each other there—the army of strikers, and the other, "citizens' army" that the bosses had organized and armed (not a hired gang, my father said, the bosses themselves—businessmen, lawyers, bankers, people like that, coming from their desks to protect their world). One man reported for duty straight from playing polo at the Polo Grounds over on the Parade, still wearing his jodhpurs and a polo helmet. A striker knocked the helmet off with a length of pipe and hit him on the head. "Imagine," my father said, "going to a strike in a polo hat!" Another man, a lawyer, was chased by strikers through the market streets and tried to run into a warehouse and was caught and beaten by men with clubs, and died there on the sidewalk. KSTP broadcast the progress of the battle as though it were a ball game, and the newspapers sent reporters and photographers, like war correspondents, and printed extras with news from the front.

One newspaper photograph in particular stuck in my mind. It looks down from a second-story window onto the battle on the street below. Men rush about, some in business suits and some in

overalls, carrying clubs. In the center of the picture a man in a cloth cap is swinging a baseball bat. It's the end of a perfect swing—feet planted, wrists turned over, arms extended—like Joe Hauser's swing when he hit sixty-nine homers for the Millers. But the ball is a man's head. The man who has been hit—one of the citizen soldiers—hangs suspended in midair, facedown, still falling toward his shadow on the cobblestones of the market street.

Hearing the stories and the radio news, seeing the pictures, I began to imagine the strike—not all of it, but scenes and episodes, like fragments of a movie I didn't know the plot of. I could see the gas pump bumping down the street with its glass tank shattering and the gas splashing out, and the ice cream melting on the hot tar of the street into a great puddle of chocolate chip and tutti-frutti and Neapolitan, and the terrified lawyer running for his life, and sinking to the sidewalk in a pool of his own blood, and I could feel the swing of the bat, and hear the bat-on-ball crack it made when it hit the man's skull. And I could see who the two armies were: the men in cloth caps were the strikers, they wanted more pay; the men in suits were the bosses who paid the truck drivers, along with their rich friends and the police, they wanted the drivers to stop striking and go back to work. I could understand all that. But I didn't know which side I was on.

It wasn't until later that my father told me his own strike story. He worked for Shell Oil as a salesman, driving around the state dressed in a white shirt and a suit, selling oil to businesses. Shell was dead set on keeping up deliveries to their stations, strike or no strike, and to make sure that happened the company assigned one man from the sales or office staff to go along with each delivery truck, driving his company car.

My father's assignment was to follow one of the big yellow-and-red tankers to a station on Eighth Street near the center of town. He did what he was told to do, and pulled up behind the truck in the gas station's driveway. He didn't know that the Central Labor Union headquarters was in the next block. As he got out of his car he looked up the street and saw a flood, a sea of strikers pouring out of the union building and running toward him waving clubs and bats and ax handles as they came. What should he do? How could he protect the truck from that roaring mob all by himself? He turned and ran into the station and into the toilet, climbed out the back window, and bolted for his car. The strikers were busy bashing the truck, the pumps, and the station windows; by the time they saw him he was starting his engine. They turned then and rushed after him as he drove off. They were so close, he said, he could see their screaming faces in his rearview mirror.

It wasn't an adventure for my father, or a funny story to be told. It was a humiliation. He had been given a job to do, and had tried to do it, as a man should. But he couldn't, he had to run away. He had failed his employer, and that mattered to him. But more than that, he had failed himself as a man. That was why he hadn't told me his story. He was ashamed.

I began to understand my father's distressful place in the strike. He was on both sides, and on neither. He respected the authority of the employers—they had a right to tell their workers to go back to work—but he despised their upper-class ways, their jodhpurs and their polo hats and their rich men's arrogance. He thought workers should be loyal to the men who paid them, but he understood why the truck drivers wanted more money; fifteen bucks a week wasn't much to feed a family on. And he hated both sides when they acted violently in mobs, like the one he had seen in his rearview mirror. He believed in independence and dignity and human kindness and hard work, the qualities that had kept his ancestors going halfway across America. But what good were those values in the middle of a strike in an American city in 1934? Whoever won this war, something he believed in would lose. It was sad, losing like that, and I felt his sadness. I knew which side I was on; I was on my father's side.

The truck strike wasn't the only news that summer. In July, John Dillinger was shot dead by FBI agents outside a movie theater in Chicago, and for a day or so his death took over the front-page headlines, pushing the governor and martial law to the inside pages. My father saw the picture of the death scene in the *Tribune* and said he knew the theater, it was the Biograph, up on the north side, he'd been to a movie there in his Chicago days (with my mother, I thought, but he didn't say so). That was the thing about the notorious crimes in our part of the country then;

they happened in familiar places. Banks were robbed in small towns in Minnesota and Iowa and the Dakotas and grown-ups said, "Oh yes, Owatonna, that's down below Faribault, I've been there"; a rich beer maker was kidnapped in St. Paul, and men said, "He's Hamm's Beer" in a proprietary way, as though by drinking his beer they had connected themselves to him, and had a claim on his front-page fame.

Crimes like those couldn't happen on West Thirty-fifth Street; we didn't have any banks, and who would kidnap Mr. Genakopolis, or the man who worked for the Northfield and Southern? But gangsters came close to our lives sometimes. A few weeks before he was shot dead, Dillinger rented an apartment on Thirty-third and Girard; that was over by Lake Calhoun, I could have ridden there on my bike and maybe seen him walk by. And a few weeks before that he shot his way out of a police ambush in St. Paul, just across the river.

We knew them, the kidnappers and the bank robbers and the murderers. Their pictures were on the front pages of the papers. We knew their names—Pretty Boy Floyd, Babyface Nelson, Ma Barker, Clyde Barrow, Bonnie Parker—and the stories of their lives. We knew that Pretty Boy Floyd's girlfriend was the daughter of a Minnesota farmer (my stepmother looked at her two daughters and crossed herself; I tried to imagine Eileen and Rose Marie as gun molls with rolled-down silk stockings and six-shooters on their hips, smoking cigars. Fat chance). We knew that John Dillinger carved a wooden pistol while he was in jail and used it to escape (Crown Point jail, my father said, up in Lake County; it was his part of Indiana). A girl I knew (but that was later) lived in an apartment down on Portland that had a bullet hole in the wall. Her mother said it was from John Dillinger's gun. She wouldn't let the superintendent cover it over; it was the only valuable thing in the whole place, she said.

I read about the robberies, and the car chases along country roads, certain that the criminals would eventually be caught, or die in roaring gun battles. Partly I wanted them to lose, because they were criminals; yet I was stirred by what they did, against the law and the odds. Grown-ups felt that way, too; the victims of the crimes—the banks, and the rich men who were kidnapped—were the powerful people, the ones who had everything. The robbers were more like us—poor nobodies from farms and small towns, people who owned nothing and had no hopes. In their crimes they were halfway to being Robin Hoods: they took from the rich; and if they kept what they stole, or spent it on guns and pleasures, well, that didn't seem so bad.

They were outlaws, of course. But outlaws were part of the country's story. Every kid knew about Billy the Kid and John Wesley Hardin and the Dalton boys and the James brothers. Jesse James was a part of Minnesota history; he robbed a bank down in Northfield, and was betrayed by a man he trusted. I could sing a sad song about him, about how the dirty little coward shot Mr. Howard and laid poor Jesse in his grave. Nobody sang songs about the cops and sheriffs who chased the robbers and sometimes killed them and sometimes got killed themselves.

So when Buck or Birdy or Cliff stood outside my kitchen screen door and said, "C'mon out, let's play guns," I knew how the game would go. We'd be the robbers: "Look at me! I'm Dillinger!" We'd find little kids to be the cops.

When we went out to play we went armed—with cap pistols from the dime store, which had the advantage of making gunlike noises, but more often with homemade rubberguns, because they cost nothing, and because you could shoot somebody with one.

This is what a rubbergun looked like:

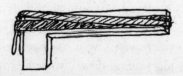

Here's how you make one. First, ask Mr. Kooihuizen, who runs the grocery store over on Nicollet, for an orange crate. He'll give you one, he has lots. It may not have contained oranges—all rectangular wooden boxes from the grocery store are called orange crates—but it will have half-inch wood ends, which are what you need. Cut an end piece into the shape of a handgun with a grip small enough to get your hand around. Steal a spring clothespin from your mother's clothespin bag and tack it onto the back of the handle. Go to a gas station—Pure Oil at Thirty-fifth and Nicollet or Standard Oil at Thirty-sixth—and ask the man for an old inner tube. He'll have one; you can only patch an inner tube so many times. Cut a wide rubber band from the tube and stretch it lengthwise around the barrel of the gun and back around the top of the clothespin, holding it shut. Cut a narrower rubber band and stretch it around the end of the barrel and pinch a fold of it in the jaws of the clothespin. When you squeeze the handle of the gun you'll release the stretched rubber band and it will fly at your target— not fast like a bullet, but slowly, like some flapping bird, and only about as far as you can spit. Still, it will be a real shot, and you might hit the kid you aim at.

Armed with such weapons, we lurked among the garages and garbage cans of Apple Alley, firing from ambush, shouting "I got you! I got you!" and "You never did! You missed me a mile!" staggering and falling when we were hit, clutching our wounded bodies and dying slowly, gasping last words—"You got me, you rat!"—and the gurgling sounds that dying villains made in the movies, long, fading "A-a-r-r-r-gh-ghs." And then jumped up to shoot and die again.

Sometimes we played our killing and dying games on an empty half block on Thirty-fourth Street that we called the Lot. Long ago, before the town grew, it had been a farm. Now it was just a city vacant lot, sloping down from the top at our end to a deep hollow at the other end, where people dumped garbage and cinders and landfill and kids hunted for broken things they could treasure. At the far corner, what was left of the farm's buildings stood: a ramshackle unpainted barn, a roofed-over cellar hole where the house had been, and a few trees that might once have been a sheltering grove. We climbed on the barn roof and played games in which it was a gangster's last hangout, or a mountain. For one long summer it was a Foreign Legion fort in the desert; we wore white painters' caps with handkerchiefs pinned down the back, and died perilously on the slooping roof. Through cracks in the roof we could look down on dusty farm machines—dead tools of a past farm life, just sitting there, waiting to rust into earth, into nothing.

We didn't use the cellar in our games. The glass was gone from the windows, we might have climbed through them, but we didn't; the darkness inside was too deep—how far would you fall, and what was down there? We peered in, and dared each other to climb through; but then we ran away into the sunlight to play some other shooting game.

Summer grew old at the end of August. The days were still hot, but nights were cooler; crickets chirred, and leaves at the ends of the longest branches of the trees turned autumn-colored. In backyards along Apple Alley the trees were heavy with fruit—green and hard looking, but apple-sized now. As we played Kick the Can we looked over the fences into the branches, and asked each other if the apples were ready, and finally, unable to wait longer, rushed into Old Man Lundstrom's yard and shook his tree wildly till apples fell in a drumroll to the ground, and shoved them into our shirtfronts and ran off and hid behind a garage and ate them.

The apples were hard and sour. They puckered my mouth and made a ball of gripe in my stomach that was sometimes so severe I had to go to bed. My father came and sat beside me.

"Colic," he said. "You get colic from eating apples before they're ripe. You have to learn to wait for things." I couldn't explain to him that of course there was no pleasure in the eating; the pleasure was in the stealing. When the Reverend Nelson told us in Sunday School about the Fall of Man, I understood the story at once; Adam and Eve had stolen God's apples—not red, ripe ones but like Old Man Lundstrom's, green as sin and with the tart taste of the forbidden. The stealing had made them ordinary humans with stomach-aches, like me.

If kids could steal apples it was still summer, and they were free. But September came, the earth tilted toward winter, school clothes came out of closets—woolly knickers smelling of moth-balls, and long stockings that wouldn't stay up—and apple steal-ers waited gloomily for the day when they would be sent to school again, where everything is rules.

In the first days of fall there was nothing to do. The season of summer games was over, nobody wanted to play ball or Kick the Can, and it was too early and too hot for football. We sat on Birdy's front steps in the September sun naming cars as they drove by, and were bored.

Birdy knew what we could do: we could go down to the dime store on Lake Street and snitch something. A toy car, maybe. Snitching was easy, he said. The toys were out there on the counters in front of you, you just took one. Dickie D. said everybody did it; he'd snitched lots of things. Nobody said it was *stealing:* it was snitching, swiping, hooking something. But we knew that stealing from the dime store wasn't like grabbing Old Man Lundstrom's apples. If we did it we'd be breaking the law, like Jesse James and Dillinger; we'd be outlaws.

And what if we were caught? I knew what would happen then; I'd been in trouble before. Once in the boardinghouse days before my father got married again, I had sneaked into an empty house with some other little kids, and one of them said, "I can pee higher than you can," and peed up the dining-room wall, and another kid tried, and I did, too (but I wasn't the highest), and then we all ran away. But somebody saw us, and that night a policeman came to our door, and my father stood talking to him in his deepest, most serious voice, and then he called me over and he and the policeman just looked down at me. And once over on Bloomington Avenue I teased my brother until he threw a stone at me and I ducked and the drugstore window I was standing in front of shattered and fell in pieces around my feet. It wasn't my fault, I didn't throw the rock, and it's natural to duck—or Chuck's either, he didn't mean to break the window. But he did, and my father had to buy a new window, and he was sore. So I knew what happened when you got into trouble.

We walked down to Lake Street, taking the route that kids took—not along the sidewalks but up Apple Alley and through the Lot and around the old barn and through the yards by the car barn where the streetcars stood waiting, and along the ballpark wall, and turned into Lake Street, past the New Lake movie (cardboard icicles dangling from the marquee said ARTESIAN COOLED, even though it was fall) and into the dime store. Except Dickie D.; he stayed outside—to keep watch, he said.

There seemed to be nobody there, only a woman sitting on a raised platform in the middle of the store playing the piano, demonstrating the sheet music that was for sale there, songs like "Red Sails in the Sunset" and "The Isle of Capri" that my stepmother sang in the kitchen while she worked. We drifted along the empty aisle, stealthy as bandits, to the toys. Cap guns. Dolls. Lotto games in boxes. Jump ropes. Roller skates. And cars: sports cars, racing cars, police cars, ambulances, dump trucks, fire engines. I looked left and right. Nobody. My hand crept up over the glass edge of the counter, closed on a little truck, and retreated to my pocket. Birdy was right, snitching was easy.

I didn't so much see as feel the huge presence looming beside me. A hand big as a catcher's mitt fell on my shoulder and a voice said: "What's that in your pocket?" I looked round and saw Birdy held as firmly by the other big hand. The manager: where had he come from? He began to talk about stealing, and how much we cost the store. We were thieves. Criminals. Birdy began to sniffle. We could be sent to reform school—to Glen Lake, or Red Wing! Birdy sniffled louder. But the man didn't say anything about calling the cops, and I began to think that maybe this wouldn't end with another policeman at my door.

The manager led us through the store, which was suddenly full of women clerks watching us with hard, disapproving stares, and down a flight of stairs into the basement. There he dumped us down on two boxes with a carton of brightly colored pencils between us and a ball of red string, and told us to tie a string to every one of the pencils. What for? A back-to-school display, he said. When you've done all the pencils I'll let you go.

There were hundreds of pencils. We tied and tied, not saying much. When we had finished we crept up the stairs and through the store past the staring eyes, past the piano player, out of the door to freedom. We had been caught stealing; and yet in a way we hadn't, since my father would never know. I hadn't succeeded in snitching a car; but then I didn't really want a car. What I wanted was wrongdoing without consequences, and I had managed that. So you might say, the Dime-store Job had been a success.

A week or so later I went to the movies and passed the dime store. There was the back-to-school display in the window, with our pencils hanging on their strings like a many-colored curtain behind the stacks of notebooks and lunch boxes. I thought the window looked very bright and appealing, and I felt a certain artist's pride that I had tied the strings that made the display so colorful. Even though no one would know.

CHAPTER FOUR

M y father and my stepmother were country people, born and raised. He grew up on a farm in La Porte County, Indiana, she came from Chickasaw County, Iowa. They lived in a city now, and would until they died, but their lives and habits remained country. They lived by the seasons, as farmers did, growing vegetables in the backyard in the summer and storing them in the fall, and they spoke the language of farms, talked about crops and weather, and used country measurements—a peck, a rod, a bushel. They knew the colors of the horses that pulled carts through the streets—bay, sorrel, dapple, roan, chestnut—and the varieties of country apples—Wealthies, Russets, Jonathans, Northern Spies. Their speech was flavored with country sayings: a hard row to hoe, plain as a mud fence, sucking the hind teat, flying the coop, locking the barn after the horse is stolen, give him a rod and he'll take an ell.

Together they ran the house we lived in like a farmer's house. They gave us all jobs to do; but they didn't call them jobs, they were *chores.* My chore was to empty all the wastebaskets every Saturday morning and burn the stuff in the wire incinerator in the backyard. Standing there poking the fire and watching the smoke lift feathers of ash and sparks, I was earning my twenty-five cents a week. I didn't get an allowance, like city kids; I worked for my money. We all did. Chuck swept the basement and mowed the lawn; my stepsisters washed the dishes and helped with the ironing. Only my stepbrother, Bill, was excused household chores because he went to the U and had a job in a Red Owl grocery store. His whole life was a chore.

You worked, in our house, and you never spent any money. Or if you did, it was because you had to, not because you wanted to. If you needed new sneakers because your little toe stuck right through the canvas of your old ones, you'd be taken downtown to buy a pair. But if you wanted long pants because all the other kids had long pants, you wouldn't get them; what difference did *wanting* make if you didn't *need?* My stepmother had a rhyme for such occasions:

> *Eat it up,*
> *Wear it out,*
> *Make it do,*
> *Or do without.*

We did all those things in my new house, until doing without became a habit, like sleeping with the window open in winter, and not wanting became easy, and spending difficult.

Spending isn't a gift you're born with; you have to learn how to be extravagant. On my birthday, one of those kid years, I was given two dollars and told to buy a toy. I walked all the way to the Sears store on Lake Street and spent an hour or more moving slowly along the counters of the toy department, looking at every single thing there. I didn't want any of them, any more than I really wanted the toy truck I stole from the dime store. But I was supposed to spend my two dollars and so finally, desperately, I bought a Detective Set—a badge and gun and handcuffs—and walked the long walk home crying, because I had spent my money for something I didn't want and didn't need, for a dumb old detective set. But that must have been earlier; I didn't cry when I was ten.

We lived by small economies at 104. When I came into the

bathroom in the morning, I would find an empty teakettle in the bathtub. My father had heated his shaving water in the kettle rather than light the hot-water heater in the basement, which would use more gas. On a bathroom shelf an old jam jar held slivers of soap too thin to wash your hands with. By adding a little water you could make a soapy goo that would do for washing your hair. Then you rinsed it with vinegar, which was cheaper than lemons and got the soap out just as well, but left you smelling like a pickle jar. In the evenings when the folks sat in the living room listening to "Amos and Andy," my stepmother mended socks, leaning close under the table lamp by her chair, pulling a sock over her wooden darning egg and poking at the holes with a big needle. When I wore through the soles of my school shoes, my father bought rubber half soles at the dime store and stuck them on with glue, like a patch on an inner tube.

Nobody bought pretty, unnecessary things for the house. We didn't have houseplants, except for the pot of mother-in-law's tongue that stood in the front window, or cut flowers, except in summer when zinnias and cosmos and asters were brought in from the backyard. In winter, when there were no free garden flowers, you could make a Depression Flower instead. My stepmother said it was easy. All you need is a biggish clinker from the furnace ashes, some salt from the kitchen box, and the bottle of iodine from the medicine cabinet. I put the clinker in a bowl, covered it with salt, and poured iodine over the top. Then I put the bowl in the pantry, and waited. After a long time crystals began to form on the clinker—green, blue, pale purple, all the cold wintry colors. I didn't think my Depression Flower was very pretty, or very much like a flower, but my stepmother said that wasn't the point; we had a decoration to put in the middle of the dining-room table; and it hadn't cost anything.

That's why my father smoked Raleigh cigarettes—a whole pack every day. He smoked when he got up in the morning, and after breakfast, he smoked when he read the paper, when he watered the lawn, and when he just sat on the back steps at the end of a summer day watching the light fade. He smoked at bedtime, and if he couldn't sleep at night he went into the bathroom and sat on the toilet and smoked. You could smell the stale smoke there the next morning. The first two fingers of his right hand were stained yellowy brown from cigarettes.

They were always Raleighs. He didn't like Raleighs much, he said they made his mouth taste like the ash pit in the furnace. But he smoked them anyway, because there was a coupon in every pack, and if you saved enough coupons you could get something nice for your house. Our inlaid-wood card table came from Raleigh coupons, and so did the 1847 Rogers silverware.

My stepmother was proud of her card table and her plated silver. And of other household objects, too: the upright piano in the corner of the living room; the black marble clock on the mantelpiece that struck the hours with a bong too deep for its size; the painting of *Old Ironsides* in full sail above the clock; the picture of a little girl listening to a robin over the sofa; the knight in armor, with hair as long as a girl's, standing beside his horse above the piano; the silver candlesticks on the dining-room table; the Haviland china—shiny white with a gold rim around the edge—that she'd bought by mail order when she was still a farm girl waiting to be married. A family that owned such treasures couldn't be called *poor*. But most of all she was proud of the two silver pheasants that stood, big as life (or almost), on the sideboard. Except for the pictures on the walls (and you *had* to have pictures, the way you had to have lace curtains) the pheasants were the only objects in the whole house that weren't useful for anything. Candlesticks hold candles, in case the lights go out; clocks tell the time; dishes are for eating from. But the pheasants just stood there, spreading their long silver tails, being beautiful.

Country-thinking folks don't buy anything they can make, not even their bedclothes. From time to time my stepmother summoned the women of her tribe of country Catholics to the house to make a quilt. They came bustling up the sidewalk, chattering and waving like emigrants off a ship: red-faced Aunt Gert, who was married to a German butcher; tall Aunt Margaret from La Crosse who didn't like small boys; Aunt Vera the nurse; Great-aunt Nellie, who drove a Packard big as a hearse and never stopped at stop signs. Irish as Paddy's pig, my father said when they came, and he withdrew to the basement or the backyard.

For days the quilting frame filled the living room, and around it the women sat stitching and gossiping, mostly about other women's ailments:

"A teacup of pus came out of it!"

"The tumor weighed fourteen pounds, and it had *hair* on it!"

"And *teeth!*"

"Her womb dropped, and she was never the same after that."

"And then she just took sick and died."

Where, I wondered, did these remarkable ailing women live? I didn't know any. Probably back in Iowa, on the farms from which the quilters had all come.

Sometimes the quilters stayed overnight. At supper they told stories as they ate, and because they and their kinfolks were all Catholics and had lots of babies, the stories were often about pregnancies and births and complications—how Cousin Norah conceived in her tubes, how Mary Margaret Kearney was three weeks overdue and still waiting, how somebody else had a breech birth and the doctor thought he'd lose them both. My father sat at the head of the table looking down at his food, not saying anything.

Aunt Vera had the best birthing stories because she was a nurse. "The delivery was terrible," she said, "it went on for twelve hours . . ." and "they took her to the delivery room and she hemorrhaged right there . . ." *Delivery,* she said, and *delivery,* as though a baby was a package the mailman brought. At the word my father looked up from his plate. "I delivered a baby once," he said. Aunt Vera stopped talking. "It was when I was in Wyoming working on Will McIntosh's ranch." (That was when he was a cowboy. I knew what he looked like then, there was a picture of him and his horse in the family album.)

"My sister, Elva, was married to Will. She was expecting her first child in late September, so early in the month Will took the buggy and drove to Laramie to buy what supplies we needed so he could be at home when the baby came, to go for the doctor and all that. Well, no sooner was he out of sight than Elva began to yell. She'd gone into labor. There was nobody else around for miles, not a soul. So I had to be the doctor. I did everything." (He didn't say exactly what *everything* was, though I'd like to have known.) "And now that baby is Young Will McIntosh.

Over six feet tall!" He looked around the circle of women triumphantly. They stared back, silenced by the impossibility of the true story they'd just heard.

I wasn't surprised, though; of course my father could deliver a baby. And it would make sense, too; you'd save money on the doctor. Doctors cost money; that's why we never called one to our house. For the ailments we had, my stepmother was the physician, with my father as consultant if things got serious. Between them they treated colds, fevers, flu (my father called it "the grip"), stomach-aches, ringworm, cuts, bruises, sick headaches, growing pains, mumps, chicken pox, and nosebleeds.

For the commonest kid-sicknesses they had handed-down rules:

Starve a fever, stuff a cold.
No solid food till the fever goes.
One full day in bed after your temperature is normal.

And handed-down remedies:

Vicks on a flannel rag on your chest for a cold.
Milk of Magnesia for constipation.
Sloan's Liniment for sore muscles and growing pains.
Honey and lemon for a sore throat.

If I had a bad cold or the flu I stayed in bed, and my stepmother came and sat beside me. She didn't stick a thermometer in my mouth, she simply laid her hand gently on my forehead, feeling the difference between her cool palm and my hot skin. If I had a fever she put me into a deep steaming bath until I was boiled pink all over, and then hurried me back into bed and piled blankets on top. "Sweat it out," she said. "A good sweat will cure you." When I had sweated the sheets to clammy wetness, she wrapped me in a blanket, carefully, as though I was a valuable parcel, or a baby, and left me in a big chair while she changed the bed. When I got back in, the clean sheets were cool and dry. Clean sheets on a Thursday!

Sick-kid diets were handed down, too. When I had the flu my stepmother brought me cambric tea. It was really only hot water with milk and sugar in it, but because I was only given it when I was sick, it seemed a special treat, a privilege of the bedridden. I sat up in bed in my blue plaid bathrobe, propped against pillows, and sipped the tea and read Tom Swift. After the fever went I was given food that was solid, but just barely: junket, and tapioca pudding that looked like fish eyes, and then milk toast, and after that poached eggs, and Jell-O, and then I was well and ate what everybody else ate and nobody spoiled me anymore.

The folks had absolute confidence in their doctoring. When I cut my leg fighting with Birdy over whose turn it was to play with my sheath knife, I ran bleeding and yelling into the house and my stepmother calmly poured some Mercurochrome over the wound and wrapped it in a bandage. Why see a doctor about just a cut? And so it healed not as a faint scar but as a raised welt like a pink caterpillar. Nothing wrong with scars on a boy, she said. And when I came home from the Lot with an aching, swollen finger I'd hurt reaching wide for a grounder after the sun had gone down, my father said at once, "It's out of joint," and gripping the finger in his big fist he gave it a sharp pull and let go. "That'll fix it," he said. But it didn't, because the finger was broken. He had to take me to the doctor, who put a splint on it and charged him ten dollars.

My teacher said I had ringworm. When I told my stepmother she said I couldn't have that, only poor children had ringworm. But my father said it was ringworm all right, but he knew how to cure it. He took a piece of shiny brown wrapping paper and made a funnel and held it upright with the pointed end down over a spoon, and lit the top edge. Brown liquid dripped from the hole at the bottom into the spoon. He smeared the liquid on my sore, and after a while the sore went away. My father didn't say anything about the treatment, but I could see he was pleased and relieved, after the finger.

It was my stepmother's cookery that showed most clearly how frugal we were in my house. It was an odd kind of cooking, sometimes country-made from ingredients grown in the back-yard, or home-preserved and brought up from the cellar, or bought by my father from farmers' roadside stands, and some-times city—put together out of grocery-store cans. We ate many kinds of casseroles: tuna, chicken, chipped beef. Here is one of her recipes:

CHIPPED BEEF CASSEROLE

2 cans mushroom soup
2 cans water
4 hard-boiled eggs (sliced)
¼ lb. sharp Cheddar cheese (grated)
2 pkg. dried chipped beef (cut up)
1 7-oz. pkg. Creamettes (uncooked)

Mix all ingredients day before and refrigerate overnight. Bake one hour at 350 degrees. Serves 10–12.

There's a lot of my stepmother in that recipe: the canned mushroom soup, an ingredient in most of her casseroles; *creamettes* rather than just noodles (she was always turning brand names into common nouns: *frigidaire* for refrigerator, *kodak* for camera, *bissell* for sweeper); the confident belief that this dish would feed twelve

people. And the cheapness of it: she'd get all the ingredients at the
Red Owl for a dollar, and you could make it even cheaper by
cutting down on the chipped beef and increasing the amount
of creamettes.

All my stepmother's everyday recipes were as cheap and plain
as that one, though some had foreign names that suggested (quite
inaccurately) that her cooking was international: Swiss steak,
Hungarian goulash, and, most exotic of all, African chow mein.

AFRICAN CHOW MEIN

1 lb. hamburger
1 chopped onion
1 cup celery chopped
½ cup raw rice
1 can mushroom soup
1 can chicken rice soup
2 cups water (use soup cans)
4 Tbsp. soy sauce
2 Tbsp. Worcestershire sauce

Brown hamburger and onion together. Mix all ingredients in large bowl. Bake in small roaster—stir often.
Put in casserole and chow mein noodles on top.

I asked her why it was called *African*. She laughed and said it
just was.

Sunday was special, it was a feast day. We had beef most Sundays, Swiss steak, or a pot roast; when I came home from Sunday
School I could smell the cooking meat as I came in the door, and
hear my stepmother in the kitchen, stirring pots and singing.

There were always two graces said on Sundays, one for the
Catholic part of the family and one for the Protestants. My father spoke first. He addressed his God in a special, high-pitched

voice, the same voice he used when he talked long distance on the telephone; he seemed to believe that the phone was a hollow tube, and the farther away your listener was the higher you needed to pitch your voice to reach him. God, being farthest away, was at the top of my father's scale, almost a falsetto. His grace was always an extemporized message, like a family letter, giving God the news of how things were going on West Thirty-fifth Street, and expressing gratitude when he could think of anything special to be grateful for. Then he turned the occasion over to his wife, like a man handing on the telephone.

Her grace was different, a Catholic formula that never varied, spoken in a flat conversational voice, as though God was very near, under the table or in the kitchen watching over the Swiss steak. She briskly asked for His blessing, and wound up—or I heard it this way—with "through Thy bountiful crest, amen." I imagined God's bountiful crest to be a sort of cornucopia, like the one in the picture on the dining-room wall, from which flowed fruits and vegetables and a dead pheasant, all supplied by Him in return for our double-barreled thanks.

Then we settled down to eating. The beef, however long it had been cooked, covered with stewed tomatoes and onions or just sitting there in its own juices, would be tough and gristly. My father would chew and chew, his false teeth making a little pop at each movement of his jaw because they didn't quite fit, and finally he would say, more in resignation then resentment, "Seems like the longer I chew the bigger it gets." There were also mashed potatoes and gravy and vegetables, and sometimes homemade Parker House rolls. My stepmother didn't bake bread—Wonder Bread was perfectly good, she said—but Parker House rolls were to her mind festive. It must have been the shape; they tasted pretty much like Wonder Bread.

At Thanksgiving and Christmas we ate turkey, like everybody else. On those days my stepmother brought out her Haviland china and the Irish tablecloth and napkins, and I wore a necktie and was at my place at the table early. The turkey, roasted brown and steaming, was carried in from the kitchen in a procession and placed in front of my father at the head of the table. After the two graces (longer than usual because it was a holiday) he began to carve, asking each of us "Dark meat or light?" and making sure that the two youngest at the table (my brother and me) got drumsticks. Then he gave himself the neck. It seemed odd to me that he should prefer that piece, since it was nothing but bones and skin, but he said a turkey was tastiest at the top end and worst at the bottom (he called that part the pope's nose). When I was older I realized that he had been denying himself for the sake of the rest of us, but even then I didn't give him much credit. I just assumed that self-denial came easily to him, that he didn't have a greedy Self to be fulfilled and pleasured, as I had.

I never asked my father about his habit of self-sacrifice, and he never said anything about it to me. Not until the day he died. He was nearly eighty then, still a big man, but hollowed out by sickness and pain (it was emphysema). That October afternoon he lay motionless and silent in the hospital bed, and I sat silently beside him, watching him trying to breathe. Then suddenly he opened his eyes and spoke. Not to me—he was looking straight up at the ceiling—but to the world, or perhaps to God. "I gave up a lot," he said. So it hadn't been easy, or natural to him. He knew what it had cost him to be the man he was; but I never would, because I was afraid to ask him what he was remembering. And then he died.

Months, maybe years later, I found in his Bible a little cutting from some religious publication. It read:

HOW THEY DIED

Simon Peter—crucified head downward
Andrew—crucified

James—beheaded by King Herod Agrippa
John—persecuted but survived
Philip—crucified
Bartholomew—flayed alive and beheaded
Matthew—stabbed to death with a spear or a sword
Thomas—killed with a spear
James the Less—beaten or stoned to death
Jude—clubbed to death
Simon—chopped to pieces
Matthias—killed with an ax.

Twelve apostles, eleven martyrs: his heroes, his models for living and dying.

The woman who had become my stepmother was a small, percolating sort of person, energetic and country-strong. Only her eyes were weak; she wore glasses that were thick as the bottom of a Pepsi bottle and made her eyes look liquid and indistinct, like the eyes of a fish in a fishbowl. Without her glasses she could see nothing; with them she saw her world with unforgiving clarity—dust on a tabletop, an unpaid bill on the desk, dandelions on the lawn where there should be only grass—and bustled to set each small disorder right (or in the case of the dandelions sent me). Neatness and order were more than housewife's habits for her; they were moral principles. The mother-in-law's tongue stood in the exact center of the table in the front window, the roller blinds were all drawn down to the precise same length, the pillows on the sofa stood in a line like soldiers on parade. Everything was parallel or at right angles to everything else: picture frames to the floor, rugs to the wall, the sofa and easy chair to each other. Outside the walls of our house disorder swirled and crashed like spring ice in the river: debt, poverty, dirt, the loss of a job or even a house, hunger and cold were all out there. Only perfect order inside would keep our protective walls standing.

Every room had its rules. They weren't written down, but I knew what they were. In the kitchen:

Don't dry your face on the dishtowel.
Don't drink straight from the bottle of cold water in the icebox.
Don't drink straight from the milk bottle, either.
Don't walk on the linoleum when I've just scrubbed it.

In the bathroom:

Don't use all the hot water.
Turn the hot-water heater off before you take a bath.
Don't change your towel too often.

In my bedroom:

Hang up your clothes.
Don't leave anything in your pockets that will go bad and smell.
Pull up your bed. (You don't have to make it; just pull the bedclothes toward the top so it *looks* made.)

I didn't obey these rules, but I liked knowing what they were. What would be the good of breaking a rule if you didn't know what the rule was?

My stepmother saved and ordered everything: recipes written on three-by-five cards and filed alphabetically in shoe boxes; old report cards in envelopes, each one labeled with the contents; photographs—always of people, most of them family—pasted in albums, the people and places identified and the occasions dated. Life was like housekeeping: a place for every-thing and everything in its place; waste not want not; see a pin and pick it up, all the day you'll have good luck.

Her vitality wore us out. On the darkest winter morning she would burst into the bedroom I shared with my brother, cheer-fully reciting lines from a poem she'd learned in school, "The lark is up to meet the sun, the bee is on the wing," when we knew there was no lark and no sun, it wasn't even daylight; in summer she swept us down to the basement after breakfast to pick over bushels of Concord grapes that she boiled to make grape jelly (I scraped the big boiling pot with a wooden spoon and ate the sweet purple goo, and made myself so sick I could never eat grape jelly again). When we all went to Minnehaha Park for a picnic, she challenged us kids to a footrace and beat us all and flopped on the grass at the end, puffing and laughing because she could run faster than anyone. She didn't run the way most women and girls ran, with their knees together and their legs kicking out at angles, but like a boy, striding.

There were times when her energy failed her, when she lay on the bed in her darkened room, motionless, like a body in a funeral parlor. Her daughters brought cold compresses for her head, and she said nothing—sometimes for days. Migraine head-aches, my father said. We tiptoed on the stairs, and spoke in whis-pers, and the bustling life of the house stopped, as though the machine that drove it had broken down. Blown her gaskets, I thought, not knowing exactly what gaskets were, but only that when they blew, the machine stopped.

My father told me to call this woman "mother"; but I couldn't. I knew she wasn't my mother. My mother was dead. When I was away from home, at school or in somebody else's house, I referred to her as my stepmother; at home when I needed to speak to her I planted myself in front of her and looked in her face, thus avoiding the need for any form of address at all.

If I *had* to call her mother, because my father was there, or some nosy relative, I would, but I'd mentally cross my fingers so it didn't count. In my mind I had no name for her at all, except *her*.

Perhaps she felt that denying space between us, and accepted it. She didn't try to be affectionate in physical, demonstrative ways that I might shrink from; she wasn't a hugger and kisser. (But that was true of most of the mothers I knew; the language of affectionate gestures wasn't spoken much on West Thirty-fifth Street.) Instead, she treated me as though I were a kid in her one-room schoolhouse, and made teaching the bond between us.

Some of the things she taught me were straight from the schoolroom. She made spelling bees into parlor games, and competitions to name the capitals of all the states: when I was ten I not only knew that Montpelier was the capital of Vermont, I knew it only had one *l* in it.

She taught me other things, too, things she'd learned along her way. When she first came to Minneapolis, a farmer's widow with three small children, she took a course in a beautician's school down on Hennepin Avenue, hoping to support her family by working in a beauty parlor. She didn't, but she remembered her lessons, and one winter evening she taught me how to give a manicure: how first you soak the fingers in warm soapy water, then you trim the cuticle and push it back with a little piece of wood called an orange stick, then you paint the nails with polish, and finally you shove some white stuff under the edge of each nail to make it look clean. We sat facing each other at a card table in the living room, the bowl of soapy water between us, the table lamp making a puddle of light on our hands and arms, while I bent over her fingers, concentrating, trying to do it all right. And I was proud of myself when I did.

Why did she teach me that useless skill? Perhaps because she was a natural teacher, for whom teaching was a habit, or a deep need; better teach anything, any skill or fact, than not teach. Or because teaching was a kind of ordering, putting details in the right places, and in her mind all order was good. Or maybe because in her house there was a small boy who distrusted her and refused to come within the circle of her country warmth.

Manicuring was something only girls did, but that didn't bother her. She had no sense that work had gender; work was an indifferentiated heap of things to be done, like the pile of dirty laundry at the bottom of the laundry chute: don't argue about who should wash it or it will never get washed. Just do it. So she cheerfully taught me skills that in other houses on our block were done only by women: to press my own pants, to cook my own breakfast, to make my own bed. If no one in the house was ever idle, if everyone worked at something, anything, from dawn till bedtime, we might just manage to get it all done, to keep the house and our lives tidy, and hold the world outside at bay.

Sometimes while we worked together, or on Sundays when we sat around the dining-room table after dinner, she told stories from her Iowa life—about the farm, and the neighbors, and the folks in the little town, and about the one-room schoolhouse where she had been first a student and then, after her husband died, the teacher. I liked her winter stories best: how when she was a child walking to school in winter, a mile across the fields, the wind blew so fiercely out of the north that she had to walk backward into it, or hang on to George Anderson's coattails and be pulled along through the drifts; and how when they reached the school the wood-burning stove was cold, and there was ice in the tin washbasin, and their syrup sandwiches were frozen in their lard-can lunch pails.

Another wintry story came from later, when she was grown up. One day she had to go into town on some urgent errand, maybe someone was sick. She harnessed the horse to the cutter and—

What's a cutter?

A sort of buggy on runners, like a big sled
—wrapped the children in blankets and set off. It had snowed
heavily all night, and the track to the highway was drifted and
hard to follow. Ahead of her through the blowing snow she
thought she saw a great hump in the track. A drift, she thought.
If she tried to go around it she'd slide into the ditch; she had to
drive straight ahead and over it. When she was past it she looked
back, and as she did the hump rose slowly up and walked away.
"It was a cow!" And she laughed out loud, remembering. Her
laugh was like nobody else's. You could hear it from across the
street—a high whoop of delight, followed by a high-pitched
chattering, *heh-heh-heh-heh,* like a hen that has just laid a very
funny egg, or an egg that tickles.

A neighbor died one winter—winter again, as though her
imagination was an icebox stored with frozen things that memory thawed out—and his family couldn't bury him in the frozen
earth. So they stood him upright in a corner of the corncrib to
wait for spring. He stood there all winter, and when—*whoop!
heh-heh-heh-heh*—when they went out in the dark to get a pail
of cobs for the pigs, they *talked* to him!

That was a funny story, sort of. Other stories were funny
in different ways. She told us about Emma Heimerdinger, a
Bohemian woman with a cleft palate who lived on the next
farm, mimicking her garbled speech—"Idonowatdemattah, Lel-
lie, datpigwongoinnabarn!"—and weeping with laughter, not
maliciously but simply because poor Emma made such funny
noises. "She had such a brogue!" my stepmother said. For her,
every kind of speech that wasn't clear American Midwestern
was a brogue, and all brogues were funny. Indeed, most of what
was different from the life she knew was comical to her. Her
story about how, when her father slaughtered a pig, the Bohemian neighbors came running with pudding bowls to catch
the blood was a comic recital of other people's oddness. "They

made sausage out of it!" she would say, astonished and amused. And when she told us about Billy Bruekel, who ran a store in Jerico that was both a bakery and a barbershop, and how the hair got into the pastry, that was a funny story, too. She had cleaned too many barns and babies and been in at the birthing of too many calves and colts to be squeamish about eating blood, or dirt ("you'll eat a peck of dirt before you die," she said), or a hair in the strudel. It was all life.

My father's stories were less heroic and less funny. He had had his share of hard times, too, but he didn't talk about them, or tell winter's tales. Only occasionally he would recall his growing-up days on the farm, and his voice would grow warm with remembered happiness. As in the story of the horse race. My grandfather had gone to town, and my father and his brother Lee decided that while he was away they'd race the farm's two horses along the dirt road that ran past the place. It wouldn't be the kind of race where jockeys sit on the horses' backs; races like that were wicked, people bet money on them. It would be a sulky race like the ones they saw at the county fair, where each horse pulls a little cart—just two big wheels, with a seat for the driver between them. There were no such carts on the farm, but the boys improvised; Lee, being older, got the buggy, and my father drove the wagon. At the start of the race Lee and the buggy were way ahead, but then my father in the wagon began to move up (when he told me this part I imagined him on his feet in the wagon like a charioteer, yelling and cracking his whip) until they were galloping up the road side by side. And then the wheels interlocked, and the buggy's wheel flew off, and Lee fell in the ditch, and my father won. But the buggy was pretty much wrecked. The story must have ended in some stern punishment, but my father didn't tell me about that; for him it wasn't a story about boys doing something wrong, it was story of happiness, of one time, in the days when he and the brother he loved were kids, when for a little while farm life ceased to be hard work and became joyous. I felt that remembered joy; it must have been like stealing apples.

He told me about his country Halloweens. They weren't like ours, in the city. We went out after supper and rang doorbells and ran away, and scribbled on window screens with soap or, if we hated the people in house, with canning wax (which is almost impossible to get out of a screen), and we made ticktacks with the wooden spools that thread comes on, and rattled them against people's windows. It all seemed tame and sissy compared to what my father and his friends did. They stole folks' front gates and put them on chicken-coop roofs, they stole pump handles and hid them. Once they pushed a privy over while a mean neighbor was inside on the throne and it fell on the door side, so he couldn't get out that way, and there was no other way out except through the hole in the seat. My father smiled when he told that story, not a *now* smile but backward looking, to his youth, when it had been fun to be him, in the country dark on an October night.

There was another difference between my father's country memories and those my stepmother called up. For her, Chickasaw County was a place she could go back to, where her father still worked the land he had always worked and she still owned the little farm where she and her first husband had lived and her children had been born. Relatives and old friends lived down there on farms and in the little towns around; she could reenter that world of her childhood and young womanhood whenever she wanted to, and she'd be welcome. But for my father, La Porte County and Rolling Prairie, the village near the farm where he'd grown up, were lost places. No members of his family lived there now, the home place was farmed by strangers. For him, those places were Eden before the Fall.

Near the end of his life, when he was ill and tired, my father asked me to drive him from his house south of Chicago to Rolling Prairie. We drove down the expressway, around East Chicago past all the industrial junk at the bottom end of Lake Michigan, and into Indiana to La Porte, the county seat of my father's home county, the capital of his beginning.

I drove slowly along the town's main street, through the deep shade of old trees. Maples, my father said; folks used to call La Porte the Maple City. There's the Court House. That's the High School where I went. And there's the Old People's Home where your grandmother lived. Died there.

I remembered that quiet, shaded old house. I had been there before. When I was six, the time we drove east through the Great Plains blizzard, we stopped in La Porte for Thanksgiving dinner with my grandmother. She was very small and fragile looking, like an old china doll sitting there in her rocking chair. On a table beside her she kept a small glass globe with a tiny town inside; when you turned the globe over snow fell on the town. While my father talked with his mother I turned and turned the globe, watching the snow fall.

Beyond the town a country road between cornfields and orchards led to Rolling Prairie. There was nothing much there, only a few white frame houses with porches facing the road and a church and a store with a gas pump in front.

"Stop here," my father said. I pulled the car onto the grassy shoulder.

"That's the house where your mother and I were married."

It was the house in the old photograph of my parents when they were young—a tired-looking place now, needing paint, the climbing ivy and the rosebush by the porch gone, but the same house. My father sat silently, far from the moment, back in that other time when he had been happy, before all the things that would happen afterward had happened. Finally he said, "Let's go." He didn't speak all the way home.

That story has an epilogue. After his death I drove once more to Rolling Prairie, this time with my brother, to show him where our parents were married. When we reached the place, the house wasn't there. It had burned to the ground, only fire-blackened stones and the stump of a chimney remained. It was as though the house, old and tired like my father, had waited until he could see it once more, and then had given up its life.

My stepmother was an economical woman. She wasted nothing and missed no chance to add a dollar or a dime to the family purse. Her yard sales were famous: she would search the attic and the cellar and everybody's closet for anything that wasn't necessary to the family's existence—old clothes, old flowerpots, old toys, an electric iron that no longer heated, old magazines, cups and saucers that didn't match—and put the whole lot out for sale. My father said she'd fill a jam jar with rusty nails and sell it for a nickel.

In her world everybody worked. Household chores, of course. But chores weren't enough, the money you got for doing chores was family money, so it didn't count. She found us all jobs. "I've got you a job," she'd say when I came home from school. "You start tomorrow." Her words were like a judge's sentence, no appeal was possible, because of course if you had a job—even one you hadn't asked for—you had to do it. I sold magazines—*Liberty* and *The Saturday Evening Post* door-to-door. I stuck handbills under the windshield wipers of cars. On Saturdays I delivered groceries.

Among my friends in the neighborhood my stepmother acquired a reputation for finding me jobs; they saw her as a natural force, a blizzard of jobs that never stopped snowing. Buck said if she was stuck on a desert island she'd get me a job shoveling sand; "Nellie's relentless," he said. Not "your mother," or "your stepmother": *Nellie*. He must have heard my father call her by her name, and picked it up; it had the right note of irreverence toward a parent. So my stepmother became "Nellie" to the neighborhood gang, and to me, too, in my mind, though I didn't call her Nellie to her face. I didn't call her anything.

Nellie was the center of our household life; like the stove in the middle of her country schoolhouse, she warmed everyone around her. She fed us (Swiss steak and African chow mein), she clothed us (mackinaws and galoshes and hand-me-down coats that still had plenty of good wear in them), she bossed and scolded us, she taught us (the capitals of the states, manicuring). When we were unhappy she told us funny stories about Emma Heimerdinger; when we were sick she made us cambric tea; when we were well she gave us chores.

I liked her. I liked the way she faced troubles and laughed at them, I liked her rough kindness and her tolerance. But I held back from her comfortable warmth; *mothers* comforted, she wasn't my mother. Her own children were like the kids in the schoolroom nearest the stove; I was in an outer circle, my back chilly from the outside cold, refusing to be warm. (So was Chuck, I suppose, though he didn't say so.)

You can see that willed chilliness in the first book I ever wrote: *Past Present Future,* a hand-lettered autobiography done as a school assignment when I was thirteen. The book is dedicated "to my mother, whose memories I cherish." Nellie had been my stepmother for four years then, but she is not mentioned in the chapter that describes those years, until the last page.

It's obvious that I meant the chapter to end with the next-to-last paragraph on that page. The one-sentence paragraph that follows is written in a different ink.

Why the reluctant addition? I imagine the scene. My father sits in his big chair in the parlor, reading my little book. When he comes to the end of that last page, he stops and looks across the room at me. Or rather, at my feet, because I'm lying on the

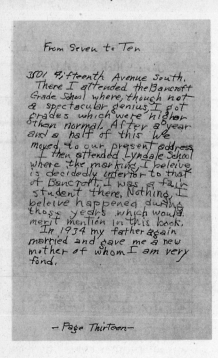

From Seven to Ten

3501 Fifteenth Avenue South.
There I attended the Bancroft
Grade School where, though not
a spectacular genius, I got
grades which were higher
than normal. After a year
and a half of this We
moved to our present address.
I then attended Lyndale School
where the marking, I believe
is decidedly inferior to that
of Bancroft, I was a fair
student there, Nothing, I
beleive happened during
those years which would
merit mention in this book.
In 1934 my father again
married and gave me a new
mother of whom I am very
fond.

— Page Thirteen —

floor with my head under the radio, listening to "Jack Armstrong," or maybe "Chandu the Magician." The radio is a tall Philco that stands on slender legs as though it thinks it's a piece of furniture. I like to lie this way when I listen, looking up into the inside of the radio, though it's mostly empty space up there, with only the speaker cone attached to the front and the little lighted dial at the top. From my position underneath the radio the sounds of the stories are round and echoing; I am closer to Jack Armstrong than people sitting in the room are.

"Son," my father says, with as much sternness as he has in him, "you can't say *nothing* about your stepmother." I say "All right," and come out from under the radio and get a pen from the desk in the dining room and write one more sentence: "In 1934 my father again married and gave me a new mother of whom I am very fond." Nothing about love, just "very fond"— a phrase you might use to describe your feeling for a distant cousin, or pickled peaches. I write it because I have to. But I write it with a chilled heart. She's still not my mother.

CHAPTER FIVE

In the photograph I straddle a bicycle that is slightly too tall for me; the toe of my shoe barely touches the ground to steady me. I am wearing knickers, the baggy kind known around school as shitcatchers, and knee-length stockings of a bold criss-cross pattern, a white shirt and sleeveless sweater, and a necktie. It seems an oddly formal outfit for bicycle riding, but the occasion is my birthday; I'm eleven, and this is my first bike, a present from my father. It's secondhand, and has skinny tires; I wish it was new and had balloon tires. Still, I'm glad I own it, you can see that in the look on my face, a kind of smiling determination. On my bike I will ride out of this safe familiar backyard with its

lilac bushes and its broken fence and its iris bed, away from the security of my house and my block into unfamiliar streets beyond, to somewhere else. As I ride, the pull of home will weaken, and I'll be free—to seek out scary dangers, to take a chance or a dare, to go where I'm forbidden to go, to get into trouble. I've passed out of one stage of childhood into the next: on my bike I'm no longer a little kid, I'm a kid.

My little-kid neighborhood, before the bike, reached as far as I could walk, from Powderhorn Park where I played to Aldrich Avenue where I went to Sunday School, and from Lake Street where the dime store and the movie were to Thirty-eighth Street where our family dentist had his office until he threw an epileptic fit on the steps of Incarnation Church, after which he retired. The folks were horrified that an epileptic had been drilling on my teeth. I wished I'd been there when the seizure came on him. I'd never seen a person have a fit.

Now that I was a kid on a bike, my neighborhood grew, became as big as the whole south side. I learned then what a sensible town Minneapolis was; there was no reason for streets to curve in such a flatland place, so they didn't; they ran straight north and south and straight east and west like the lines on a checkerboard. And they were sensibly named: the east-west ones were called streets and were numbered consecutively starting downtown by the river, and the north-south ones were called avenues and were numbered starting with First Avenue on the other side of Nicollet and continuing east all the way to Forty-eighth Avenue over by the river. In the other direction, going west, the Avenues beyond Lyndale were just as sensible, only alphabetical. Every kid I knew could recite the names in order: Aldrich Bryant Colfax Dupont Emerson Fremont Girard Humboldt Irving—mostly names of famous Americans, my teacher said, though out around the lakes, where the difficult letters were, the namers had settled for any word that began with the right letter: Queen Avenue, Xerxes, Zenith. Beyond Zenith another alphabet began, but there was no reason to learn those names, they were too far away to matter.

A kid on a bike might reasonably believe that this sensible town had been planned specially for him, so that however far he rode he could find his way home. Except for the streets right around my house. There, though the east-west streets were numbered in order, the avenues made no sense at all. Going west from my house, they went Blaisdell, Pillsbury, Pleasant, Grand, Harriet, Garfield, Lyndale. Why those names, in that order? Some I knew about: Pillsbury was on the bags of flour in our kitchen, and Garfield was a president of the United States who was shot by a crazy man and died. But who was Blaisdell? And why Pleasant? Was life pleasanter there than it was on Garfield? Was Grand grander than Lyndale? And who was Harriet? So some of the names meant something and some didn't, and the order they were in wouldn't help you if you were lost. My part of town was only *half*-sensible.

Another set of names was scattered across the city not for rational but for poetic reasons. They were Indian names: not of *real* Indians, not taken from history, but from a poem our teacher read to us in school, *The Song of Hiawatha.* "By the shores of Gitche Gumee, by the shining Big-Sea-Water": I liked the rhythm of it, like girls playing hopscotch, and the long Indian words—Mudjekeewis, who killed the great bear Mishe-Mokwa with his war club, and the south wind, Shawondasee, and the north wind, the fierce Kabibonokka—words that were like savage songs, or war dances. And it all happened right here in Minnesota where I lived. But different then, before there were cities or farms or even roads, only the woods and the lakes, the animals and the Indians, and the spirits that were in everything.

Back in time, when the city began to grow, when it stopped being St. Anthony's Falls and became Minneapolis, back then the men who named the streets borrowed names from Longfellow's poem and stuck them on places in town: Hiawatha the Indian brave became a long street that stretched all the way out to the river at Fort Snelling, and a school, too; Minnehaha, his sweetheart, became an avenue, a parkway, a creek, a waterfall, and a park (where there was a statue of Hiawatha carrying her across a stream, and one of her breasts was bare!); Nokomis, Hiawatha's mother, was a lake, a junior high school, and a movie theater at Thirty-eighth and Chicago.

It seemed odd at first, to name streets and schools and even churches after Indians in a poem that wasn't even true; but after a while I figured it out. *The Song of Hiawatha* was the only poem that was ever written about Minnesota; Minnesota just wasn't poetic. And the man who wrote the poem was famous, he was just about the most famous American poet there was. We read his poems in school, memorized them, recited them in class: "It was the schooner Hesperus that sailed the wintry sea," "Under the spreading chestnut tree the village smithy stands," "Listen, my children, and you shall hear." Everybody knew Longfellow's poems. Even my father, who had never read a poem in his life, would say when Nellie was frazzled after a hard day's work that she looked like the wreck of the Hesperus, and if I was grouchy he called me Old Rain-in-the-Face. Longfellow was in our language and our lives, so why shouldn't he be on our streets? Why shouldn't there be a Minnehaha Liquor Store, a Hiawatha Motor Company, a Nokomis Meat Market?

Our neighborhood was a safe place for kids; you could get into trouble there, but not into danger. But if you rode farther off there was danger enough, and plenty of chances to do what you were forbidden to do. West of us there were the swimming lakes—Calhoun, Harriet, and Cedar—a long way, but not too far for a kid on a bike. It was an adventure to set off on a hot summer morning, wearing your bathing suit under your pants and carrying a towel and a bag of lunch in your bike basket, with your mother on the porch shouting warnings and instructions after you—"Don't go in deep, don't swim for an hour after you eat, don't go beyond the ropes!"—knowing that you were going where her voice couldn't reach you and her rules wouldn't apply.

The ropes enclosed the soupy warm shallows of the lake near the beach, the part that was safe for little kids to paddle in. A kid who had outgrown that splashing, bucket-and-shovel, inner-tube-wearing stage would go—would *have* to go—beyond the ropes into the deep water and swim flailing out to the wooden dock where big kids sunbathed and laughed and did jackknife dives from the board and pushed each other into the water. Out there the pebbly lake bottom fell away steeply and suddenly. That was the drop-off. If you reached your foot down you wouldn't touch anything but water, nothing you could stand on while you caught your breath. And if you sank, there would be no one to help you. Kids died swimming in the lakes, I read about them in the paper: TWO BOYS DROWN AT LAKE STREET BEACH—and I'd read on, because it could have been me; "they went out beyond the ropes," "stepped into a drop-off," "the water was over their heads." Down in the cold dark below the sunlit surfaces, that was where you died.

There were plenty of other risks a kid could take. You could go over to Powderhorn Park. Powderhorn was the only place in the neighborhood that wasn't flat as your dining-room table. Long ago a glacier had gouged out a deep hollow there four blocks long and five blocks wide. The name came from its shape, wide at one end and pointed at the other, like the cow horns the settlers carried their gunpowder in, but if you weren't a settler it was easier to think of the park as like a bathtub, and the small stagnant lake at the bottom as a clogged drain. You could go there in early winter before the lake was frozen solid and skate out onto the ice and feel it sag and bend under your skates, and hear the crackle of breaking ice telegraph out across the surface, and see water ooze up through the cracks. Or you could build a ski jump out of snow on a hillside and plunge down the slope and out into space, your skis wobbling and your eyes watering in the wind and your arms waving to keep balance, and thump down on the packed snow below and slide on to the end of the run, or fall and reach the bottom in a tumble of snow and skis.

You could take a streetcar to the end of the Minnehaha line and flounder across the park through the snowdrifts to the falls. In summer the water over the falls was a modest piddle that fell into the pool below like water from a bathroom tap; but in winter the creek was high, and the water froze as it fell and formed ice pillars that towered from the stream bed to the edge of the falls and filled the pool with great ice fragments, like the ruins of some old castle.

Under the falls' edge the tumbling water had carved out a cave that in winter was walled in by the ice pillars. A risk-taking kid could scramble behind that wall of ice into the damp-cold cave and make his way through to the other side, boots skidding on the wet ice, thinking as he went that if he lost his footing he'd crash through the ice wall and fall to the jagged ice and the freezing pool below. That slipping, sliding journey was a dare you couldn't refuse to take. It was scary, it was dangerous, my folks wouldn't let me do it, if I asked them. But of course I didn't ask; I didn't want to be forbidden to climb the falls, but I also didn't want to be permitted to. Life without permission, that's what I wanted.

The Milwaukee railroad tracks down beyond Lake Street

were outside the neighborhood, beyond the limits of what was allowed. Parents were afraid of the freight trains. But we went there anyway to hang over the bridge rail above the tracks and watch the trains rumble by below. The smoke from the engine would come pluming up and then stop as the engine went under the bridge; if you ran across to the other side you could be there when the smoke resurrected itself with a tall puff in your face, and try to drop a snowball down the smokestack. You could climb down the side of the cutting with the other kids (absolutely forbidden, this), and dare each other to stand close to the tracks while a train passed, and yell insults at the brakeman in the caboose. Kids bigger than me grabbed hold of the iron ladder that ran up the side of a car and clung there for a while and then dropped off, or stayed on and rode across town, or even farther if the train speeded up, and one kid fell and had his foot cut off. Birdy told me about another kid who climbed on top of a boxcar and touched the power line above his head. The shock knocked him clean off the car, and his hand was all burned. Crisp, like bacon, Birdy said. But I didn't see it, and probably Birdy didn't, either.

There was more than danger in trains. Lying in bed at night, I heard the far-off moans of trains leaving town, west along Twenty-ninth Street, or south down Hiawatha, the sounds distant but clear across the flat town. In the morning when I woke up they'd be in Milwaukee or Kansas City, or even farther. Elsewhere. When I sat on my bike at an open crossing waiting for a freight to pass, I read the names on the boxcars—M & St. L, Rock Island Line, Great Northern, Soo Line, Burlington, Northfield and Southern, Canadian Pacific, Northern Pacific. And sometimes cars that had come from far away, as though to assure me that elsewhere was real, too: Baltimore and Ohio, Lackawanna, Florida Coast Line, Louisville and Nashville, Atchison, Topeka and Santa Fe, and the mysterious Route of the Phoebe Snow. You could go to those places when you grew up. Except maybe Phoebe Snow.

Airplanes, too. I always looked up when I heard one over-head: a skywriter, maybe, high above the downtown buildings, spelling out PEPSI or RINSO; or a passenger plane taking people to Chicago or St. Louis; or after dark the mail plane's running lights, like shooting stars. Every plane was worth gawping at. I rode my bike out to Wold-Chamberlain Field on the edge of town and lay in the grass outside the fence and watched the bi-planes land. They were Navy fighters, a Navy Reserve squadron was based there. A kid could crawl under the fence and go in the hangar and just wander around, the mechanics didn't mind, and look at the oil-streaked fuselages and the open gunports in the wings, and imagine brave wars.

Even streetcars could reach a kid's imagination sometimes. After the stir of evening had ended and I was asleep in the dark, I might wake to the iron rattle of wheels on tracks, over on Nicollet: the Night Owl, the night's last car, headed for the car barn or out to the lonely end of the line. Empty now. I wouldn't want to be on it, all alone with the cold and darkness around; best to be warm in bed at this time of night.

In Minnesota, winter is the hard season. Snow covers the earth for a third of every year there; people die of the cold. You can't just wait for winter the way you wait for summer, you have to get ready for it. The folks, being country people, prepared for winter in country ways. When the hard frosts came in the fall my father put up storm windows, and filled the coal bin, and brought the snow shovel up from the basement and put it by the back door.

Nellie stocked the fruit cellar. On the farms where the folks grew up, the fruit cellar was an earth-smelling, spiderwebby cave dug into the ground under the house, deep enough that the ground wouldn't freeze in winter. Fruits and vegetables that could be canned were stored down there, and root vegetables in bins—potatoes and turnips and parsnips and rutabagas—and apples, too, till they rotted. Nellie reproduced that country cave as well as she could in an unheated little room under the cellar stairs. There on rough shelves she ranged the products of her summer's canning, square Mason jars of bluish glass containing preserved peaches, tomatoes, Italian prunes, grape jelly, apple butter, watermelon pickles, each with a label in her careful Palmer-method handwriting: STEWED TOMATOES—9/15/35. Against the wall under the little cellar window my father built bins big as barrels, and in the fall when he traveled the country towns he stopped at farms on his way home and bought bushel baskets of apples and onions, and gunnysacks of potatoes with the earth still clinging to them, and brought them home and stored them in the bins.

I thought my father was old-fashioned, buying stuff from farmers when he could get it all at the Red Owl or the A & P. But when he strode into the house after one of those farm journeys carrying a bushel of apples on his shoulder as though it weighed nothing at all and tumbled them into the root-cellar bin in a bright flood of redness, it was like the Bountiful Crest on the dining-room wall, and I felt sheltered and safe. The apples were a part of his powerful protection, like the storm windows and the full coal bin; our house would be snug and warm and full of food when the deep snows came.

But the fruit cellar would be cold. In winter it was my job to go down there and pick over the apples and potatoes in the bins and throw out the ones that had rotted. Every Saturday morning, all through the long cold months, I stood there on the cement floor beneath the dusty little window, sorting the potatoes and picking off the sprouts that grew like fingers out of their eyes, and fumbling the softening apples, fingers red and numb with cold, half-sick with the smell of rotten potatoes. But doing it because it was one of my chores.

Every cold night before he went to bed my father performed the same ritual. First he went down to the cellar and banked the fire, throwing dead ashes from the furnace ash pit over the live coals and closing the draft to slow the burning, so that in the morning there would be live coals to light the new day's fire. Then he patrolled through the house, locking the back door and checking all the window latches. But before he locked the front door he went out onto the porch and stood silently for a moment looking up at the night sky, reading tomorrow's weather. It was a farmer's gesture, his father had done it, too; farmers respected the weather. "Smells like snow," he would say, and I, standing shivering beside him, would sniff the night air, smelling cold and coal smoke, trying to smell snow. Then we'd go in and he'd lock the door behind him, locking out night, cold, and the winter that was coming.

First comes the cold world. I wake at morning and the day is different; frost is crackled on the windowpanes in snowflake patterns, and the light that shines through it is brighter and colder, like splintered ice, and when I reach one foot out of the warm bedclothes to the floor, the linoleum is ice, too. Up from the cellar comes the scrape of a shovel as my father scoops coal from the coal bin and hurls it onto the sleeping fire, and the *clank-clank* of the big furnace shaker as he forces it back and forth, sifting the night's ashes down into the ash pit, reviving the fire so that it glows red and flames dance across the surface. The hot-water pipes to the radiators begin to clank and chatter as they warm, and first heat creeps into the shivering rooms. I grab my clothes and run down to the kitchen, and dress in front of the open oven door, from which heat rolls out deliciously.

Clothes change when the cold world comes. I wear long underwear now, though I don't want to; the legs stretch, and make bunches around your ankles under your long stockings, so that everyone at school knows you're wearing long underwear, like a baby or a sissy. My knickers are heavy wool, and so is my sweater. When I go to school I wear a mackinaw, red-and-black plaid thick as a horse blanket, inherited from my brother ("plenty of good wear in that," Nellie says, holding it up at arm's length), and a wool hunting hat with a bill in front and flaps that hang down over my ears. And a wool scarf, long enough to go round and round my neck. And chopper mitts—two pairs of mittens, one inside the other, the inner ones knitted wool, the outer pair yellow horsehide. Later, when the deep snow comes, I'll wear boots that lace up the front and have a little pocket sewn on the side to put a pocketknife in. I don't own a pocketknife, but the pocket is essential. You're nobody at my school if your boots don't have a knife pocket.

Outside in the cold world the trees are bare silhouettes against a gray sky; the grass is brown and dead, and the earth is frozen, stiff and rigid as iron. When Nellie hangs the laundry out the clothes freeze before they're dry, and slap her when she pulls them off the line. At night when my father puts the car in the garage, he throws an old blanket over the hood, as though the car was a horse in a barn.

On a day in November the clouds lower and the light fades to a twilight grayness. In school the teachers turn classroom lights on, even though it's daytime. A few snowflakes fall, scattered and aimless, melting on the street outside, turning the pavement black. Sitting at our desks, we look out of the darkening windows and point and whisper: "It's snowing!"

All day long the snow falls and falls. Distance disappears, a whiteness like cotton wool hangs over the roofs across the street and leans to earth at the end of the block. When school is over we run out into the new snow world shouting. Little kids hold their faces up to the sky like birds and open their mouths; snow prickles eyes and frosts eyelashes and settles in the folds of woolly hats. The falling snow is invisible now except in the soft cones of light from streetlamps at the corners, and in the headlights of passing cars. We walk home in darkness, contented. Winter has begun.

Or the first snow comes in the night, and half waking I hear the *sh-sh-sh* of flakes against the windowpanes and half think, "It's snowing," and fall again into sleep. And wake in the morning knowing before I open my eyes that the world outside is different, hearing the difference, the muffled silence, nothing stirring. Then a car goes slowly up Blaisdell, chains *chunk-chunking* against the fenders. Farther off somebody stuck in a drift tries to back out, and the engine note rises and tires whine as they spin. A snow shovel scrapes on cement—next door Mr. Westmoreland is already out, shoveling his sidewalk. I jump out of bed to look.

And see yesterday's street erased, all the details and edges blurred, sidewalks and curbs smoothed out in one wavelike drift; snow deep on the roofs like meringue on a pie and stuck to the windward side of trees, and on the spread branches of pine trees, all that white smoothness unmarked, and I want to run out and stamp the first footprints into it and shake showers of snow from the pines or just run in great circles, arms stretched wide like wings, for joy of the first snow.

But Nellie doesn't allow joy on school days; "wrap up good," she says, "and don't forget your lunch," and she stands at the front door with the cod-liver-oil bottle and a tablespoon (I get colds and flu in the winter) and sends me out as though today were the same as yesterday, into light that pours down from the morning sun and leaps up from the snow, making West Thirty-fifth Street a place without shadows.

The winter I was eleven was the coldest ever in Minnesota. Each bright frozen morning Nellie appeared at our bedroom door reciting her cheerful wake-up poem: "The lark is up to meet the sun, the bee is on the wing," always the same lines, and reporting the temperature: "eleven below today," "seventeen below," "twenty-three below!" as though such numbers were challenges that would stir us from our beds. In the kitchen the radio was tuned to "Dayton's Musical Chimes," a breakfast-time program as cheerful as Nellie, beginning with its theme song: "GOOD news! You're bound to DO me good! Come right here TO me, GOOD NEWS!" Followed by the weather: blizzard conditions in Fargo, six inches of snow in Brainerd; five below in Duluth, ten below in Bemidji, fourteen below in International Falls up on the Canadian border—all reported in the highest spirits. Lucky to live in the Northwest, in deep winter.

The morning of the coldest day the temperature was thirty-six below, but the routine was just the same—same wake-up poem, same jolly radio, same oatmeal, same open oven door. Same school. "Wrap up warm!" said Nellie, who had walked backward two miles to school in a blizzard when she was a kid, and I was out the door, into bright air so cold that it hurt when I breathed in, to walk my usual route up alleys and through vacant lots and over fences to school, rubbing my cheeks and nose to keep them from freezing, pinching my ears—can I still feel that?—the scarf across my face first damp from my steaming breath and then frozen to rime frost, toes cold in my boots, body clenched like a fist against the searching cold, thinking "This is me on a brave adventure, nobody has ever walked to school on such a cold day before," thinking "I'm Admiral Byrd!" and feeling heroic, defying winter.

At the supper table that night I heard Coldest Day stories. The news on the radio said the temperature was still twenty-five below, and would stay below zero all week. The temperature in Owatonna had dropped fifty degrees in sixteen hours; that was a record. The wind was drifting the snow so you couldn't drive on country roads. My father read us a story out of the *Tribune*: over in the river by the Ford Bridge a seventy-one-year-old man was found frozen in the ice—upright, with his head and shoulders sticking out, like a fisherman's bobber, my father said. And down at Red Wing a young girl left a party at midnight and never reached home, and in the morning they found her stretched out in a field, stiff and blue, only a hundred yards from her front door. Hearing these tales, I felt even more heroic; I had survived a day's weather that had *killed* an old man and a girl.

But in fact the coldest day had been like any other winter day. None of the kids I knew had stayed home from school, or been driven there; and none of them had been frostbitten. We did our lessons, we played on the playground at recess, we walked home. What was the difference? We lived with cold all the time.

That coldest winter Nellie got me my first paper route. It looked simple enough: after school you just pick up your bundle of *Star-Journals* at a tin shed up an alley, roll each paper into a shape like a short baseball bat, and stick them all endwise into a canvas sack in your bike basket. Then you ride along the sidewalks on your route (mine would be Stevens Avenue) throwing papers onto porches or front steps. On Saturday you collect the cost of the week's papers from your customers, take your share, and give the rest to the man in the tin shed. A paper route would be easy. A cinch.

Except on Sundays. Then you'd have to get up early and leave before the house was awake. In summer it would be fine going out like that into the new morning, the sun just rising, the air fresh and cool, and nobody else up. But winter was different. Then you'd rise into blackness and cold and the streets would be frozen and the houses dark and hostile. On Sundays the papers would be too thick to roll and toss; you'd have to carry each one to a front door, and your fingers would get numb in your chopper mitts, and your feet would freeze in your boots.

The first Sunday was the worst (all first times are the worst). When I left home in the still-night darkness the temperature was below zero, and the ice on the streets was black, and slick from passing cars, and the sidewalks were rutted with frozen snow. I collected my papers, but when I tried to ride with the load of them in my bike basket, I skidded and fell and the papers slewed out across the snow. I tried again, and fell again. It was no good: out there alone in the frozen dark, I had a job I couldn't do.

One house among the sleeping houses had a light on in the kitchen: someone who couldn't sleep, having coffee and a lonely cigarette at the kitchen table, the way my father did. I tapped at the front door. A man in a bathrobe opened it. Could I use his phone to call my father, please? Sure. I phoned, and after a while my father answered. Where was I? He'd be there in ten minutes. The man went back to his coffee. I waited alone in the dark hall by the front door, looking down the street into the gray dawn. Nothing stirred except the windblown snow. Then the lights of a car turned the corner and crept toward me and I ran out to the curb. "Well, son." Together we delivered the papers, and by then it was day, the eastern sky flushed, the snow pink where the slanting light hit it. The wind had died down, and smoke from chimneys rose and stretched along the air. The houses were waking. We put my bike in the trunk and drove home to breakfast.

———

Winter went on through its own seasons, each with its own weather, its own special snow: the late autumn months when the first snow falls, windlessly, softly, not a sound but a perfect silence; midwinter, the darkest months, when blizzards rattle like buckshot on windows; and late winter, when the wind swings sometimes to the south, and melting snow slides from roofs, and the days stretch out toward evening in long, cold-colored sunsets, and the snow falls in fat flakes like the flakes in the glass ball my grandmother had in her room at the Home. "Wet snow," my father said when we stood on the front porch at bedtime looking out into the night. "Winter's over when the wet snow falls."

It wasn't, though. In late March snow still lay deep on yards and the roofs of houses, and was piled in ranges along the sidewalks where men or their kids had shoveled it—old, soiled snow, gray with soot and yellowed at corners where dogs had pissed. Along the top of the sidewalk piles the feet of little kids had worn black trails on their way to school (who would walk on sidewalks when there was a mountain path to follow?). But the hard season was growing soft. In Powderhorn Park the ice on the hockey rink was porous, my skates cut into it, and on south-facing hillsides snow melted from toboggan slides and ran in streams, and patches of wet earth appeared, steaming in the sun.

Buck and I rode our bikes to Lake Calhoun, and stood on the shore looking across the lake. Two weeks ago there had been skating rinks out there; now ice floes pitched and tilted, grinding together and tossing up water in bright sprays, making the lake surface seem at once solid and restless. We eyed the span of open water between the beach and the nearest floe. "Go on," Buck said. "I dare you." And because I was afraid to, I jumped, landing unsteadily on the raft of ice, feeling it begin to tip and settle, the water lapping over the ice surface toward my shoes, and jumped to another floe and stood there balancing and shouting, and the floe began to drift away from the shore, and I made a desperate leap and landed calf-deep in icy water, and went home with wet feet, again, and Nellie said, "Take those wet shoes right off and stuff them with newspaper!" But not angrily, because when kids' shoes are wet, spring is coming.

Old winter retreated slowly. Long after mild days had come and the sap was rising in the trees, snow still lingered on the north side of houses and in the narrow spaces between the garages in Apple Alley. In a game of Kick the Can I could just squeeze myself into one of those crannies to hide. The air was cool and damp there, like the breath from an open icebox, and when I thrust my hand down, my fingers sank into grainy snow.

And then, so suddenly that you miss it when it happens, spring comes in the morning. Nellie washes the dust of winter out of the lace curtains and stretches them on frames to bleach white in the sun and washes and polishes the windows and throws them wide open, and I'm sent into the backyard to smack the winter dirt out of the carpets with a beater shaped like a banjo. My father carries porch furniture up from the basement—the swing that will hang on chains from the porch ceiling, the glider, the Mission oak table that my mother bought from Grand Rapids, the fake Tiffany lamp, the rockers, the straw summer rug. I help him put the porch screens up; they make the porch an outdoor parlor full of sun and soft winds. My father sits back in a rocker and looks at our work with satisfaction. "Spring," he says.

CHAPTER SIX

The summer after the coldest winter was the hottest summer ever. For two whole weeks in July the temperature was above ninety degrees, even at night, and for five days in a row it went above a hundred. I woke every morning on sweat-soaked sheets, and washed in water that ran warm from the cold tap. The ice in the icebox melted, the milk was warm on my Wheaties. When I went outside after breakfast the heat was a blanket and the sun pressed down on my head and in on my eyes, I was blinded by it; and when I retreated into the shadow of a roof or an awning, the shade blinded me, too.

There was no wind, no clouds; the empty sky hung motionless above the town. "Hot enough for you?" folks asked. "Hot enough for you?" I went swimming in Lake Calhoun and the water in the shallows was warm as bathwater; you had to dive way down into the dark below to find coolness. Old people died in the heat, and their names were in the paper. When neighbors met on the sidewalk they stopped in the shade and told heat stories. My father knew a man at the Ford plant over across the river who lost seventeen pounds that July, working on the assembly line. Just sweated it out, my father said.

The tar on the street melted and caught at my bike tires, and the sidewalks were too hot to walk on barefoot. Sprinkling trucks drove slowly through the neighborhoods, spraying water over the pavement and into the gutters, and children splashed along behind them, cooling their feet in the spreading stream. But when the truck had passed the street steamed and dried in the sun, and the tar melted again. Small boys pulled lumps of warm tar from the street and chewed it. The tar tasted of gasoline, but a kid chewing it could spit black spit, and pretend to be a grown-up man chewing tobacco, or snoose.

At night families gathered up old blankets and sheets and went to the parks to sleep outdoors on the grass. We went to Powderhorn; surely, my father said, there'd be a breath of air on the hills. But there wasn't. Lying on the hillside in the dark, I could see ghosts of families all around me, dark figures against white sheets, and sometimes a wink of light far off on the hill across the lake: someone lighting a cigarette, or looking at his watch. Or a flashlight would move up the hill toward the pump by the street, and I'd hear the pump handle creak. A hot, thirsty night. The artesian water would be good, so cold from the deep earth. All over town sleepers lay out in city parks those nights.

That was a drought summer. Dust clouds blew up out of the west, turning the sky earth-colored and obscuring the noonday sun until it was only a veiled red ball in the sky, half-seen through the thickened air. Dust blew along the city streets and lay in drifts on sidewalks at the edge of the grass, like first snow.

Dust was everywhere. It entered houses like a brown ghost, through closed doors and windows, and covered the furniture and got into the food; you could feel it between your teeth when you ate. Even your spit was brown. Nellie, for all her fierce housewifery, couldn't keep her lace curtains white. She washed them every week and hung them for drying in the basement (no good hanging a washing outdoors, it would come in brown). But dust crept into the basement, too. My father said it wasn't our dust, it came from dry prairies way out west. Farmers out there had plowed the plains, and now their topsoil was blowing away. There was no rich earth left there for anything to grow in, he said; they had made their land a desert.

Sometimes dust storms blew in on fierce west winds, like summer thunderstorms but without rain, breaking windows and uprooting trees. The wind-driven dust erased distance—you couldn't see the house at the end of the block—and stopped cars and buses. Tumbleweeds blew down the streets. No one had ever seen a tumbleweed in our town; where had they come from? Not from anywhere in Minnesota. North Dakota, maybe, or even Wyoming, rolling and bouncing all that way in the dry wind and the dust. Grasshoppers, too, dust-colored like the air they flew in. They swarmed out of the west in clouds like the dust, darkening the sky, and settled on the dry earth so thick they crunched under your feet when you walked. If you caught one and held it in your hand, it would look at you with its buggy eyes and spit tobacco juice on your fingers. The plague of locusts became imaginable, and the preacher at church preached on that text. Were the grasshoppers a punishment? He said they were.

All that dry, hot summer I played ball at the Lot. There wasn't a real baseball field there, just an empty space at the top end of the slope with a worn spot at the corner for home plate and a track through the weeds that was the base path. Kids put their shirts down for bases, and a foul ball was anything you couldn't catch. The field wasn't even level; the ground sloped so sharply toward right field that you could hit an easy grounder past first base and it would roll all the way to the junk heaps down by Nicollet Avenue and turn your single into a home run. The infield earth was hard and cracked and full of sandburs, grasshoppers jumped and chirred, and the sun shone red and burning in the dusty air.

The kids I knew in the neighborhood came to the Lot most mornings, bringing their gloves and their cracked, nailed-together bats and their friction-tape-wrapped balls. Buck came, tall and freckled and sandy-haired; he was the best player, he could throw and hit farther than any of us. Birdy came, black hair greased down under his skullcap; he could run fast but he couldn't hit. And Dickie D., a small kid who yelled a lot—"Pitch to him, he can't hit," and "Swing, batter," stuff like that; he wouldn't field grounders because he played the accordion and he might hurt his fingers. Cliff came, skinny and narrow-shouldered, with big hands and feet; he wore glasses, and was apologetic because he was no good at baseball, but he lived next door to Rosy Ryan, the Miller pitcher, and that somehow gave him a right to be there. Sometimes Rosy Ryan's kid came; he was going to be a pitcher like his father, he already knew how to throw a curve.

If a lot of kids came we chose sides and played a team game. But it was best when there were only a few of us and we played Bounce Out. In Bounce Out everybody plays all the positions in turn, moving up from fielding to pitching to catching to batting, and the batter stays up until he hits a fly and it's caught, or he hits a grounder and runs for first and a fielder throws the ball between the runner and the base. Then he's out, and he goes to the outfield and the catcher becomes the batter and all the players move up. What I liked about Bounce Out was that there was only one team, so you didn't keep score and nobody won and nobody lost and there wasn't any end; the game just went on, all that hot summer long.

Summer has only one date when you're a kid—the Fourth of July. That was true in the country on the Heggs' farm and it was true in town. But the way you celebrated it was different. The town Fourth began a long time before the date, when fireworks stands appeared along highways beyond the last houses, the junkyards and the used-car lots. That was because it was against the law to sell fireworks inside the city limits. Buck and I rode our bikes out Cedar Avenue to where the hasty sheds and tents stood with their red-white-and-blue "Fireworks" signs, and there bought skyrockets, Roman candles, pinwheels, cherry bombs, torpedoes, ladyfingers, half-inchers, inchers, and even two-inchers, and rode back into town with our stuff in paper bags in our bike baskets, the sticks of the rockets standing up like flagstaffs.

Morning comes early on the Fourth of July in town. I wake in the half dark before dawn to the sound of the day's first explosions, a distant rattling stutter; somewhere in far-off backyards other kids can't wait. I dress and take my sack of firecrackers downstairs and out to the back steps. Chuck is already there, sitting silently, with his own sack. We can't begin yet; there has to be a period of waiting, like Christmas morning, until the folks are awake. The best times are always delayed by adults, every kid knows that. Then the lights go on in the kitchen and the pots rattle and the radio begins to play, and we can begin.

I start with my littlest crackers, the strings of ladyfingers; they go off together in a rattling rush, *pop-pop-pop-pop*. In other backyards I can hear other kids doing the same thing, making the neighborhood crackle. When the little ones are gone I build a miniature village out of strawberry boxes in the dirt by the back door, carefully digging a little lake beside it that I fill with the garden hose. Then I put one-inchers under the houses and blow them all into the air. I rebuild the village and do it again. The destruction is very satisfactory, like being God when he's angry. I like the drift of the smoke and the smell of burned powder. But Nellie makes me stop, not because of the noise or the splintered village but because I'm making a puddle where she hangs the laundry to dry.

After lunch I meet my friends in Apple Alley. We find empty tin cans in garbage cans, set them up in the alley with a two-incher or a cherry bomb underneath, and blow them high into the air. Cherry bombs under cans make parents nervous: "What if the can explodes? Don't stand too close! If it doesn't go off, don't pick it up!" We know fireworks are dangerous, we've read about accidents, and will find them again in tomorrow's papers: ANOKA BOY LOSES FINGER IN FIREWORKS ACCIDENT, GIRL'S DRESS CATCHES FIRE FROM SPARKLER, ROCKET BURNS GARAGE DOWN. It's the danger that makes it fun, that and the noise.

At Powderhorn Park the Fourth of July is an all-day carnival, with running races and music and speeches by politicians. We don't go to the daytime part—that's the time for kids in the alley with their own fireworks, and anyway my father doesn't like speeches, he says they're all lies—but after supper we walk together to the park for the fireworks, a family among other walking families, slowly because there's lots of time, it's still daylight, joining folks who converge out of side streets, the crowd thickening until it flows into the park and onto the hills that circle the little lake, making a great bowl of waiting people.

The sunset slowly loses its color behind western trees, and the high sky turns a darker blue. Birds settle in the trees, bats swoop low in the half darkness and girls squeal and cover their hair because a bat might make a nest there, and the families wait quietly, except for the children, who stir restlessly and ask, Is it dark enough yet? *Is it?* and light sparklers that burn like lightning bugs on the far hills. Down below on the island in the lake shadowy figures move, and flashlights blink. And the crowd, denser now, waits.

The last light is gone from the sky, and stars are out—it *must* be dark enough now! A sudden sizzing streak of fire and smoke climbs the night air and the first rocket bursts overhead, and the crowd on the hillside sighs one "Ah-h-h-h," because it has begun. And then another and another, each one bursting as the one before fades in a scatter of sparks, all the possible varieties of rocket, surprising us, delighting us—"Ah-h-h," "Ah-h-h," "Ah-h-h-h"—the ones that burst and spread fingers of smoke that burst again at the fingertips, the ones that spread bright worms of fire, the ones that explode with a bass thunder that rumbles and echoes in the hollow of the hills, the ones that open and linger like chrysanthemums, the necklaces of lights that float slowly down, fading from brightness as they fall, the blinding white ones like a million flashbulbs or the end of the world that catch our rapt white upturned faces on the hillsides and hold them for a moment fixed in pure light, and then return us all to the darkness.

The last rocket is always the best of all—burst after burst, the echoes rebounding, and then another burst just when you think it is all over. And then it is. The families rise slowly in the sudden silence and fold their blankets, and walk home through the dark, still streets, not talking much, purged by the high splendors they have seen, satisfied that another Fourth is over, another summer has been celebrated with a proper hullabaloo.

But not quite over, even then. When I have gone at last to bed, and lie there half-asleep thinking about the day and the rockets in the park, kids who have a few firecrackers left are still setting them off, finishing the long day. I can hear them through my open windows, far off across the flat dark town: *pop-pop, pop-pop-pop.*

Pop.

I didn't expect anything to change in my West Thirty-fifth Street world, now that we were settled there. We had a house that was ours, with a father, a mother, and children in it. We did things together—walked to the park for the fireworks, went fishing (the girls sat in the rowboat in their summer dresses and shrieked when fish nibbled their lines), and had picnics (like the one where Nellie outran us all). We had become a normal, ordinary family. We'd go on in this house in this neighborhood, permanent as trees and lampposts, the same persons sitting down at the same dinner table and sleeping in the same rooms up-stairs—always. It wouldn't be like the boardinghouses.

But there were changes in our house, too. My stepbrother, Bill, graduated from the University and moved up to North Dakota to be a manager for Red Owl stores. He wore a dark suit now when he came home to visit, and though he was still friendly and smiling he wasn't as much fun, because he was a grown-up.

My stepsisters were becoming grown-ups, too. They fin-ished high school in June of the hottest summer and went downtown and found typing jobs in offices and went to work on the streetcar every morning. That's what they expected, what we all expected; girls took typing and shorthand in high school and belonged to the Commercial Club so they could be typists in offices and maybe eventually secretaries, and make good money, and then get married.

Eileen, the bright one, wasn't satisfied with that. One night at supper she said she wanted to go to the University, like Bill.

Where would she get the money? Nellie asked. Tuition alone was a hundred dollars a year, and she only earned twelve dollars a week, typing.

Eileen thought that maybe if she lived at home, and didn't have to pay board and room . . .

But she *would* have to. Bill paid B&R all the time he was at the U, and Rose Marie was paying B&R now. So it wouldn't be fair if Eileen didn't, would it?

So Eileen stayed at her typing job, and for a whole year saved what she could, and the next fall she enrolled as a fresh-man. She had to keep her job, though; she went to school in the mornings and typed every afternoon, and did her homework at night. In the winter of that year she got sick, so sick that for weeks she had to stay in bed, not doing anything. I heard Nellie talking to Rose Marie about Eileen's illness: "It's gone to her lungs," Nellie said, savoring the medical details, as they all did. "It's pleurisy. Maybe TB!"

It wasn't tuberculosis. She recovered slowly, but she had to quit the University and go back to being just a typist. The folks were relieved; she'd been working too hard.

The next summer Bill came home for a visit. That surprised me; he didn't usually come home in the summer. Even more surprising, a girl came up from Iowa to stay while he was home. Her name was Theodora. She was the most beautiful girl I'd ever seen: her hair was corn-colored (sweet corn, the kind you eat, not the white kind you feed to the pigs) and her skin was like the top of the milk and her eyes were sky blue; everything about her was like the country. She sat in the parlor in the summer heat, smiling and looking cool, and Bill sat looking at her all the time, and smiling, too. She was a friendly girl; she didn't mind me being not quite thirteen years old, she talked to me, told me stories about the farm where she lived, down in Iowa.

Nellie was very polite, she always was when there was company. She got out the Haviland china and the 1847 Rogers silver plate and put the two silver pheasants in the middle of the dining-room table, and roasted two chickens. But she didn't laugh or even smile at dinner, and the talk was full of silences in which the only sound was the popping of my father's false teeth as he ate his corn on the cob. After supper Bill and Nellie and Theodora sat on the porch together. I thought they must be arguing. Bill wouldn't like that; he hated arguments, worse than spaghetti, he said. They stopped talking when I came near; kids aren't supposed to know when something's going on.

Next morning Theodora left, and then there were more talks, whispered behind closed doors, the whole house hushed as though someone was sick. Then Bill went back to North Dakota. After he left I asked Nellie if Bill was going to marry Theodora. "No," she said, "he's not. She's *Lutheran*."

The attic was my private place. Nobody else went there; the windows were never opened, and the air was still, like the air in a church when there's no service going on, and the sounds of the street below rose faintly, like whispered secrets. I spent a lot of time up there by myself, playing elaborate games that I made up, with trucks and tin soldiers, or just looking out of the window. From that high place I could be a watcher of the street. I watched the neighbors coming and going, the Genakopolises from the house on the corner, and Miss La France next door, and Charlie Butts, and Mrs. Ford, and Alf De Smidt, and Mr. Delmore and his black-haired daughter, Denise. I watched the mailman go down the street, and the milkman, and the man who delivered laundry. And the strangers to the block: the man with the goiter, and the woman who always wore white (even in winter), and the old lady with the blue-tongued chow on a leash.

The attic was where things were stored: suitcases (my father called them "grips")—cracked cowhide, woven straw, cardboard painted to resemble leather—the tired companions of two families' poor journeyings; and cardboard boxes tied with string and labeled in Nellie's handwriting: "old photos," "children's clothes," "wedding dress." And a dressmaker's dummy, a torso covered in white muslin representing a woman's body, but nothing like the shape of any female in our house. All that stuff was history. You could tell the story of our family lives from what was there, pushed back under the eaves.

My father gave me a Lionel electric train for Christmas when I was twelve, and set it up in the attic on a trestle table that was our old ping-pong table turned upside down, so that its top was a flat plywood surface with a wooden edge round the sides like a wall. On the table he mounted the tracks, carefully tacking down lengths of gray inner tube for a roadbed, and connected switches and signals that turned from green to red when the train passed, and a control for separating cars from the engine and for backing the train up, and a crossing gate that closed when the train went by. I painted the table grass-green, and stained bits of sponge green and stuck them around for trees; I built a station and little houses out of cardboard, and made a sand road for the crossing gate. And so gradually the tabletop became a small world entire in itself, a private reality where the only sound was the small, companionable *clickety-clickety* of the train running on its track, around, and around, and around.

Even after I stopped playing with the train because I was too old for such toys, I liked knowing that it was up there in that other world that my father and I had built, and that I could reenter that world if I wanted to. Then Nellie sold it. "You never used it," she said in her practical way, missing entirely the difference between using and having. I felt my loss bitterly. It wasn't grief, exactly, not like the feeling when someone you know dies; more like what you feel when a favorite thing is smashed, or swept away by a stream, or dropped from a moving car onto a highway, or just left behind in a place you'll never go back to. Something that was yours is gone forever; and if that can happen, if this thing you treasured can be taken from you, then everything can.

There was another change in the house that year: Nellie hired a maid. We'd never had a maid before; why would you hire a woman to do your housework when there was a strong farm wife in the house to do it, and two grown girls to help her? But Nellie had a full-time job now working for Mr. Spradlin, who ran a mothproofing company over on Hennepin ("Everything wool mothproofed in your home"), and the girls were working. And so Gladys appeared. My father closed off a space at the top of the attic stairs with plasterboard and put a narrow bed in it, and a chest of drawers, and a rag rug, and called it the Maid's Room. It wasn't a very private room; I went through it every time I went up to play with my train. It had no lock on the door and no toilet of its own. But for an out-of-work woman it would be a refuge, a place to go at night when the supper dishes were done, a place to sleep alone. With it she would get five dollars a week and Thursday evenings and Sundays off.

Gladys was a pale thin woman with big front teeth. She was probably not much older than my stepsisters, but in her starched white maid's uniform, with her straight black hair pulled back in a tight bun, she looked very grown up, like someone who had a natural authority over kids. Every time she spoke to me it was to give me an order: "Don't track dirt in here, go wipe your feet"; "Don't walk on the kitchen floor, it's not dry yet, step on the newspapers"; "Don't bring those smelly sneakers in the house, leave them on the back porch."

The week, for Gladys, had a strict order: washing on Monday (damp smell of soapsuds up from the basement), ironing on Tuesday (smell of starch on the hot iron and steaming cloth), clean the furniture on Wednesday (polish and wax). So did the food she cooked: on Monday hash from the Sunday roast, on Friday fish (because of the Catholics), on Saturday Boston baked beans and Boston brown bread. She must have been a good cook, most of the time; my stepsisters thought her white cakes were wonderful. When she wasn't, when something in the kitchen went wrong, she wouldn't apologize, she'd argue; the breakfast toast wasn't burned, it was just a nice brown, and Nellie would stand at the sink with the toast in her hand, not saying anything, just scraping the black surface, certain that beneath the charred outside there was a perfectly good piece of toast that somebody could eat.

On Thursday evenings Gladys went to a Lake Street dance hall. My father disapproved of this—no good ever came to anybody from going to a dance hall—but he couldn't prevent her from doing what she liked on her night off. My stepsisters thought she must be rather fast, going off like that on her own, without a date. Aside from the dance-hall evenings she seemed to have no life at all; she appeared in the kitchen in the morning before I was up, and disappeared at night, up the bare stairs to her narrow room. I could hear her heavy shoes on the stairs and on the splintery floor of her room. So tired they sounded. So tired.

One afternoon I came in from school while she was scrubbing the kitchen floor. As I stood in the doorway considering how to get to the icebox, her scrubbing slowed and stopped, and she gripped her stomach with both hands and began to rock back and forth, kneeling there on the linoleum and moaning, not loud but steadily. I stood and looked at her; I didn't know what you did when a maid moaned. Just then Nellie came home from work. She knew what to to; she bent over the kneeling woman, gently raised her to her feet, and led her up the stairs to her room and put her to bed.

What's wrong with Gladys?

Nellie said she had a stomach-ache. But I'd had stomach-aches, they weren't like that; I hadn't moaned and rocked back and forth on the floor. What Gladys had was different, and worse.

For a day or two she remained out of sight in her room while my stepsisters did the housework and I walked freely across the kitchen floor in my dirty Keds. Then she was gone, just disappeared while I was at school, the room at the top of the attic stairs cleared of the few things she owned, empty and desolate again. There was a connection, I knew, between the pain and moaning on the kitchen floor and her swift departure, but no one would tell me what it was, and my father frowned darkly when I asked. Maybe the dance hall was part of it, and my father was right; no good had come to her there. She had lost her job, and her room, and her five dollars a week. She remained in the family memory as a fading black-and-white presence, and for her sentence about the toast: It's not burned, it's just a nice brown. We said it of anything that came to the table too overcooked to eat. And then ate it.

After Gladys came Olga. She was a country girl from a farm somewhere out near Dassel, in the city for the first time and in her first job, undomesticated and untrained, more like some small barnyard creature than a person you'd meet on the street. Short and round, she seemed made of red rubber balls: her hair was the color of Christmas-stocking tangerines, and bounced on her head as she bounded through her work; her face was perfectly round and red, and grew even redder when she blushed, which she did all the time, and her mouth was an open red O, as though she has just seen something astonishing. Her eyes, round and staring, were a startling blue in all that redness. Her rubber-ball body was squeezed into a maid's uniform of a vivid pink that clashed with her tangerine hair and her red face. Nellie said Olga looked like a hen she'd had once, back in Iowa, a Rhode Island Red; she treated her not in the city way, as a maid, but in the country way, as a hired girl.

There's a photograph of Olga in the family album. She stands in the backyard in her maid's uniform. It must be early spring; the lilac bushes by the fence are bare branches, and last scraps of snow lie scattered on the ground like white chickens. Olga's face is clenched in what she must have meant to be a smile but is more like a grimace. Her arms are blurred; Nellie's Kodak has caught her raising her hands in a characteristic gesture, an expression of her continual astonishment at life.

I wondered if Olga had been pushed from her family nest, or whether she had chosen a new life in the city for the adventure of being alone. On hardscrabble farms like hers parents kept their sons at home to help work the land, married off what daughters they could, and sent the unmarriageable ones out to work. Was Olga marriageable? I thought the odds were about a thousand to one against—or maybe a thousand to zero.

If that was true, it didn't bother her. She seemed to think it was a happy fate to be herself, with a warm bed in an attic room and three meals a day and five dollars a week to spend; and maybe it was better than the life she had come from, the farmhouse with too many kids crammed into too few rooms, and work that was as hard as any draft animal's, and no five dollars at the week's end.

Olga wanted to be a good maid and do everything right, and all that wanting made her nervous, and especially when she served dinner. She would blush scarlet as she hipped her way through the swinging door from the pantry into the dining room, thinking perhaps that she was about to drop the Swiss steak into somebody's lap, and stand nervously behind my father's chair trying to remember whether you served from the left or from the right. If my father or Nellie spoke to her she would rise on her tiptoes, as though she thought—or hoped—that a taller Olga would be a more credible waitress. If she had to speak, her voice might suddenly change pitch and volume in midsentence, as (brandishing the percolator): "Can I give you some more coffee (normal voice), MISTER HYNES?" (high uncontrolled shriek). Chuck and I would snigger at that, which made my father angry; he didn't approve of laughter at the dinner table; laughter was for things you knew in advance were funny, like Jack Benny on the radio.

It was during Olga's reign that I became aware of the way our family order was beginning to stretch and splinter. We lived our lives by separate schedules, like boardinghouse folks: in the morning we woke and ate breakfast and left the house at different times, and there was no more cod-liver oil at the front door. The weekday timetable was now something like this:

6:30. My father is up and in the basement, shaking the furnace and rattling us all awake.
6:45. Olga is in the kitchen, yawning and cooking the oatmeal and making the coffee.
7:00. Nellie appears at my bedroom door: "The lark is up to meet the sun." The girls rush into the bathroom before I can get there.
7:30. My father drives off to work.
7:45. Nellie leaves for the mothproofer's, shouting over her shoulder "Don't forget your homework!"
8:00. The girls leave for their jobs downtown.
8:15. Chuck leaves for school, carrying his trombone (he's in the Bryant Junior High School Band, and they practice before school).
8:30. I leave for school.

Around 8:14 one morning I heard an odd noise from the basement; Olga was down there doing the washing, so it must have been Monday. It was her voice I heard, but the words weren't words: "I ant et y ow oze! I ant et y ow oze!" She came up the basement stairs into the kitchen, her blue eyes staring and her mouth a wider O than ever, and strange words issuing from it: "I ow ih uck o'en!" I looked at Chuck, standing by the front door; everyone else had left, he was the older brother, he should take charge.

"She can't get her mouth closed."

Chuck considered the situation. "Well, then," he said at last, "I guess she'll have to do the washing with her mouth open." He picked up his trombone and left.

I phoned Nellie at Spradlin's and told her what had happened. Stay right there, she said, she'd call the doctor. Olga and I stood in the front hall staring silently at each other; I had nothing to say, and she couldn't say anything I could understand. After what seemed a longish wait the doctor arrived. He took one look at Olga, thrust both his thumbs into her mouth, and gave her jaw a sharp sideways push. It snapped shut, biting his thumbs. I left for school. I'd be late, but I had an excuse. But would my teacher believe it? "I'm late because our maid got her mouth stuck open." Probably not.

CHAPTER SEVEN

Minneapolis was full of churches. Big ones: the Episcopal cathedral up on Loring Hill, and the domed Catholic basilica down below on the other side of Loring Park (the only Catholic church ever built at the *bottom* of a hill, my father said), and the Methodist Episcopal church farther up behind the cathedral, looking even bigger because it was higher. And little ones: storefront Holy Rollers and corrugated iron Evangelicals, roofed-over-basement churches waiting for their first-story sanctuaries, brick churches and stone churches and wooden churches, churches with carillons of bells that lifted the pigeons into flight, and churches with loudspeakers that broadcast organ hymns into the Sunday air, and churches with nothing but a piano and faith.

Many churches and many religions: Adventist, African Methodist Episcopal, Baptist, Bible, Catholic, Catholic Greek, Christian Disciple, Christian Science, Church of God, Congregational, Episcopal, Evangelical, Evangelical Free, Evangelical Synod, First Church of the Brethren, First Church of the Nazarene, First United Brethren, Four Square, Friends, Full Gospel, Greek Orthodox, Latter-day Saints, eleven kinds of Lutherans: Lutheran-American, Lutheran-Augustana Synod (divided into Swedish and English congregations), Lutheran-Danish, Lutheran Eilzen Synod, Lutheran-English, Lutheran-Finnish, Lutheran-Free, Lutheran-Norwegian, Lutheran-Slovak,

Lutheran-Synodical, Lutheran-United, Methodist Episcopal, Presbyterian, Swedish Evangelical, Unitarian, Universalist.

We had two religions in our house—Nellie's Catholicism, which was everyday, audible, and public, like the radio, and my father's Presbyterianism, which was silent and private. Nellie and her children went to the Church of the Incarnation at Thirty-eighth and Pleasant. Incarnation was tall as a barn, and red: red-brick walls, red tile roof, tall redbrick tower. The front doors were wide as barn doors; when they were open you could smell the sweet smoky smell of the inside. Mass was on Sundays, but Catholics went to church on weekdays, too. My stepsisters went to Confession, and to sodality meetings, and to weekday Masses on specially holy days. I heard their Catholic words around the house all the time: Easter Duty and Ember Days and Days of Holy Obligation and Vigils and Encyclicals and Confraternities and Hail Marys and Father This and Sister That and the Holy Mother of God. Catholicism was a religion that kept you chattering and bustling and praying all the time; and it had a vocabulary of its own to do it in.

Catholics were everywhere in the city's daily ordinary life. During the football season their school teams played each other, and got into the headlines in the *Star-Journal:* ST. JOSEPH CRUSHES OUR LADY OF FATIMA. Ordinary schools were named for famous Americans, or for the streets they were on or the part of town they were in; Catholic schools had saints' names, or the names of religious notions that Protestant kids didn't understand, like Immaculate Conception and Sacred Heart of Jesus and Our Lady of Perpetual Sorrows. When Catholics had a church holiday there were pictures in the paper of priests and bishops and processions streaming out of churches into the street. But even on ordinary days you'd see them, the priests in their black suits with their collars turned wrong way round, and the nuns who taught in the Catholic schools in their long, flapping black robes with stiff white cloths like bandages framing their faces so you couldn't see their hair. Catholics were different from us, and they were always there, a visible presence in the neighborhood. The rest of us, the Protestants, were only visible at our church doors on Sunday mornings.

Maybe it was all the popish talk in our house that made my father decide to send my brother and me to Presbyterian Sunday School. Maybe he thought he should have our ears filled with good Protestant words at least one day a week, even if we did nothing on weekdays that you could call religious—didn't say our prayers, or read the Bible, or mention the name of God at all except in vain. My father didn't try to teach us his own religion; he seemed to find talking about God as embarrassing as talking about sex (which he never did, either).

The church he chose for our religious education was a mile west of our house—along Thirty-fifth Street, the other side of Lyndale. "Walking distance," he said, with his wide country sense of what a boy could do on his own two feet, and so it became. But on the first day he drove us there, and led us in. He wouldn't go to church himself, except on very special occasions like this one: his Presbyterianism would always be a religion-in-exile. In his mind he was a Protestant who had married a Catholic, and so banished himself from the company of faithful believers. But he would send us, and we would grow up on the inside of our religion, among Protestants who belonged. I didn't question the rightness of this decision: I was what my father was. Presbyterianism must be in my blood, like being a Hynes, like being American.

Aldrich Avenue Presbyterian Church sat squarely and certainly on its piece of the earth. It was broader than it was tall, and had a short thick tower at the corner; it looked more like a fort than a church, I thought, or like a broad-shouldered, thick-necked policeman directing traffic. It was made of red brick, like the Catholic church where my stepfamily went, but the effect was the opposite: Incarnation was tall, and its tower thrust upward toward the emptiness where maybe God was, and it was named for a Holy Mystery that nobody could really understand; Aldrich was heavy and earthbound, and was named for the street it stood on.

We entered the church and stood for a moment at the back under the balcony. I had never been there before, but the room seemed familiar: the pale-painted walls, the varnished oak paneling, the smell of furniture polish, the murmur of voices all made it like the assembly hall at school. Oak pews stood heavily in rows. Sunlight filtered through the custard-colored glass of the windows and filled the room with pale, shadowless light. In the two biggest windows pictures had been painted on the glass. In the pointed window at the far end of the church a man with a beard knelt with his hands clasped on a big rock. That was Jesus. He was praying. In the big window at the side He was floating up in the air and people were staring up at Him. There were no other decorations in the room, no flowers, no pictures, no figures, not even a cross.

Nothing religious was happening. Grown-ups and children stood or sat around in small groups talking, and at the front of the room a gray man in a gray suit seemed to be waiting for something. My father said that was Reverend Nelson. He took us by the hands and led us down the aisle to be introduced, and stood for a while with his big hands on our shoulders, making us easy in that strange place, talking politely to the Reverend. Then he turned and strode back up the aisle and out the door, hurrying, as though he felt wrong being there.

My Sunday School class sat on little chairs in a circle near the front of the room. The teacher smiled round the circle and began:

"Now we will each recite our favorite Bible verse. Who'll be first?" All hands shot up except mine.

"Arthur?"

"Jesus wept." Arthur looked around triumphantly at the rest of us. He had got in first with the shortest verse in the Bible. The other kids would have to work harder.

I only knew one verse, not even all of that, only part. When my turn came I began: "Suffer the little children to come unto me and forgive them not . . ."

That was wrong, the teacher said; it's *forbid* them not. But *forgive* makes more sense, really, if you're a Presbyterian.

When we weren't quoting Bible verses we prayed and sang. Praying was embarrassing, even more than the Bible verses; you had to talk out loud to God while everybody listened, and then you had to listen, or pretend to, while the other kids prayed. Singing hymns wasn't so bad, at least you didn't have to sing by yourself. There were special hymns for Sunday School, with words that kids could understand: "Brighten the Corner Where You Are," "Bringing in the Sheaves," "Jesus Loves the Little Children of the World," "Jesus Loves Me, This I Know," "Peal Out the Watchword," "Love Lifted Me." I sang when told to sing, but I had no sense of what I was singing; Jesus had no real existence, I didn't know what you did when you pealed the watchword (and I got *peal* and *peel* mixed up, which made it worse). I especially disliked "Love Lifted Me," because it was in waltz time. I knew God didn't waltz.

I hated Sunday School, but I went, for the same reason I went to school—I had to. I went so regularly that after a while I was given a little gold pin with an inscription on it—"One Year in God's House," something like that. After another year I got a gold wreath that fitted around the pin, and a year after that a little bar that dangled below it, and then another and another until the whole pin looked like one of those sharpshooter's medals that soldiers wear—each bit a testimony to another stretch of resentful presence in that cold place. I was confirmed there, and my father

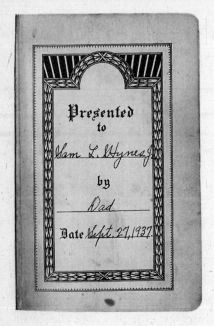

gave me a Bible, inscribed in his strong, regular hand: I had just turned thirteen.

Sometimes the Sunday School stayed on for the eleven o'clock grown-ups' service, and my father occasionally came to one of those, perhaps to see me receive my sharpshooter's medal, or to be confirmed. At those services Communion might be served, though not very often, because Communion was something Catholics did. At our Presbyterian Communion the congregation sat stolidly in their pews while the choir sang, and ushers like waiters in a restaurant brought around little trays with holes drilled in them. In each hole was a tiny cup like a thimble, full of grape juice. In the middle of the tray were some fragments of bread. You drank the juice and ate the crumb of bread and then put the thimble in a rack attached to the pew in front of you. I didn't think the Presbyterians had got the Communion service quite right; surely on that last Thursday night of His life Jesus didn't give His disciples grape juice to drink.

After Communion we sang hymns. My father sang with great confidence and volume, certain that he was a natural bass singer. I was impressed that a man who could speak in such a high-pitched voice when he talked long distance on the telephone could drop so low into the bass clef in church. When we sang a hymn he knew and liked—"The Church in the Wildwood" or "Onward, Christian Soldiers"—his voice, strong and completely unmusical, would wander rumblingly along the bottom of what's audible, in what he believed was harmony. He especially liked the part in "The Church in the Wildwood" where the basses sing "Come, come, come, come" very deep, and continue after the sopranos and tenors and altos have gone on to other words—"come, come, come" like a bass drum in a marching band. He sometimes kept it up right to the end of the hymn, never hitting a right harmonious note, and very happy. Standing at his side, I felt protective of him, so confident in his singing and so wrong; he could sing that way if he wanted to.

Worship at Aldrich was a wintry duty; even Christmas was a bleak occasion there. Nellie and Bill and the girls would go to Midnight Mass on Christmas Eve; I'd hear them coming in late long after I was in bed, laughing and chattering. But there was no Midnight Mass for Presbyterians. Our service was early on Christmas morning, so early that we trudged to church in darkness, hunched in our mackinaws, woolly hats pulled down against the wind's sharp edges. Up ahead we could see the church windows casting their paleness across the snow, the only lights in the dark street. Inside, as we sat in our pew, the windows were still night-colored and opaque, and shadows gathered in the corners of the room and under the high roof, in spite of the hanging lamps.

The Christmas service was always the same: the familiar carols, the manger story from Luke, a sermon that was last year's sermon. The Reverend Nelson must have felt the worn familiarity of what he was doing; one year he tried to give the service new life. At the end, after the sermon and the collection, he asked us all to stand in a circle round the aisles and then to come forward in turn, receive a small candle, and light it from a big candle by the pulpit. Slowly the rotating circle of the congregation became a circle of little lights, shining up into faces and making them warm and bright. When it was complete we stood holding our winking candles and sang "Silent Night." It was pretty, but it was something more—it was a kind of ceremony, a ritual such as I had never seen in that church before. For a moment, we had made our Presbyterianism beautiful.

By then dawn was breaking, leaking into the church through the tall windows; I could see the ascending Christ floating grayly against the cold half-light. Reverend Nelson stepped into the pulpit. "These candles," he said, "are the light of the Christmas spirit. Take them out of this church into the world to spread that spirit wherever you go." We filed obediently to the doors at the back, holding our little flames, and out into the winter grayness. Every candle was immediately blown out by the whipping wind. We walked home toward the morning, each carrying an extinguished candle stub.

The other part of Christmas—the part that was Jesus' birthday party and a winter festival, too, the feasting and present-giving part, the part that chooses the dark time of winter as a day when winter-dwelling folks can turn to each other and say, "Eat, drink, this won't last forever, spring will come," and give each other presents that aren't birthday presents but promises of bright, warm days coming—that part began as we walked home. The sun was up by then, and the sky was a cloudless palest blue. Through windows along the block I could see lighted Christmas trees; in our house a fire would be burning in the living-room fireplace. As we came in, stomping the snow from our feet, noisy with expectation of presents, Nellie would say firmly: "Breakfast first, everybody needs a hot meal in the morning!" One more duty before pleasure, adults making kids wait. But endurable, because from the dining room I could see the presents in a drift of bright paper and ribbons under the Christmas tree.

There are no particular Christmases in childhood, all Christmases are one, all happy in the same way: the same excited anticipation, the same joys of having on this day more than you expect or really want—more presents, more food, more affection (that's what the presents and the food express in reticent families). For one day the make-it-do-or-do-without rule doesn't apply. In one long tinseled, colored-lighted, tissue-paper-wrapped morning I am given: a toy furnace that melts lead and casts toy soldiers, a chemistry set, Tinkertoys, Lincoln Logs, an Erector set, Big Little Books, Tootsie Toy cars, a dump truck that really dumps, skates, crayons, a magic blackboard that erases itself, a Lionel train, skis.

The skis are special: long, grown-up skis, so special that Nellie takes my picture with them, and notes on the back: "Sam Jr., Christmas 1936. New 7 ft. skis." I stand by the front steps, dressed for skiing—knitted hat, warm jacket, wool knickers, mittens. The bright winter sun casts shadows of tree trunks across the snow. With my right hand I hold the skis upright, the tips two feet higher than my head. They are of dark wood, and heavy looking, with a leather toe strap to hold them on my feet. I will cut two thick rubber bands from an old inner tube and run one under each toe in front of the toe strap and around my heel, and these will be my bindings. With them on I will ski the slopes of Powderhorn, and try the lower, easier jumps. But for the moment of the picture I stand,

proud and determined, older and more courageous than I was before Christmas because I own seven-foot skis.

When the Reverend Nelson preached to us about Christmas, he got one thing wrong, I thought; Christmas isn't a time of giving, it's the year's great feast of getting, a day when things pile up around you, more than you can ever play with, or read, or eat. Of course you have to give presents or you won't get any, I could see the justice of that. But buying presents was easy, you just gave people the same thing you gave them last year: bottles of Evening in Paris perfume from the drugstore for my stepsisters, a Big Little Book for Chuck, a tie for my father, a handkerchief for Nellie. It didn't matter what you gave them, a present was a present.

One gift I gave that Christmas when I was twelve was different. I didn't buy it in a hurry, any-old-way, I *chose* it, and took pleasure in the choosing. And it was a grave misjudgment. Walking through Dayton's in the present-buying season, I wandered into the picture department and was struck by a framed motto:

> A friend is not a person
> Who is taken in by sham:
> A friend is one who knows your faults
> And doesn't give a damn!

The special beauty of it was in that "damn!" Frank, blunt, a little daring—like Nellie. Just the right present for her, I thought, and I bought it. On Christmas morning she opened the package, read the motto, thanked me, and went to hang it on her bedroom wall. It hung there for a day or two, or possibly three, and I went up to admire it. Then it was gone, and in its place was a motto that my stepsister Rose Marie had given her:

> A mother's love is like a precious rose,
> With sweetness in every fold.

That, I saw, was what you did with a present you didn't like; it was how natural kindness dealt with mistakes.

After the presents, after the blizzard of torn tissue paper ("save that piece, we'll use it next year"), after the carrying off of new possessions to bedrooms to be gloated over, Christmas dinner: turkey with bread stuffing and giblet gravy, mashed potatoes, candied sweet potatoes, cranberry relish, watermelon pickles, pickled peaches, pickled crab apples, homemade rolls. No green vegetables, of course, and no salad: it's winter, and this is farmhouse winter food—at its grandest, but still farmhouse, still winter. My father sits silently for a moment gazing down at the turkey, thinking perhaps how much it cost, or how he'd like a drumstick this time, just for a change, or maybe that this is how life should be all the time, this generosity, this bounty that loads our table. He looks round at the faces of his family, shining with gifts received. Then he launches into his grace: "Lord, we're here today . . ." I lower my head as I'm supposed to, but peep out at the steam rising from the dishes, the turkey and the gravy, the potatoes (two kinds), the rolls. He finishes his prayer, waits while Nellie rattles through hers, then stands, solemn as a preacher in a pulpit, and begins to carve. I am very happy: happiness is this rich having; having is happiness.

By now it is midafternoon, the sun low in the elms on Pillsbury Avenue, the shadows on the snow blue cold. Adults go to their bedrooms for a nap; children run out into the fading day to try out skis or skates, or up into the attic to put the train together, or into the cellar to make lead soldiers and chemical stinks. Christmas has passed its highest moment, gone beyond the excitement of expectation to the diminished, because real, excitement of fulfillment. What I wanted, I have. But having is never as good as wanting, I know that by now. The day will end soon, the last light will fall into darkness; there will be another meal—the same food, but less wonderful now because it isn't Christmas dinner anymore, it's only leftovers—and then something on the radio, or a family game in the living room, and then bedtime, the year's best day done. But not completely, the happiness still floating in the air, the day's special affection still enclosing us. We have had another Christmas, just like the other ones, or so nearly like as to be indistinguishable in memory, a ritual that will be performed again next year, and every year. I take it for granted that this is the right way to celebrate Christmas, the only way there is to act out with food and gifts what we feel, or ought to feel, for each other.

I was a Presbyterian because my father was, but I didn't know what that meant, and his example didn't explain much. He didn't go to church (though I had to), he didn't do anything religious, like praying, in front of other people, except for saying grace on Sundays, he didn't talk about God and Jesus, and if he read his Bible he did it privately, as though religion was a secret.

I could work out a little of what his religion was if I thought about the hymns he liked best. One was "The Old Rugged Cross." He sang it to himself sometimes while he stood at his workbench in the basement, working with his hands, mending a screen or planing a board for a new shelf:

> On a hill far away stood an old rugged cross,
> The emblem of suffering and shame . . .

He sang the words very softly, in a voice that was higher than when he sang in church, as though his bass singing was only something he did to help the choir out:

> To the old rugged cross I will ever be true,
> Its shame and reproach gladly bear . . .

And at the end of the chorus:

> *And exchange it someday for a crown.*

His other favorite was "In the Garden." Someone goes to a garden alone; it's early in the morning, the dew is still on the roses. He hears the voice of Jesus, and they walk and talk together, and Jesus tells him he is His own. That's all.

They were sad, lonely hymns: one man alone, in a garden or on a hill, nobody else around, no preacher, no congregation, no church, just the person who sings, and the cross, and the man who died on it. And suffering and shame, and burdens, and solitude. Only Jesus to talk to. Was that a religion? It wasn't Presbyterianism, those hymns weren't in the hymnal at church: Baptists sang them, and Seventh-Day Adventists! But my father wouldn't mind that; he wasn't an orthodox man, not even in his hymn singing. He had made his own faith out of enduring life's burdens. Salvation didn't seem to enter into it.

Neither did Sin. He hated the same hymn I hated, "Love Lifted Me," but not for my reason, that it was in waltz time. The hymn began:

> *I was sinking, deep in Sin,*
> *Far from the peaceful shore . . .*

What offended him was the idea of Sin as a big body of water, like Lake Michigan or the Atlantic Ocean, with folks just floating around in it—not swimming, not even treading water, just floating, until they were pulled out by Love. Or drowned. I don't think he believed in Sin, not really. For him the problems that tried human hearts and tested human strengths weren't matters of moral failure, they were just troubles—health troubles, money troubles, accidents, crop failures, bankruptcies, fires and floods and storms and winter cold. God gave you strength to face your troubles and you struggled and survived them; or he didn't, and you struggled and sank. Sin didn't come into it at all. There were things you shouldn't do, of course, like drinking, and dancing on Sunday; but they weren't *sins,* they were more like bad manners.

My father's other beliefs were less clearly religious, but he held them with the same quiet certainty. He never put them into words, but I understood what they were, so clearly that I could have carved them on tablets, like Moses with the Ten Commandments.

A man should work. Work is valuable in itself; work is salvation. The worst thing that can happen to a man is to lose his job; out of work is out of life. Men came to our back door, shy men in worn, shabby clothes, and knocked politely and asked if there was any work they could do. There never was—my father did what man-work there was round the house—but he would go out and talk to them, and give them a little money, a quarter or fifty cents, or maybe a dollar bill, and my stepmother would offer them a little plain food ("plenty of nourishment in good bread and butter," she said), and the men would say "thanks" and back off down the steps and go to try next door, where there wouldn't be any work either. I was a little scared of those men, I said they were hoboes; but my father said no, they weren't. They weren't wanderers by choice, they were just out of work. They came to our door because they couldn't think of anything else to do with their time and their hunger. It's a terrible thing, my father said, to be without work.

A man should maintain his property. He should mend what was broken—a screen or a windowpane or a cupboard door. He should plant his own garden and harvest his crop. He should make his house snug and safe for his family. When my father put the storm windows up in the fall, he was doing something more than saving on heating bills, he was putting barriers between us and the cold, like a caveman barricading his cave against saber-toothed tigers. And when he took them down in the spring, he was letting life in, telling us we had survived another winter.

A man should have his own tools, and know how to use them. My father didn't have many tools, and those he had were old, but they were reverently cared for. The blade of his wood-handled plane was always sharp and shiny, and his crosscut saw was silver-toothed and ready. His spirit level was beautiful: waxed oak and polished brass, with little glass tubes on the top and the side full of oil with a bubble in the middle. There were other tools he didn't use much—a ball-headed hammer, some chisels too big for any household job, a pipe wrench as long as my arm: probably they were family tools, what was left when his father gave up the farm. When I watched my father at his workbench, sliding the plane softly along a board, turning up a curl of wood as easily as Nellie peeled an apple, I saw that working with your own hands, with your own tools, on a part of your own house might be a kind of ceremony, maybe even a religion.

A man should meet his obligations. Obligations are a blessing. That meant that a man paid his debts when they came due; to be in debt was almost as shameful as being out of work. A family was a bundle of obligations; a man didn't walk away from them, not any of them, though sometimes he might be tempted. On a damp evening in early spring my father takes my brother and me for a ride in the car. I'm maybe eleven. It's dark, and in the little houses of the neighborhood lamps are lit and cast their squares of light on the gray end-of-winter snow. We drive up and down the streets on the other side of Nicollet—up First, down Stevens, up Second—slowly, as though we are looking for something. My father is silent; his face is in shadow. Finally he says: "How'd you like it if it was just us three again?

Snap, Crackle, and Pop?" I remember his joke on our winter journey through the Nebraska blizzard, and the memory gives me a good feeling; but I don't want to do it again, I don't want to be out there in the cold darkness, I don't want to go back to the shared rooms and the boardinghouses. What about my train in the attic? What about my initials in the cement? I hold my breath, I can't answer. Chuck is silent and motionless beside me, holding his breath, too. My father doesn't say anything more. After a while he drives back home and puts the car in the garage, and we go back into the house. Whatever happened is over. I don't know what it was, and nobody tells me; but when you're eleven you can feel trouble without understanding it. The memory remains, a small seismic shock that makes my world less solid, less secure.

And yet, my father and Nellie seemed genuinely fond of each other. Sometimes at night after I'd gone to bed I'd hear the low murmur of their voices from their room, and Nellie's high stuttering laugh. And when she cooked something he specially liked, Brown Betty or an angel food cake, he'd look up at her as he ate and say, "You're the best cook alive!"

Nellie and I are in the kitchen, just the two of us. She stands at the counter by the sink peeling an apple in one long snake of peel, which I grab from the sink and eat from one end, letting the rest hang down from my mouth like a long green tongue. She glances round at me over her shoulder and asks: "How would you like a little brother?" There's a shy excitement in her voice, as though she's bought me an expensive present and isn't sure I'll like it. I'm shocked: I don't want a little brother, what would I do with one? I make some vague reply. She seems disappointed, but says nothing more, just goes on peeling apples. The subject doesn't come up again, no little brother appears, and I remain the youngest member of the family.

A man should stand on his own two feet. He shouldn't depend on others, he shouldn't move with a crowd. My father didn't believe in joining clubs, he wasn't an Elk or a Moose or an Odd Fellow, he hated the idea of all that fraternal stuff, hanging around in a clubhouse somewhere smoking and telling dirty jokes. There was one exception, though: he was a Mason, always had been. I suppose the Masons, being a *secret* society, seemed all right to him; or maybe it was that they hated Catholics the way he did. He had joined a South Chicago lodge while he was still living there, before my mother died, and he went on paying his dues all through his travels and troubles. He never went to a meeting, but he wore a Masonic ring on his finger, and let me look at it; when I asked what the letters round the edge—KSHFHWSST—meant, he laughed and said: "King Solomon Had Five Hundred Wives, Some Say a Thousand," which I knew wasn't the real secret answer.

When he died, in a suburb south of Chicago, Nellie looked around for pallbearers, and thought of the lodge. Why not? He'd paid dues all those years, and got nothing out of it. On the day of the funeral six strangers in black suits appeared at the funeral parlor and carried the coffin to the hearse, and from the hearse to the grave, and lowered it into the earth. Then they disappeared—just gone, like ghosts from his other life.

Because my father didn't believe in joining groups he didn't like team sports; the all-American, father-and-son-pals-together games weren't part of our family life. He never took me to see a baseball game (though Nicollet Park, where the Millers played, was only four blocks away), or a football game (though the University's team, the Gophers, was the best in the country, and you could get to the stadium on the streetcar). He never taught me the team-sport skills—how to throw from third to first, how to catch a pass, how to dribble and shoot. We didn't even play catch.

Probably he didn't know how himself, probably he had never in his life hit or thrown or carried a ball in a team game; when the other boys in his high school ran out onto the playing field for practice, he went back to the farm to do chores. He'd have been a good football player—a lineman, maybe, or a fullback; he was six feet tall and broad at the shoulders, and he was strong. I could imagine him in the uniform football players wore then: moleskin pants, a tight wool jersey with a number on the back, and a helmet made of leather and felt. If he had played, maybe he'd have learned to join together with other people, and to desire the approval of his teammates and coaches. But he didn't; he stood alone, on his own, and did what he thought was right.

I suppose that's why his favorite sport was wrestling, where one man struggles against another man. He admired the old-fashioned classical wrestlers, Abe Kashey and Strangler Lewis and Bronco Nagurski, strong, straightforward men who fought and won honestly (or so he believed) by strength and skill alone.

He took my brother and me to wrestling matches at the Auditorium. From where we sat, high up in the banked seats, the wrestlers were indistinguishable to me: they were all big, and all wore the same dusty black tights and undershirt tops, more like workers on a building site than athletes. When they wrestled they worked slowly and effortfully and without theatrical effects: they didn't throw each other through the ropes, or pound on the canvas in mock agony, they just leaned together in the center of the ring under the staring lights, straining and grunting, until one pinned the other to the floor and the referee tapped the winner on the shoulder. I liked being there with my father, high up in the blue smoky air among the shouting men, but I didn't understand why they shouted, since nothing much seemed to be happening down in the ring. My father followed the wrestlers' exertion with tense concentration: "Look!" he'd exclaim. "He's got a hammerlock," or a half nelson. He was back in La Porte High School then, the strongest kid in school, who could have been a wrestler, maybe a famous one, if things had been different.

A man shouldn't complain. It wasn't just that complaining wouldn't do any good; it was that a complaining man was less of a man. And being a man was the best you could do. A man stood alone, did his duty, lived the life he was given. He endured.

My father was a Republican. I knew that, but I didn't know what it meant, any more than I knew what a Presbyterian was, and he never told me, or talked about politics when I was around. He didn't believe in talking about such things; beliefs were simply there, in what you were. His politics wasn't a matter of words and slogans and partisan acts: he never put a campaign poster in the front yard, or went to a political meeting, or listened to a political speech, not even on the radio, and I don't suppose he ever gave a candidate a single dollar to help him. His Republicanism was in fact not much more than the frontier self-reliance of his ancestors. It was a faith that would never benefit him in the world he lived in—how could it?—but he believed it would benefit his country, if only enough decent people shared it. Every election day he went to the polls and loyally voted Republican and came home and told us he had.

Nellie went with him and, being a good Catholic, voted straight Democratic, thus canceling his vote, and said nothing.

My father was a Republican, so I was a Republican. And because I was I fought my first real fight. The spring I was eleven Floyd B. Olson was governor of Minnesota. He was Farmer-Labor, so I was against him. My friend Duke was for him; he wore an "Olson for Governor" button on the skullcap he'd made from his father's old felt hat. As we walked home from school one afternoon I looked at his hat and said he shouldn't wear a button like that; Floyd B. Olson was a bad man, I said; he was for the truck drivers in the strike.

Duke said he was for the workingman.

"My dad says he's a Communist."

"Your dad's full of shit!"

So then there had to be a fight. We should have argued more first, chest to chest, trading insults and denials: "He's a crook!" "He isn't!" "You're a liar!" "No, *you* are!" But we didn't; Duke just shoved me backwards into a pile of dirty snow. I lay there looking up at Duke standing over me with his fists clenched. I could fight him, or I could cry. I fought, because I was a Republican, because my father was a Republican, for our family honor.

It wasn't a fistfight—kids don't fight with their fists much—it was more of a wrestling match like the ones I saw at the Auditorium, the two of us grabbing and grunting and rolling around in the wet March snow. I didn't want to hurt Duke, he was my friend; I just wanted to overpower him, shove him down with his shoulders on the ground, and sit on his chest with my knees on his arms until he said, out loud so the other kids could hear, "I give up."

That fight was the peak of my life as a Republican. A new political life began the next fall. It is afternoon in late October 1936, the sun is low in the west, the air is chilly. I stand on the curb on Nicollet Avenue and Thirty-fourth Street in front of Mr. Tenvold's drugstore, part of a crowd that lines Nicollet three or four deep in both directions as far as I can see. Up the street from the south comes a procession of black closed cars, the occupants invisible behind steamed windows. Then an open one, a convertible sedan, the first I've ever seen. It looks like a long black lifeboat. In the back seat sits a big man with a full, smiling face and a thrusting chin. He wears glasses without earpieces pinched on the bridge of his nose, and a gray hat with the brim rolled over all the way round. He turns from one curb to the other, smiling and waving, and the people in the crowd cheer and cheer. Then the procession is gone, north toward Lake Street. I have seen the President of the United States, my first Great Man. I am twelve years old, and I have just become a Democrat.

CHAPTER EIGHT

Easter 1937. Easter is an important feast day in our house: spring has come, Christ has risen, we all have new clothes. This Easter I have been allowed to choose my clothes myself. After church Nellie takes my picture. I stand at the foot of the front steps squinting into the bright sun (it's spring), beside a heap of winter-blackened, half-melted snow (it's Minneapolis), wearing a gray snap-brim hat like the one my father wears, a plaid cardigan sweater, long pants (also plaid), and gray suede shoes with rubber soles. For the picture I have assumed an odd, stiff posture, back rigidly straight, arms linked behind me, feet together—a personal version of standing at attention.

The reason for the stiff attention is the occasion: I am wearing my first pair of long pants, which, with the hat, make me seem a small replica of a grown man—or a midget. I'm aware that this dignity has come to me later than it should; I'm twelve years old, I'm in the seventh grade, other boys in my class have had long pants for a year, or even more. Until now, when I mentioned this fact to Nellie, she replied that I was younger than they were (which was true, I'd skipped a grade), and besides, my knickers had a lot of good wear left in them.

Nellie doesn't understand. Little kids wear shitcatchers, and go to grade school, and sit in the same room with the same teacher all day, and when they go out to the playground at recess they play little kids' games: they run around in flocks like birds, swooping and squawking, or they separate and the girls play jacks and hopscotch and the boys play marbles and mumbly-peg. I don't do those things anymore; I'm in junior high school, I'm not a little kid. And today at last I wear the visible sign of my change—long pants.

Everything changes in junior high school. You're in a room and then the bell rings and you're in the hall going to another room where there's a different teacher and after an hour another bell and another room; the whole day is bustling and bumping and kids yelling. There are more rules here: Walk up the stairs on the right-hand side. Don't run in the halls. Don't go out in the hall during classes without a pass, even if you have to pee. Stand in line in the lunchroom and don't shove. Rules multiply, it seems, as you grow older.

But the more rules there are, the more spaces open between them. At lunchtime you can escape the lunchroom and the rules and go across the street to Carpenter's Candy Store and spend your lunch money on a caramel apple or a devil's food cupcake or a fold of sponge cake filled with yellow goo that tastes a little bit like bananas and smells like airplane glue and squirts out the end when you bite it. You can do what you want.

On the sidewalk outside Mr. Carpenter's store Filipino men no taller than I am demonstrate yo-yos. They can do amazing tricks—"Around the World," "Walking the Dog," "Sleeping," "Spank the Baby"; the yo-yos leap and spin in their brown hands, go away and obediently return. Kids buy the yo-yos, but they can never do all the tricks, not the way the Filipinos can.

Back at school there are other skills to learn: woodworking, printing, electric wiring, metalworking. The school calls them Manual Training, every boy had to take them. They're practical, they get you ready for grown-up jobs. Learn your trade early. But I think they're more like wearing long pants; having these skills will entitle you to enter the world of grown men. A man should know how to work with his own two hands.

In Mr. La Berge's woodworking shop the floor is carpeted deep in sawdust, and wood dust hangs in the bars of sunlight that slant from the high windows, and the air is sweet with the smell of wood. Mr. La Berge shows me how to sharpen the blade of a plane. He wears a blue carpenter's apron with a folded-up wooden ruler in a pocket on his chest. He holds the bright plane blade carefully in his hands and moves it in small steady circles on the sharpening stone. Concentrating, doing the job right.

I make a clothesline reel in Mr. La Berge's shop—everybody does, it's the easiest job a kid can do, just two dowels connected by short lengths of wood. I give it to Nellie. She smiles and thanks me and sends me out to put the clothesline up. I move on to a more difficult project, a boat: not a sailboat, which would be prettier and more fun, but a speedboat because it looks easier. I shape the hull slowly and laboriously, holding a spokeshave in both hands and pulling it toward me over the wood in the vise, turning block into boat. With a coping saw I cut windows in the wood for the cabin. I sand the hull and the cabin and nail them together, and paint the hull shiny white. I make a stand. When it's done I take it home and launch it in the bathtub; it floats lop-sidedly. I give it to my father and he puts it on top of the Philco in the living room. It's there in its stand in family pictures, a decoration and a point of fatherly pride: "Sam made that."

The print shop has a different smell—of ink, which is everywhere, and gets on your hands and face and clothes. I stand at a type case. In my left hand I hold a stick, which isn't a stick at all but a metal rack for holding type as you set it. With my right hand I pick up type one letter at a time from the case and set it in a line in the stick, writing my name backwards:

senyH maS

When I've finished setting I slip the set type onto the stone, lock it into a form (slugging and tightening it so it won't fall out when I lift it), place it on the press bed, and pull a proof. Now I can read what I have set the right way round:

Sam Hynes Junior
104 West Thirty-fifth Street
Minneapolis, Minnesota
United States of America

The black italic lines march leaning across the proof, real, physical. I have printed my own calling card: that person is me. The card won't be of any use to me, I can't imagine handing one to anybody ("Here, take my calling card"—why would I do that?), but I've made it, with my own two hands.

I loved the shops, their sounds and smells and the way the light came in. I loved the sure movements of the teacher's hands, the gestures of habitual skill, and the tools, the way each one was special for the job it did, the heft and shape of them in my hands. I loved the words, too, that named the things we worked with: spokeshave, fretsaw, miter box, brace-and-bit; slug, font, galley; circuit breaker, fuse box. Those words were a world, where men worked.

Typing was different; it was a girls' skill, it didn't even have any tools, a typewriter isn't a tool. Nevertheless I learned to type; it might be useful some day, Nellie said, you never knew. I sat in a room full of girls and clattering typewriters and wrote without looking at the keys: "The quock brown foc jymps over the laxy dog." That sentence used all the letters on the keyboard. Then I tried to write it again faster and with fewer mistakes. At the end of the course I had nothing I had made, nothing I could hold and touch and look at. But I could type, if I looked at the keys. Maybe Nellie was right, maybe typing would get me a job in an office; but the wood, the ink, the tools, the lively wires, they were better.

Musical instruments are tools. Not the kid instruments we had in grade school, the mouth organs and jew's harps and sweet potatoes that little kids carry in their pockets but can't play, but real, grown-up instruments. I took trumpet lessons, and joined the junior-high-school band. My brother was already there, playing the trombone. We wore red-and-white uniforms, and played strutting soldiers' music, and when the weather was fine we went out on the school playground and practiced marching up and down and playing at the same time. I didn't understand why we marched; our school had no sports teams, there were no big games with other schools, and we weren't good enough for the Fourth of July parade. We just marched.

It wasn't easy, keeping step, following the person ahead of me, turning smartly at the right place and on the right foot without knocking my horn against the sousaphone in the next rank, all the time trying to read the music in the little lyre-shaped clip fastened to my trumpet. But I was happy marching there in the bright autumn air, the sun blinking and flashing on the bells of the horns, the white legs of the marchers moving, and the music blaring. I liked the noise we made, the loud brass and the rattling drums and the high tweeting fifes and flutes, and the way the trumpets all played one stirring phrase, like an army going to war—

TUM-ta-ta-TUM-ta-ta-TUM-tum-TUM

—and then some of them played it a third higher, and then some higher still, and then we played it all together in brave chords that ended with a fortissimo TAH-TUM! I liked seeing my brother up ahead among the trombones pumping his slide in and out, and meeting him coming back when we wheeled and turned, his face red and his eyes popping with the blowing, both of us playing the same tune and marching to the same cadence, with nobody watching us except the little kids in the backyards beyond the playground fence.

I liked it all. But I couldn't really play the trumpet, not well enough to be out there marching in the band. I held my horn to my lips, and when I knew where we were in the music, I blew, and the rest of the time I just marched and twiddled the valves. Marching in a band without actually playing the music was something you could get away with, in junior high school.

The little kids who watched us as we marched around the playground were Negroes; they lived in the houses along Clinton Avenue. Their mothers hung out their washings when we played, paying us no mind. Bigger kids from those houses were in school with me. I had never met a colored person before; there weren't many in Minnesota, and most of them lived across town on Sixth Avenue North, where I had never been. But a small Negro neighborhood, only a few blocks square, had grown up around Fourth Avenue and Thirty-eighth Street. If you rode through it on your bike you couldn't tell where it began and ended, the houses were just like all the other houses in our part of town, small and neat, each on its narrow lot. But then a man would come out and stand on his porch and watch you riding by, and you'd feel you were wrong to be there, this was a hostile country you'd blundered into.

I was afraid of the Negro boys in my school. They were bigger than I was, and tough looking; and they knew more than I did—not about school matters, maybe, but about everything else. I stayed away from them, and they stayed away from white boys like me. They sat together at the back of every class, they played together at recess, they ate their lunches together; they never talked to us, or even acknowledged that we were there. Except in the swimming pool.

The pool was in a long, low-roofed room by the gym. Everything was white there—white painted ceiling, white tiles on the walls and floor, no color anywhere except for the ice-blue water. Lights from the ceiling fractured and blinked on the pool's pitching surface and threw moving patches of reflection on the tiles; sounds—the slopping of the water, the teacher's whistle—echoed from the walls. It was always cold in the room where the pool was, even before you jumped into the water.

Boys and girls swam at different times. Girls wore bathing suits when it was their turn (but boys weren't allowed to see them); boys swam naked. On my first day at swimming class I crept out of the locker room, trying to conceal my private parts without seeming to, and stood, shy and cold, at the pool's edge. The Negro boys in the class stood on the opposite side, close together by the white wall, like generals planning an attack in a war that hadn't quite begun yet. Their bare, black-all-over bodies were strong and muscular, more like men's bodies than boys', more developed, more male. The cluster of black bodies didn't break up into separate ordinary kids like us, horsing around and trying to push each other into the water; they stayed aloof, silent and motionless, closed in their common identity.

The coach blew his whistle. First, he said, you're all going to swim a race, just to show me how well you can swim. Line up against the wall. Now the first eight boys to the end of the pool. They shuffled up and stood in an uncertain row. Except for one Negro boy: he crouched at the very edge, knees bent, arms stretched back, toes gripping the tiles. The coach blew his whistle and the Negro kid plunged flat out into space and hit the water swimming in a long, fast crawl, barely turning to breathe, feet beating up a wake behind him. He was at the other end and turned and coming back before the other kids had begun. Like a fish, I thought or Johnny Weissmuller in the Tarzan movies.

I knew that kid, sort of, he was in my homeroom. I didn't know his name, or even his face, really; what I recognized was his hand. All over the back of his right hand the skin was shiny and cracked looking, like the crackling on roast meat, as though someone had pressed a hot iron down on it and held it there. But how could that happen to a kid? Who would do such a thing?

Afterward, in the locker room, I talked to him. I said I wished I could swim as fast as he did. You should swim down at the Y, I said, you could be on the team, and win a prize. He turned toward me, fiercely, angrily; they won't let me, he said. I almost asked why not? But I knew. We walked to our next class together. He said his name was Nelson Peery.

Away from school the Negro boys were freer, and sometimes they seemed threatening. They used ugly-sounding words I didn't know: *motherfucker*, and *cocksucker*, and they stared angrily, and took offense at things. You had to be careful. In winter after supper they came sometimes to skate under the floodlights at Nicollet Field, and we met them there and mixed and even played together on the ice—hockey or tag or Crack the Whip—but tensely and cautiously, as though the color line that was drawn between us was a no-man's-land where war between Negroes and whites might begin any time.

On a cold night I sit on a pile of snow in the half darkness at the edge of the rink, putting on my skates. My friend Duke has his on and is idly making patterns on the ice, skating backwards, making circles and figure eights. A Negro boy named Sharp skates by. "Hi, Sharp!" Duke yells. "Where you been, you old sonovabitch?" Sharp stops skating. I stop lacing. Duke stops his figure-eight skating and stands motionless on the ice, like someone who has just pulled a trigger he didn't mean to pull. Sharp skates up to him, very close, and says in a voice so low I can hardly hear it: "Boy, you talkin' 'bout my mama." The silence is abrupt and absolute. Duke looks down and begins to kick the point of his skate blade into the ice, again and again, making a *chip-chipping* noise that is the only sound. Then he turns and skates away and Sharp skates in the opposite direction. I have seen something dangerous happen, or almost happen, a moment of emotion higher than acts or words. There will be no war this time. But no peace, either.

At about the same time that I got my first long pants, I discovered sex. There's a connection: you can't enter the world of sex wearing knickers. But discovered is the wrong word; sex began to happen. It came mostly as an embarrassment. A guy with his first pair of long pants sits at his desk at school with a hard-on (for no evident reason except that he's twelve or thirteen), and when the teacher asks him a question he can't stand up to answer it, or go to the blackboard to do the problem, but has to say he doesn't know, when he really does. He wakes up in the night and finds his pajamas damp and sticky, and wonders what has happened to him, and what his mother will say; but she just puts the pajamas into the washing machine and says nothing, as though an explosion of sperm in the middle of the night was as ordinary as ironing. He learns to masturbate, and feels guilty, and is shocked that other boys in school talk about it frankly. "See that guy?" Dickie D. whispers in the hall, "That's Frenchy. He jacked off seven times in one day!" And we look at Frenchy with a kind of admiration, as though he were a star athlete, a fullback or a long-distance runner.

A guy in his first long pants knows that sex is everywhere. Only what does it look like? He doesn't know, he has never seen it. There are no models of the sexual life in his house; he can't imagine his parents doing whatever it is that men and women do, and his sisters can't be objects of anybody's desire, they're just sisters. But there are girls in his school, they pass him in the halls and sit near him in classes. He begins to realize that underneath their clothes girls are *naked*. He'd like to see some of that nakedness, but when he tries to peek down their blouses or up their skirts, they catch him looking and are offended, and tell him he's a dirty boy. Or don't catch him, and he has a glimpse, a wink of underclothes, and is excited. Seeing a girl's underwear has been a game for boys for as long as he can remember; even back in grade school, if a girl tripped on the playground or had her skirt blown up by the wind, little boys would dance around her chanting "I see London, I see France, I see Nancy's underpants!" Just the sight of that last thin covering of nakedness was enough, then.

But not when you're thirteen. Now you want to see, to have seen, nakedness itself. It seems impossible, but you have to try: when you have seen a girl's bare body you'll be different. Kids pursued that naked goal in desperate ways. A boy I knew at school climbed out of his bedroom window onto the porch roof one night and watched through the bathroom window while his sister took a bath. Then he told us what her body looked like. He had seen what none of the rest of us had seen, an entirely naked female, and he must have expected to be envied and praised. But we turned away, embarrassed. His own sister! That was *dirty!*

Dirty was looking up girls' dresses and peeping at your sister bathing, but it was more than that: it was a language, a whole vocabulary of jokes and sniggers. Dickie D. could speak Dirty. That was probably because he played the accordion. He performed for all kinds of grown-up clubs—the Elks, the Moose, the American Legion, the Odd Fellows, the Shriners—and the men at those club meetings talked dirty among themselves and told dirty stories, and Dickie D. listened. When I saw him on the playground during recess, he'd have a circle of boys around him, and as I approached I'd hear the last line of a joke—"Wrecked 'm, hell, it damn near killed 'm!"—and he'd grin and look round the circle sideways from under his drooping blond hair, and the boys would laugh uncertainly because they didn't get the joke but could see it was a joke and if they didn't laugh they wouldn't belong to Dickie D.'s dirty world.

Dickie knew dirty-word jokes, too, like "I'm not a fig-plucker nor a fig-plucker's son . . ." that you were supposed to say over and over again, faster and faster, until you were talking dirty without meaning to. And he made puns with words, making clean words dirty; a word like *whom* was dirty-funny to him because it sounded like something inside a woman's body. And he would look round and grin.

I'm on the ice at Powderhorn Park on a winter afternoon. Dickie D. and Birdy skate up, skidding to a sudden stop in a spray of ice chips. Dickie D. whispers in my ear; he has figured out how we can peek into the girls' toilet in the warming house. He dares Birdy—poor dopey Birdy—to try it out, just to see if the scheme works. We skate across the frozen lake and climb the splintery wooden warming-house steps, still wearing our skates, making the thumping bumping sound that skate blades make on wood, into the boys' toilet. Birdy peers under the doors of the stalls; nobody there. He opens a stall and sits down on the toilet to take off his skates. The walls and door are scribbled with names and initials and drawings. And with rhymes:

> *Here I sit, brokenhearted*
> *Paid a nickel and only farted!*

and

> *A man's ambition must be small*
> *Who'll write his name on a shithouse wall.*

and

> *No matter how much you shake and dance*
> *The last drop's always in your pants.*

A record of what kids (and adults, too, for all I know) think about when they're in there, what they think is funny about toilets.

Birdy doesn't pause to read the messages on the walls. He climbs onto the seat and from there to the top of the stall. Balancing there, he stretches above his head and dislodges the grate on the ceiling air vent and moves it to one side and pulls himself up into the darkness above until only his kicking legs and stockinged feet are visible. Then they, too, disappear. I stand around below; Dickie D. is outside, as usual—keeping watch, he says. Birdy is gone a long time; what's he doing, what's he seeing, looking down through the vent in the ceiling of the girls' toilet? What does he know now that I don't know?

His face appears in the opening above my head: Is the coast

clear? He kicks his legs over, reaching blindly for the stall frame, and lets himself down. He is covered with dust and cobwebs. Dickie D. comes in to hear what happened.

Birdy doesn't look as triumphant as I expected, not like a guy who has seen a girl with her bottom bare. Why doesn't he grin and strut, why doesn't he say anything? Finally I ask him:

What happened? What did you see?

I could look straight down, he says, right into the can.

But what did you see?

Well, Donna Nelson came in to take a leak, and she pulled her snow pants down . . .

And what did you see then?

See? I saw the top of her head, and the shoulders of her snowsuit, and the knees of her snow pants.

And?

That's all. *You can't see nothing from the top!*

You could learn some things about women's bodies from the magazines in Mr. Tenvold's drugstore, when Mr. Tenvold wasn't looking. *Esquire* was a big shiny magazine full of colored drawings of women in bathing suits, or lying on beds in negligees with their breasts almost bare and their legs sticking out of the covers. You learned from those drawings that sex was funny. But they weren't drawings of real female bodies; they didn't tell you anything about the girls in the eighth grade.

Farther along the rack were pulp magazines like *Spicy Detective.* They had their visual images, too: on the cover, a man in a trench coat and a snap-brim hat reached for a girl who was coming out of her clothes. There were more illustrations inside. The stories were better than the pictures, though, because sex wasn't about girls just lying there, however close they came to nakedness; it was what people *did*. Sex had a plot.

Dickie D. stops me in the hall at school and whispers, "Come in the can, I want to show you something." His pockets are full of little comic books, and he pulls them out one at a time and shows them to me: Ella Cinders, Popeye, Andy Gump, Mr. & Mrs.—all the comic characters I read about every Sunday morning lying on the living-room floor. But they're different here. In these comics they take their clothes off, and display their private parts, and do sex things with each other. Someone comes into the can, and Dickie D. stuffs the books back in his pockets and walks out whistling. But we read them again after school, up an alley or in somebody's garage on the way home, sniggering and nudging each other. The drawings are crude and exaggerated (so are the drawings in the Sunday funny papers), but they teach us a little bit about the sexual act, how the woman lies down (mostly) and the man climbs on top, and how their bodies meet. You couldn't do it yourself with only these comics to guide you, but they're a start. And they're forbidden— we know that without being told—and that in itself makes them worth reading. They don't spoil the Sunday funnies—I go on laughing at Popeye and Olive Oyl as innocently as ever—but they show me the other side of the imagined world, where even Mr. & Mrs. fuck.

Birdy's father was manager of the Ford garage on Lake Street. Birdy hung around there a lot—he liked cars and wanted to be a mechanic when he grew up—and one day he found dirty books of a different kind hidden on top of a locker. These were dirty books for grown-ups, with a story printed on the left-hand page and a photograph facing it. "Printed in Paris," the title-page said; some mechanic who was a soldier in the war must have brought them home and hid them where he worked, away from his wife and kids. And Birdy found them.

He showed them to me, one afternoon in his room—slewed the whole pile out across his bed like a big deck of cards. He chose one and sat on his bed, and I chose another and sat on the chair by the window, and we read. When we had finished the books we had we exchanged them, not saying anything, and read on. We read all that afternoon until the daylight faded. It wasn't like ordinary reading, it was more like staring—at the photographs, but at the words, too, words we'd never seen written before except on the walls of the Powderhorn toilets.

The French books were dirtier than Dickie D.'s cartoon books, because real people were in the photographs—lots of naked people combining and intertwining in ways that were sometimes hard to figure out: dingy-looking people, with plain, tired-looking bodies, not smooth and inflated like the *Esquire* girls, or extravagantly sexual like Popeye and Olive Oyl, just people doing dirty things for money. Looking at them was like being in a smelly toilet; but I looked, tossing one book aside and taking up another. They were all different, but they were all the same; sex had plots, but not very many.

It was our silence that made Birdy's mother suspicious; it wasn't natural for boys to be quiet together. She came to the top of the stairs.

"What are you doing in there?"

"Nothing." That was always the best answer to a mother. "We're not doing anything."

After we'd left, his mother searched Birdy's room. He wasn't any better at hiding the books than the mechanic at the garage had been; she found them under his mattress. She went sort of crazy, Birdy said, stomping around the house waving the books and yelling, sometimes at him and sometimes at his father, who had just come in from work. It wasn't the books that bothered her so much, Birdy said; she wanted to know what we *did*. But we hadn't done anything, not what she meant; we had simply stared at the books in remote astonishment, the way we looked at half-naked African women in the *National Geographic*. What did dirty French people in old pictures have to do with two kids in a house on Blaisdell Avenue?

Birdy's mother was right, we did want to do something. But not with each other; with girls. We wanted to know everything about girls—how they looked, and smelled and felt and tasted, everything.

All these disturbances of life in the eighth grade belonged to the world of men, the long-pants world I had just entered. You could set them down as natural laws in that world:

> *A man likes to look at women.*
> *A man wants to see women naked.*
> *A man wants to touch women's bodies.*

And maybe add:

> *A man likes to talk dirty about women to other men*
> (but not, of course, to women).

My father wouldn't accept these laws, not for a minute; but I knew they were true.

A soft spring evening: I am out on a restless ramble, down side streets and up alleys, searching for something without knowing what it is. I take a shortcut across the high-school grounds, diagonally up the terraces that form the school's front lawn. When I reach the second terrace I stop for breath. I am level with the second-story windows of the house across Fourth Avenue. The windows are dark, except for one. In that lighted room a girl stands before her dresser. I am held by her solitude, which I have ignorantly entered. She pulls her sweater over her head, and tosses her head to shake her hair back into place. She drops her skirt to the floor, and I imagine the sound of falling leaves. She reaches both hands behind her back to release her bra, and tosses it onto the bed. She slips her underpants down and steps out of them, one foot and then the other. For a moment she stands in front of her mirror, examining her reflected body, approving it. She raises her hands to her hair and then cups them beneath her breasts. Then she turns toward the window, sees that the blind is up, and reaching out toward me, slowly draws it down, turning the window into a blind bright rectangle, like the screen in a movie when the film ends.

And I on the dark terrace am motionless, rapt, like a worshiper in a church when the service has just ended, or the audience at a concert in that instant of silence after the last chord of a great work of music has faded, the silence that separates the world of art from the ordinary coughing, shuffling life of people. For the first time in my life I have seen a girl in the perfection of her nakedness. Her body is beautiful, but I am held by more than its beauty. I have been witness to something rare and private. This bright vision is not like what my friends have told me about, or what I have seen in the dirty books, or heard in dirty words. It is more like a story out of some old book, in which a hero meets a goddess, and knows her divinity by her majestic nakedness.

I turn and run on across the terrace, leaping and shouting.

CHAPTER NINE

The Philco in the living room was mine until six o'clock: Dick Tracy at five, Tom Mix at five-fifteen, Jack Armstrong at five-thirty, Renfrew of the Mounties at five-forty-five. I didn't lie with my head under the radio anymore—the emptiness inside the box had lost its magical presences—but I still listened, when I was thirteen.

At six, when the news came on, the Philco became my father's. He sat in his big chair smoking a cigarette, not lounging but straight upright, facing the radio as though he was in church and the radio was the pulpit, while voices told him of the world's distresses and disasters: in Spain a civil war was being fought; in Germany the Chancellor threatened other countries; in Abyssinia Italians killed Abyssinians; in Hawaii Amelia Earhart crashed a plane. The reports came, one after another, from places I had never been, where no one I knew had ever been. They were about reality, I didn't doubt that, but in another world than mine; Barcelona and Berlin and Addis Ababa were places in stories that the radio told to grown-ups every evening, after it had told my stories. The events in those grown-ups' stories were serious—I could tell that from the look on my father's face as he listened—but to me they seemed all of the same order of seriousness. They were like the crises that came at the end of every episode in my kids' serials—an Oriental fiend, an earthquake, an Indian war party, a poisonous cobra, a gangster, a foreigner with an accent—necessary dangers to keep the story going, but surmountable by heroes who ate Wheaties and drank Ovaltine.

It was different when the news story happened in Minneapolis or St. Paul. When rich brewers from across the river were kidnapped and held for ransom, when gangsters fought gang wars in the streets and shot at policemen from apartment-house windows, those stories were real in the same way winter weather and city streets were real; they had happened in the world I walked in.

When a newspaper man named Liggett was killed in a downtown alley, that was real. His daughter Marda went to Lyndale School, where I had gone. The day he died he picked her up after school and drove her to the Lake Street library (I got books there, too), and then home to South Second Street (I knew where that was, way over east in the bend where the river turns south). He drove up the alley (like our alley, all alleys are the same) and got out of his car to open the garage doors. And as he stood there a car pulled up beside him and a machine gun poked out of the backseat window and fired five bullets into his body, and he died there in the alley right in front of Marda's eyes. Kid Cann, my father said; it was Kid Cann and his gang killed him. Liggett was writing things about the Mob in his paper.

Violence and death didn't happen often on the South Side of town where I lived; all the shootings and the stabbings went on somewhere else—on Sixth Avenue North were the poorest Negroes lived, down on Bohemian Flats under the Washington Avenue Bridge, and among the drunks and bums on Washington Avenue at the bottom of downtown. Not in our neighborhood: on West Thirty-fifth Street folks didn't lock their doors or their cars in the daytime, and kids and women walked around alone and nobody worried. By daylight we were all decent folks in my part of town.

It was different at night. After my father had banked the fire he walked through the house, locking the doors and checking the window latches. I liked to see him on his rounds, night after night, making our homestead safe. I wasn't afraid, exactly; but outside in the darkness and the cold there might be something, some creature frightening in a way I couldn't even imagine, that would come out of the night and silently enter our sleeping house, and do a terrible violence without a name. I wanted night locked out.

The death of Laura Kruse was like that, an act of night that was more frightful because it happened in a corner of my part of town, and so was not only terrible but also possible—not evil done in the distance, or in the movies, but right here, where decent folks lived.

It happened on the last day of winter. In Minnesota that date doesn't mean spring has come, it only means that the long cold season is exhausted. March is the naked time between winter and spring; the piles of soot-stained snow are shrinking, the air is clammy and penetrating, the earth is a blank page: no buds on the trees, no birds, nothing green anywhere. A dead, gray time to die in.

I read about the murder on the front page of the *Journal* I delivered on my paper route, and I saw the photograph at the bottom of the page, the dead girl lying facedown beside the

Attacker Kills South Side Girl Outside Home

Beauty Operator Slain After Leaving Party—Dragged Across Street— Car Following Trolley Checked

foundations of a house, half on, half off a patch of dirty snow. Her skirt had been pulled above her waist, and her white under-

Body of Slain Girl as It Was Found at Rear of South Side Home

Brutally beaten, the body of Laura Kruse, 18-year-old beauty academy student, was found Saturday at the rear of a vacant house at 5125 Fourteenth avenue S. Photo shows body as found by Wallace Perlich, 5129 Fourteenth avenue S.

clothes were disarranged, and there were stains—dirt or blood—on her legs. I couldn't see her face. I didn't know her, of course. And yet I did. A country girl, from up near Pine City, who had come to town to learn how to be a beauty-parlor operator. She went to the DeGuile School of Beauty Culture down on Nicollet and Eighth ("That's where I went to beauty school," Nellie said). She was eighteen, just out of high school (like my stepsisters), and she had to find a way of supporting herself (like my stepsisters, like our maids Gladys and Olga). It could have been any of them lying dead on the snow, out on the South Side.

That's what they said at Sunday dinner the next day:

It could have been one of us.

Nobody even heard it happen.

A person's not safe anywhere anymore.

(But they didn't mean a person; they meant a girl, a young woman. There were men out there in the night.)

The story that the paper told from the testimony of wit-

nesses—neighbors, a streetcar conductor, beauty-school friends—
was certainly enough to frighten girls on their own. Laura Kruse
had been living with a couple she knew in their house on Fourteenth Avenue South, out at the end of the Bloomington streetcar line. I knew that neighborhood; Nellie's sister Gert, the one
who was married to the butcher, lived out there. It was yesterday's farmland, flat and treeless, row after row of little one-story
houses, all alike on their narrow lots, laid out on identical
straight streets. An anonymous anyplace.

On the night she was killed she had been to a party downtown with girls from the school; they'd just finished their course,
they were celebrating being real beauticians. After the party she
and some of the other girls caught the night-owl streetcar home.
One by one her friends got off, along with other late travelers,
until she and one couple were the only passengers. Then the
couple left. It was past midnight then, the city was asleep. I could
see it all in my mind—the streetcar moving along Bloomington
Avenue between the dark rows of houses, screeching and tossing up sparks when it crossed over switches (sleepers woke and
thought "the Night Owl" and fell asleep again), sliding the light
from its windows along the piled snow at the curb. I could see
the motorman at the front staring ahead along the tracks, glad it
was his last run. And behind him, sitting alone on a yellow-straw
seat, the girl, looking out without seeing the sleeping houses and
the deserted side streets, thinking about the party, and about going home to Pine City in a day or two to work in the beauty parlor there and marry and have a home and a family; but maybe a
little frightened by the darkness beyond the streetcar's cold light.

Because the streets were empty the motorman noticed one
car—a black Ford coupe. It passed him first around Twenty-
fourth Street, blowing its horn to get by, and again just beyond
Lake Street, and around Fortieth, and at Forty-ninth, where it

stopped and turned off its lights, and let the streetcar pass. At Fiftieth it caught up with the streetcar again and drove along beside its front doors, and the man at the wheel peered in.

When the streetcar stopped at Fifty-first Street to let Laura Kruse off, the Ford stopped, too, and watched her go. The motorman was suspicious by then, and tried to read the Ford's license plate, but could only make out a few numbers. The car pulled ahead for two blocks and then turned right—the direction the girl had taken—and when the motorman reached that corner he slowed down to see where it went. He could see it turning again, back toward where Laura Kruse was hurrying toward her house. He was worried about the girl alone in the dark and the hovering Ford, he thought he should have warned her. But he had his schedule to meet, and he drove his streetcar on to the end of the line, and turned round and headed back for the car barn and the end of his shift.

By then Laura Kruse was dead. Her murderer had caught her at her front door (her keys and purse and a box of cake from the party lay on the snow nearby), and had struck her there (that's where the blood was). When she fled around the house into the backyards of the block, he followed and caught her beside an empty house, and there he raped and strangled her. Some of the neighbors heard a cry—a short, shrill scream. One man opened his back door and let his dog out, but saw nothing, though the dog ran back and forth barking; another man heard the scream and woke his wife to ask her if she had heard anything, and when she said no he went back to sleep. The body was found at morning light, when the people on the block went to work.

I read everything the papers printed about the Kruse case: the motorman's story, the testimony of the neighbors, the promises of the police. A man was arrested with blood on his clothing and bruises on his face, but was released; Ford coupes with the license numbers the motorman thought he had read were searched

for and examined; a statewide hunt was begun for persons sus-
pected of sex crimes, some of which I had never heard of: ped-
erasts, exhibitionists, masochists, auto-eroticists were gathered
up and questioned. Folks from all over the Northwest wrote to
the police to report suspects: a seventy-year-old Indian man in
Savage had a reputation for bothering women; a man in Bemidji
was a confirmed masturbator; a man who lived near Shakopee
exposed himself to children. Police departments in other states
sent photographs of their favorite perverts. Every girl and woman
in Minneapolis who had ever been approached or frightened by
a strange man was interviewed. People sent checks to be added
to the reward offered for finding the murderer.

The investigation went on—a week, two weeks, a month—
reported now in shorter articles on the inside pages of the *Journal,* and then not reported at all. But I wasn't worried, the police
would catch him. They'd find the overlooked clue, the one mis-
take every criminal makes; they'd track him down. The story
would end like a crime in a movie, or in *True Detective*.

But it didn't. It just stopped. And he was still out there, the
undiscovered murderer, walking the sidewalks I walked, or driving slowly past in his Ford car. He would always be there, like
the Pig Woman of La Porte.

I remembered Bernice Rosen—sort of. She was the small dark
girl who sat at the back of my sixth-grade room at Lyndale
School and never said anything, or stood at the edge of the playground during recess, silently watching the other kids playing
Pum-Pum-Pullaway and Red Rover—a sharp-eyed girl, bright
looking but in a wary, vulnerable way, like a squirrel that had
wandered too far from its tree. I never spoke to her. Kids have a
ritual of silence that is stricter than adult reticence: if they don't
know another kid they don't speak; they just stare and move

away. That silence, that turning away can be cruel; but kids are cruel, cruelty is a part of their world.

Out on the playground in the swoop and chatter of play, there were lots of ways of being cruel. Boys' ways were mostly physical: they pushed each other off the teeter-totter, making the other end crash down, bumping the kid sitting on it; they hurtled down the slide feet first, into the little kid who slid before them; they threw balls and stones and cinders at one another, and in the winter snowballs with rocks in them. If you were a boy you could hold a little kid's head locked in the bend of your arm and rub the knuckles of your clenched fist back and forth on his scalp, hard (that was Dutch rub); or grip his forearm with both hands and twist in opposite directions (that was an Indian burn). Or a bunch of you might grab a solitary boy and hold him and pull his pants down, for no reason except that there was a gang of you and only one of him, and leave him standing alone with his knickers down around his ankles. Maybe he'd cry, and if he did you'd chant, "Crybaby! Crybaby!"

Little girls were different, their cruelties weren't physical. They whispered, two girls together looking at a third; they pointed; they teased. When they played their girl games—hopscotch, jacks, jump rope—

> *Cinderella, dressed in yella,*
> *Went downtown to meet her fella,*
> *How many kisses did he give her?*

—they always left one girl out—the plain one, the small, sad, shy one—because if you don't leave somebody *out,* how can you think of yourself as *in?*

Bernice Rosen was one of the lonely ones. I didn't speak to her, but I knew who she was. But then the school year ended, and

I moved on to Bryant Junior High School and she went to Jefferson, over on Hennepin Avenue, and I forgot about her, until the summer I was thirteen, the summer I became a library haunter.

The library I haunted was down on Lake Street. I followed my usual route when I went there—across the Lot, through the yards of the car barn, and along the bleachers wall of Nicollet Park, where the Millers played. On home-game afternoons I'd stop and hang around on the sidewalk behind home-plate corner for a while, listening to the game sounds—the yelling crowd, the shouts of men selling beer and hot dogs, the wooden smack of a hit—hoping the batter would hit a foul so high it would clear the grandstand roof and fall at my feet. If you got to the ball first and turned it in at the gate, the ticket man would let you in free to watch the rest of the game.

So I always gave luck a chance. If I got in I might see someone hit a ball over the fence into Nicollet Avenue: maybe Dutch Hauser, the first baseman, down from the Majors with legs so tired fans said he had to hit a home run to get on base at all; or Buzz Arlett, an outfielder who had once played a season with the Phillies. Buzz only had nine fingers. I'd seen a picture of his batting grip in the *Tribune,* and one finger of his left hand was just a stub, with a little cover over it like a short, one-fingered glove. Forty-one homers in a season with only nine fingers seemed to me heroic. But Buzz had quit baseball by the time I began to haunt libraries, and had opened a bar (a saloon, my father said) on Lake Street around the corner from the ballpark. So I wasn't supposed to admire him anymore.

Lake Street was the bottom edge of my neighborhood. On our side, folks lived in houses with clean curtains, and grass in the yard; on the other side there were railroad tracks and factories and people lived in furnished apartments and rooming houses and didn't pay their rent. For these two neighborhoods

Lake Street was Main Street. Sears and Roebuck was there, and the New Lake Theater where I watched Tom Mix and Flash Gordon on Saturday afternoons, and the White Castle hamburger stand where Nelson Peery and his friends broke all the windows because the manager wouldn't sell hamburgers to Negroes, and the Idle Hour Pool Hall, and the dime store where I was caught stealing.

Most of the Lake Street buildings looked alike: yellow-brown brick, two or three stories high, with stores on the street level that sold stuff you wouldn't ever want to buy: parts for old cars, marked-down clothes, secondhand vacuum cleaners. Entryways between the stores led to apartments upstairs. A film of dusty failure lay over everything—the store windows, the goods they showed, the curtains in the upstairs windows.

Bars along the street breathed out the stale smell of beer and a mumble of voices and jukebox music. They were wicked places. I peered into the dark interiors as I passed, curious to see what wickedness looked like; but I only saw shadowy figures along the bar, sagged over their drinks, doing nothing. Sometimes I saw men along the sidewalk who had been in those bars. They wore dirt-stained clothes—not work clothes, not overalls, but old suit coats that didn't match their pants—and they were drunk. Their movements weren't anything like what kids did when we played at being drunk, staggering about and falling down and hollering with laughter; these men walked with a fierce, concentrated unsteadiness, staring and muttering to themselves. They must live desperate lives, beyond what West Thirty-fifth Street could imagine.

The Lake Street library didn't look like a library, but like what it was, a half-converted store in a block of stores, next to the auto-parts store and across the street from the White Castle. You walked into it the way you would walk into any store in the row, like a shopper, without reverence. Nothing inside was inviting—there were no soft reading lights or upholstered chairs, nothing to suggest permanence or comfort, or to invite quiet reflection; only books, lined up against the walls like the stock in the dime store. But the books were enough: I went in like a thief entering a bank vault, not knowing what anything was worth, or what to take first, but feeling riches around me.

The best thing about the library was nobody told you which books were the good ones, you had to find them yourself. The librarian was only there to keep you from talking, or stealing. When I found an author I liked I camped there; I read all the books of Albert Payson Terhune, all of Arthur Ransome, all of Jack London, all of Ernest Thompson Seton, all of Booth Tarkington's Penrod books, all of Richard Halliburton, and every book in a series about children in other places and other times: *Og, Son of Fire,* and *Young Fu of the Upper Yangtze.* I pulled books off the shelves for any old reason—because I liked the cover, or because they were illustrated, or because of their titles, or their thickness, and carried them home and read them straight through and took them back and got another armload.

None of the books I read had anything to do with me or any place or time I knew anything about. But the worlds inside them were real—as real as West Thirty-fifth Street, as true as street signs. I liked the maps in Arthur Ransome's books because they seemed to prove their book-reality; the children in them, John and Susan and Titty and Roger, would always be where Ransome said they were, you could look them up on the maps. I didn't know that the places were real English places with real English names—Coniston Water and the Norfolk Broads—but it wouldn't have mattered if I had; to me they were imaginary places that were true. The same with Richard Halliburton's endpaper maps, they didn't chart the earth's actual geography: Carthage and Mount Olympus, the Taj Mahal, the Matterhorn, the Alhambra were only real when the books were open, but they were real and true then. Other books would have different realities, they might happen in deserts where genii lived in jars, or in a grimpen where an enormous hound roamed, or at the center of the earth, or in a country where a toad drove his own motor car; I didn't care, so long as the world the book said was true stayed true to the last page.

Trips to the library were solitary journeys; why would you go with someone else who'd only interrupt your haunting? Bernice Rosen went there alone, too. I knew she lived on Lake Street in one of those shabby apartments above a store, alone with her mother. She seemed to spend a lot of time in the library, sniffing along the shelves like a mouse in a pantry, running her fingertips along the books as though they were pickets in a fence, sometimes taking one down and putting it right back, as if touching, not reading, was what you did there. I never spoke to her. But I remembered her when I read in the papers what had been done to her.

In the winter we ate breakfast in the kitchen with the oven lit and the oven door open. It was snug and warm there when the rest of the house was still cold and dark. My father read the morning *Tribune* while he ate, and if any of the rest of us were in the kitchen, he reported news items to us between bites. One morning he said two women had been attacked in their Lake Street apartment. No (as he read further), not two women, a woman and her little girl. Savagely beaten. With an iron bar. As they lay in their beds. Near death, he said. Rosen, their name was. Goldie and Bernice.

"I know Bernice Rosen," I said, forgetting that I had never spoken to her. "She went to my school." I felt somehow important, knowing somebody who was in the paper, who was almost dead; and I began to construct in my head the fearful scene, the two victims lying in their beds, blood everywhere, and the intruder just standing there over them, breathing hard, still gripping the iron bar.

By the end of the day the story had changed: Mrs. Rosen was dead, and her daughter was unconscious in General Hospital. Bernice had been found in her bed, covered with blood—that part of the morning paper's story was true; but her mother lay at the foot of the cellar stairs, her head crushed by blows from what turned out to be a furnace shaker like the one my father used every morning to wake the fire up. I had hefted our shaker, I knew how heavy it was. To be hit on the head with it! You'd have to be strong to lift it up and then crash it down.

I imagined a new story. Late in the cold night Mrs. Rosen hears a noise in the cellar, two flights below her apartment, and because she is a brave woman, and because it's her building, she goes down into the darkness to investigate, and finds a man there, a strong man who grabs the nearest weapon, the fire shaker, and strikes her down, and then hits her again, and again. And Bernice, upstairs in her bed, hears her mother's cries, and comes fearfully down the stairs, barefoot (there was dirt on her feet), in her flannel pajamas (because it's cold, it's January), and meets the man coming up. He throws her down the stairs with one sweep of his arm, follows her to the bottom, and strikes her, too, with the shaker—many times, she has thirteen head wounds—and then runs up the stairs and out the front door, leaving it ajar. Bernice tries to lift her mother, but loses consciousness—for how long? It seemed important to the story, but I couldn't guess—and falls across the body of her mother. Then she wakes, and crawls up the desolate stairs to her room (where else would a child go, broken as she was, and her mother seemingly dead?), and falls onto her bed, unconscious again, soaking the bedclothes with her blood.

For days after the crime the papers said Bernice was "near

death." Policemen waited at her bedside to question her if she recovered consciousness. But she didn't, not for a whole month, and then when she did she wasn't strong enough to be interviewed. That wasn't news, and gradually the case dropped from the headlines, replaced by more customary crime stories—bank robberies, kidnapping, J. Edgar Hoover and his G-men. I forgot about Bernice Rosen.

Then in April the Rosen case was in the papers again. Bernice had recovered—not completely, the *Tribune* said, her speech was still slurred, and one of her hands hung drooping from her arm, but enough to identify her attacker. She was taken to the police station, there was a picture of her there, on the front page: a thin, frail-looking girl wrapped in a heavy coat too big for her (though the day was warm), a scarf covering her head (to hide the thirteen terrible scars, I thought), half smiling, because she was having her picture taken, but with sad, shadowed eyes.

When she was led to the room where the police lineup had been arranged, she couldn't go in; she was afraid to be in the same room with the man who had killed her mother. Two large detectives had to stand in the doorway, and she crept up behind and peered between them. But even with the detectives protecting and concealing her, she couldn't speak when she saw the man who had hit her; she could only squeeze a detective's hand—meaning *that's the man.* I could imagine the shy small girl of the school playground and the library, hiding and peeping out like some little animal, speechless with fear in the presence of such evil.

Weeks passed while the suspect was charged and the trial was arranged. The baseball season began, and I read the sports pages on my paper route instead of the front page. The Millers opened in Indianapolis with a new right fielder, a nineteen-year-old kid named Ted Williams who was supposed to be a slugger, and I watched the box scores for his numbers. In three games in Indianapolis he went 0 for 12: some slugger. But when the team came to Minneapolis he began to hit—a home run in the first game that cleared the right field fence and landed in Nicollet Avenue and almost hit a streetcar, and two more in the next game that carried even farther—and I had a new hero. Then it was June, and I graduated from junior high school and escaped into summer.

It was after school was out that the Rosen case finally came to trial, and back onto the front pages. I dawdled along Stevens Avenue on my paper route reading the testimony of the witnesses and the accused man, and now I could imagine the other story of that night, the murderer's tale.

His name was Kenneth Palmer, and he, too, lived on Lake Street, in another of those soiled-looking apartments above a store, with his wife and child and mother-in-law. He was a casual laborer when he worked, a bully who threatened to kill his wife if she left him but still went with other women ("a womanizer," my father said with contempt in his voice), a petty criminal who had been in jail, a drunkard who never had enough money to pay for his own drinks.

On the night of the crime he had drifted along Lake Street from one bar to another, from the Right Spot to Lyle's and eventually to Buzz Arlett's. Buzz and his wife testified that by the time he reached their place he was broke; he had to write an IOU for fifteen cents to buy a pack of Camels. A man he knew remembered seeing him on the street after dark that night, walking west with his coat collar turned up and his hat pulled down, "slinking along like he was afraid of something," and I could imagine that furtive figure hurrying along past the dark stores and the bars, stony broke and thirsty for another drink. And then he thought of the Rosens' basement, where he had once repaired the furnace. Under the stairs he had seen little barrels of wine that Mrs. Rosen stored there.

"Because they were Jews," my father said. "Jews use wine in their religion."

I didn't know what Jews were, exactly. That is, I knew what they were in the Old Testament, I'd heard enough about them in Sunday School; I just didn't know what they were *now*, in Minneapolis. Bernie Kravitz was a Jew. My stepsisters went to high school with Bernie; his father had a dry-cleaning and furrier's business over on Nicollet, and the family lived above the store, like the Rosens. There weren't any other Jews in our neighborhood that I knew of.

The family talked about Jews over dinner. Somebody said they didn't have Christmas because they didn't believe in Christ; somebody else said they had a different New Year's. And they went to church on Friday night. My father said he admired them: "They know how to make a dollar," he said, and there was respect in his voice, because he didn't. Nellie regarded Jews as she did all foreigners, as odd, eccentric people who couldn't help not being like us, and who should be treated with an amused kindness. You should never call a Jew a Jew to his face, that was rude because he couldn't help being what he was. But you could use *jew* as a verb: it meant to bargain hard, which was a good thing to do, in our family. When Nellie said she had jewed down the farmer who sold vegetables from his truck, she meant she had bought more potatoes for less money, and she expected to be praised for her sharpness. The Jewishness of individual people didn't seem important to her; it takes all kinds, she said.

So Jews drank wine because of their religion, not in church the way some Christians did, but at home, and they kept their wine in barrels in their basements. Kenneth Palmer knew where Mrs. Rosen kept hers. He crept into the dark entryway of her apartment that night and knocked on the outer door, and saw through the frosted glass the blurred figure of a woman descending the stairs—Mrs. Rosen, a little nervous because it was nighttime, but angry, too, because nobody should come knocking at such an hour. The furnace, he said, he had to check the furnace, and she let him in; but followed him, suspicious of this night visit, down the stairs into the dark cellar. I could imagine it all, except the ending, when the murderer raises the iron shaker and strikes the woman down.

The testimony of witnesses at the scene—the police, the lodger, the ambulance men, the emergency-room doctor—was vivid, and I read it all: about the furnace shaker clotted with blood, and the bloody handprint on the cellar wall, and the bloodstained bed Bernice lay on, and how Mrs. Rosen's glasses had been driven into her skull by the blows. And I stared with fascination at the crime-scene photographs—the cellar with cobwebs in the corners and rubbish on the floor and a large irregular dark stain at the foot of the stairs that was blood—and at the pictures of the accused man, handcuffed to a policeman and hiding his face with the other hand. That was what a real murderer looked like. But I couldn't see inside his head, I couldn't see what would allow a man to smash a woman's skull.

The Rosen case ended the way crime stories should end—the way they always ended in my other reality of films and detective stories—in appropriate justice. Kenneth Palmer was found guilty and sentenced to life imprisonment in the state prison at Stillwater. But Bernice's story didn't end; it simply stopped. She didn't appear in the library anymore, and that fall, when she should have entered Central High School with my class, she wasn't there. Some family member must have taken her in, perhaps in another city, in another state; nobody knew. Did she recover clear speech and the use of her right hand? I wondered. Did her thirteen scars fade and disappear? Did she forget that January night? And if she didn't, what was it like to remember?

. I didn't wonder very long, though. Her story became like the other stories in old newspapers, faded and forgotten, replaced by newer headlines. But whether I remembered or forgot, the place I lived in was changed by the deaths of Laura Kruse and Goldie Rosen, and the near death of Bernice. Not suddenly or melodramatically, but changed. Now the neighborhood included a different Lake Street, where murderers crept along in the shadows with their caps pulled down, and a different South Side, where killers drove Ford cars at night down empty streets hunting for solitary girls. Nobody could feel secure, not ever; because there were other human beings who might kill you, anytime, right now. Life was perilous, in the darkness of the world.

CHAPTER TEN

"How'd you like to live in Litchfield?" My father had just come home from traveling the county towns out in the middle of the state, he should have been worn out from all that driving, but he seemed oddly cheerful, sitting there at dinner, and excited, too, like a kid with a secret.

"I've just been there," he said. "Do you remember it?"

Sure, I remembered Litchfield from my farm summer: the flat little town with its one block of redbrick stores, the grain elevators by the railroad tracks, the park with its bandstand, the white houses looking blue in the shadows of the elms.

"Well," he said, "we might just move there!" And he began to talk about what it would be like, how he'd be manager of the Shell distributorship there, and we'd live in one of those white houses by the park, and Chuck and I would go to Mercer County High School and swim with the other boys in the lake and maybe learn to sail a boat, and we'd have picnics by the bandstand on concert nights in summer, and he'd walk along Main Street in his good suit, saying hello to the people he met, being Someone in Litchfield because he was the Manager.

I said it was all right with me. I'd go to Litchfield if he wanted me to, and be a small-town kid. But I felt sad as I said it. I liked living on West Thirty-fifth Street; I liked the house, and the neighborhood, Apple Alley and the Lot, I liked my school, I liked my friends. I didn't want to start over again. But we'd moved before; another move wouldn't kill me.

Nellie didn't say anything. Neither did Chuck. Or if they did I didn't hear them. Neither did my father. He just went on telling his small-town story.

After that night he didn't talk about Litchfield anymore. He didn't explain why, he just stopped. Maybe he'd hoped to be offered the job and he hadn't been. Or maybe he'd never had a chance, and the talk had only been a daydream he'd dreamed of a new life in a country town like the ones he knew when he was a boy, where the folks all knew each other and were happy. It sounded fine when he talked about it that evening at supper, the way dreams are fine, and stories in books like *Swallows and Amazons* that make you feel good while you're reading them, but couldn't happen, not to you.

Then, when school ended in June, we moved; without warning, with no long preparations or farewells, we just packed up and left. Nellie wrapped up her chiming clock and her silver pheasants and put *Old Ironsides* and *The Age of Innocence* and *Sir Galahad* in boxes, and men came and carried out the piano and the furniture. Nobody told me why we were moving, and I didn't ask, we just moved. But not to Litchfield, only a mile or so across the South Side.

Our new house wasn't a house, really, it was just the ground floor of a duplex on Columbus Avenue: living room, dining room, kitchen, and two bedrooms, or three if you counted the storeroom off the back hall, a room so small my father said he had to back out of it turn around. In came the furniture—the piano into the front hall, the Philco (with my model boat on top) to a corner of the living room, *Old Ironsides* above the davenport, the silver pheasants on the dining-room sideboard, my stuff to the small back room. When it was all in place the rooms looked familiar, but I could see this wouldn't be as good a house as the one on West Thirty-fifth Street. There was no attic, and no room for a ping-pong table in the basement, and no yard big enough to play in. We wouldn't even go upstairs to bed.

The 3800 block of Columbus Avenue was a slightly classier place to live than West Thirty-fifth Street, in Minneapolis terms. For one thing, it was on a hill. Hills were rare in our town, folks bragged if they lived on a hill. There wasn't a view from our house, just the houses across the street; still, it was on a hill. And there was a playground down at the end of the block: Chicago Field, a dusty square block with a place to play baseball and some concrete tennis courts and a warming house for winter, when firemen came and flooded the field and turned it into a skating rink. I would play baseball there and break my finger (the same one) again, and play football on a team that was nearly city champions, and watch a race riot almost happen. But all that was later.

In my new neighborhood the intersection of Chicago Avenue and Thirty-eighth Street was "the corner," it was where kids hung around. When you told someone you'd meet him at the corner you didn't have to say which one, he'd be there. The corner was like the middle of a small town. If you wanted to go somewhere else you'd start there at the stoplight. You could catch a streetcar that would take you down to the Loop, or in the other direction out to the edge of town, or a crosstown bus all the way to the river one way and over to Lake Harriet the other.

All the businesses a small town would need were at the corner: three grocery stores (an A&P, a National Tea, and a little one-man place that Nellie wouldn't go into because she said the man overcharged her), two gas stations (Phillips 66 and Standard Oil), two garages, a laundry, a restaurant, two dry cleaners, a plumber, a dentist, a luncheonette, two candy stores, a movie theater (the Nokomis), a beauty parlor, a jeweler, a hardware store, a dry-goods store, a butcher, a drugstore, two bakers, and a beer joint. There was no hospital on the corner, so you couldn't be born there except accidentally, but there was an undertaker down on Thirty-seventh Street. So once you were born you didn't really need to leave the corner for the rest of your life. Except to buy clothes; nobody sold clothes on the corner.

I sat on my front steps in the morning sun looking at my new neighborhood. I didn't know anybody. My old friends from the Lot—Birdy and Cliff and Dickie D.—were gone from my life, they might as well live in Fargo for all I'd see them. A kid came out of a house across the street and stood staring at me. He was about my age and about my size—an ordinary-sized four-teen-year-old. He wasn't ordinary looking, though. First of all there was his hair. You could call it red, but it wasn't, really; it was the color of fire, and it stood up on his head, thick and stiff looking, like a flaming scrubbing brush, or Moses' burning bush. His face was red, too, as though he was blushing, which made his eyebrows and lashes, which were nearly white, stand out like chalk marks. I could see them, white against red, even from across the street. Down the middle of his forehead from his hairline to the top of his nose a deep, dead-white scar ran. What had happened to him to mark him like that?

This startling red-and-white boy stood there for what seemed a long time—not sure, maybe, that he wanted a new kid on his block. Then he crossed over and spoke: "My name's Michaud," he said. But not like that, he drawled it out, as though speaking his own name tired him: "M-m-y-y-y n-n-a-a-m-m-e's-s M-m-m-i-sh-sh-sh-aw-aw-aw-d."

We walked back across the street and sat on his steps. Michaud told me about his family. He lived with his mother and his stepfather. His real father was called Coon.

Why Coon?

Michaud didn't know, he just was. From Wisconsin. There are lots of Canucks in Wisconsin.

Does he live there now?

Michaud didn't know where he lived. He's a sort of a hobo, he said. He likes to ride the rails. (As though jumping freight trains was a hobby.) When he runs out of money he stops, and gets married. Three times, at least. I thought there was something heroic in Coon, going where he wanted to, and getting married when it suited him, and then getting *not*-married again.

Michaud called his stepfather Fred-the-Tyrant. "He's crazy," he said. "He makes me do stupid jobs just so he can boss me around. Last winter when I'd shoveled the snow off the sidewalk he told me to shovel it off the grass, too. I said: 'F-r-r-e-e-d-d, has your mind s-n-n-a-a-p-p-ed?' He chased me around the block waving the shovel, but he couldn't catch me."

I could see why Fred-the-Tyrant hated his stepson. Fred was the grown-up and Michaud was the kid, and there were rules for that relationship. But Michaud didn't recognize them. He didn't recognize any rules. I knew kids like that. But not many. Most kids seemed to like living by grown-up rules and doing what they were supposed to: in grade school they stayed after class to clean the erasers, clapping them together out on the steps or smacking them hard against the brick school wall; in junior high they were hall monitors, they yelled at you to walk on the right side of the corridor and on the stairs, and demanded a pass if they saw you in the hall during class time; in class they always put their hands up first to answer a question, and their answers were always what the teacher wanted; they washed the blackboards; they carried the teachers' messages to the office and waited for replies; after school they were crossing guards on street corners, they wore white Sam Browne belts and held up a sign that said STOP; in high school they wore ties to class, sometimes even suits, and were on committees, and were elected to the National Honor Society. When they grew up they would work in offices, or be dentists.

Kids like Michaud didn't do those things: they walked up the school stairs on the left, they forgot their homework, they looked out of the window when the teacher asked a question, they skipped school; they didn't obey, they didn't respect, they didn't follow. They didn't join clubs or teams, or if they did they ignored the rules. If they had to march, they marched out of step. They'd cross an intersection just because the stoplight was red. There wasn't any word for kids like that that I knew of, they were just *against:* against parents, teachers, cops, preachers, scout-masters, school principals; against all signs that said DO NOT and KEEP OUT; against fences and walls and ropes at the beach; against everything that spoke for authority. If you were against *everything,* then you were free.

Up at the corner, across the street from the Nokomis and next to the beer joint, Wilma and Laverne ran a luncheonette called the White Palace. It wasn't like the White Castles that were all over town, it didn't have white tile walls and a crenel-lated roof, and it didn't sell five hamburgers the size of quarters for twenty-five cents; it was just a room with a counter and a few stools, one booth, and a pinball machine. Michaud told me about the women who ran the White Palace. Wilma was the waitress; she spent most of her time leaning on the counter, smoking and watching customers play the pinball machine. La-verne was Wilma's mother. She owned the White Palace but you never saw her behind the counter. That was because she was always upstairs in bed with Ben, the mechanic from the garage across the street. Sometimes she got pregnant, and then Ben took her somewhere to get rid of it. (How did Michaud know all that? Did Wilma tell him? I was amazed at his exact informa-tion about these grown-ups' private lives. And what did "get rid of it" mean?)

Michaud was a pinball addict. You could find him in the White Palace most afternoons after school, standing tensely at the machine, hands clutching it on either side as he tried to coax the little steel ball to roll one way or another without jiggling the machine enough to light up the "Tilt" sign and stop the game. It was a serious contest for Michaud; winning was more than just running up a score and collecting a few coins from Wilma, it was beating the rules, and the "Tilt" sign. His red face grew redder when he played, and his gripping hands went white at the knuckles. When he lost he hurled curses at the machine and the rebounding ball, and at anyone who was there to witness his defeat.

I strolled into the White Palace one afternoon when Michaud was at the pinball machine, and stopped to watch the ball knock and bound and the lights flash. Then the flashing stopped and the "Tilt" sign blinked on. Michaud pushed me away, as though the tilting was my fault.

"Do-o-o you m-m-i-i-i-nd?" he said furiously; it was a phrase he used to keep the world at bay. I didn't take the hint and leave him alone. "Michaud," I said, filling my voice with phony sympathy, "why is it you never win?" He turned slowly toward me, his red face coloring toward purple, his eyes under their pale lashes nearly closed. "Why-y-y-y don't you step o-o-o-u-t-s-i-i-de?" he said.

It was an invitation as formal as a challenge to a duel; I couldn't refuse it. I followed him out onto the sidewalk and we stood for a moment facing each other, neither of us wanting to begin the fight, neither really wanting to be there. Then Michaud threw a punch and hit me on the shoulder and I threw one and hit him on the chest, and then there were more punches. Once you start fighting it's easier to go on than to stop. I hit him in the eye and he hit me in the mouth, and then we wrestled around for a while, straining and grunting and breathing hard, not falling to the sidewalk but remaining upright, holding and turning like a couple dancing a slow dance, while a crowd of kids gathered and criticized our lack of ferocity. And then, without a signal or a word, we both let go and stepped back and shook hands. The fight was over. We had fought our duel, not very hard, but hard enough; after all, it had only been a matter of honor. Afterwards we were friends; our fight had come out even—a black eye equals a fat lip—and that somehow was a bond.

The old widow who owned our duplex lived on the second floor. Mrs. Nelson was Swedish; when she spoke English her voice went up and down in the singsong cadences that Swedish has, and she mispronounced English words. I didn't like being around her. I wasn't afraid of her, exactly—I was too old to be scared of old ladies—but I didn't like the way she watched me with her wrinkly old eyes.

Mrs. Nelson lived alone and did all the work of her house herself, both the woman's work and the man's. On winter mornings before my father was up and dressed, I could hear her down in the cellar scraping her shovel across her coal-bin floor and pitching coal into her furnace. Later she would carry her cans of ashes up the cellar stairs, one laborious step at a time, and out to the alley, grunting and muttering in Swedish.

She was an exacting landlady; my father had to keep our furnace as neat and tidy as she kept hers, and carry his own ashes to the alley without spilling any along the way. One morning Nellie came in from the backyard laughing her high whooping laugh. Mrs. Nelson had met her in the hall to complain that my father had been spilling ashes. Nellie suggested politely that the offending ashes might be Mrs. Nelson's. "Oh no," Mrs. Nelson replied, "dey couldn't be mine. You haff *black* asses and I haff *white* asses!" Nellie went off into another whoop of laughter. "She has such a brogue!" she said.

The household machinery in the cellar seemed as old as

Mrs. Nelson. In the damp, soap-smelling laundry room a contraption stood that must have been the first electric washing machine ever built. A galvanized tank hung balanced within a wooden frame on four wooden legs. You filled the tank with water and dirty clothes, shut the lid and turned on the switch, and the tank rocked back and forth in its frame like a playground swing, sloshing the clothes and the water together.

The steady rocking made the whole contraption creep across the laundry-room floor, slow and stiff-legged, like Frankenstein's monster learning to walk. When Nellie used it she treated the machine as she would an obstinate farm animal—a horse that shied from its harness, or a cow that stepped in the milk pail. I could hear her down in the cellar on wash day, shouting "Stand still, durn you!" and once I found her wrestling with the sloshing thing, trying to prevent it from walking into a corner.

The hot-water heater wasn't as old as the washing machine, but it was old-fashioned. To get hot water you had to go down into the cellar and light the heater with a match. The gas would ignite with a blue *whoosh!* and the burner would begin to glow red. Then you went upstairs and waited. After a while you went back to the cellar and felt the top part of the water tank; if it was warm a foot or so down, you had enough hot water for a bath.

You turned the heater off and went up to fill the tub; or you left it burning so there would be more hot water as the bath cooled, and turned it off afterwards.

Or, if you were me, you meant to but forgot. I took my bath one night and went to bed, and the water heater went on heating water—our water, Mrs. Nelson's water, the water of the house next door. Mrs. Nelson got up in the night to go to the toilet and the water that flushed it was so hot it scalded her bottom; in the neighbor's house it cracked the tank of the toilet. The way my father told the story the next morning, the whole 3800 block of Columbus Avenue was one great cloud of steam that night, with Mrs. Nelson in the middle, yelling about her burned bottom and offering to show her blisters. He didn't seem angry; he actually chuckled over Mrs. Nelson's fussing. Maybe by then he had grown used to the way his sons got into troubles that emptied his wallet and sometimes brought the cops to the door. Or maybe he remembered his own childhood, the chariot race and the overturned privies on Halloween.

It must have cost him more money than he had to replace the broken toilet next door and to soothe his angry landlady, because by then he was certainly out of work. He said nothing to me about it—he could no more talk to his sons about losing his job than he could about sex—but I knew. I felt it in the anxious silence that hung over the house, and I saw it in Nellie's squeezed economies. All that winter the house held its breath, waiting for a job for an unemployed engineer to turn up. And none did.

Maybe that was because my father wasn't really an engineer at all; he'd never gone to college, he didn't have a degree or a diploma or a certificate, what he knew he'd learned by doing it. But he thought of himself as one: on forms that asked for his profession he always wrote *Engineer,* or *Lubrication Engineer,* a title he'd invented to name his skills. If he was an engineer then he was like his brother, Lee, who had gone to engineering school

up at the University of Michigan and owned his own company—
a solid man, respected and successful, a professional man.

In the spring he gave up looking for an engineer's job and
leased a gas station over on the north side, and set out to support
his family by pumping gas and changing oil and patching tires,
all the small, dirty jobs that men who run gas stations do. He
wore a blue work shirt with SAM'S CITIES SERVICE stitched over
the breast pocket, and work shoes, and a cap with a bill, he who
for all the years I had known him had dressed every morning in
the white shirt and gray suit of a professional man.

I only went to the station once. My father showed me around,
not proudly but with a kind of resignation. Here was the office,
a cramped and littered room with a rack of road maps, a Coke
machine, a pay telephone with phone numbers scribbled on the
wall around it, the two toilets (my father would have to clean
them). And here was the garage. Two long holes in the floor
gaped like open graves. Those were the grease pits; when my father had to grease a car he drove the car over one of those pits,
and then climbed down beneath it, into the pit, to do the work.
Out in front two gas pumps stood in black puddles where waiting cars had leaked oil.

Grease and oil lay over everything; nothing could ever be
clean here. And there was my father, doing dirty jobs for other
men and being called Sam by every stranger who bought a gallon of gas, while idle men in work clothes lounged around inside the station, smoking and drinking Cokes. I could see that
my father was ill at ease among them, and especially when I was
there. He hated their coarseness, and the stories they told; he
didn't want me to hear them, or see him force himself to laugh
at the end because he had to, because they were his customers.

I never went back to the station, but my brother did. He
worked there on Saturdays during his last year of high school.
I'd meet him sometimes coming in from work, dressed like my

father in greasy work clothes, hands and face streaked with oil, tired and silent like a convict who has served time but has a long sentence still to go.

Chuck saw Sam's Cities Service every week, and he knew what I didn't know, that the station was failing. My father couldn't tell which of his customers were honest, when to give credit and when to refuse it, and he couldn't bring himself to demand that a man pay his bill. He was a generous, trusting man, and he took too many IOUs he couldn't collect. One customer who claimed he couldn't pay in cash offered payment in cases of canned prune juice and my father took them, and put them in the basement fruit cellar. Every morning after he'd fed the furnace he'd bring a can of prune juice upstairs and drink it at breakfast. "Good for you!" he'd exclaim when he'd drunk it. "Helps your digestion!" None of the rest of us would touch it; it tasted of the tin can it came in, and made you go to the bathroom. And as Nellie said, the man hadn't really paid his bill, you couldn't spend cans of prune juice at the A&P. They just sat down there in the cellar, reminding us of another bad debt unpaid.

That June (it was 1939) my brother graduated from Central, and quit working for my father to look for a real, full-time man's job. He must have been relieved to escape from the station. But maybe not, I thought; it must be scary to have to be a man when you're only seventeen. The job he found was with Woolworth's, assistant manager of a dime store in Wausau, Wisconsin. I thought, he'll be the man in Wausau who catches kids like me when they try to steal toys. He won't like doing that, or be very good at it. And he won't like being alone so far from home. But he went. As Nellie said, a job's a job.

The green wooden box that stood outside the Leamington Hotel on the corner of Third Avenue and Tenth Street looked as though it might contain sand or salt for throwing on icy streets in winter. But when it was unlocked and opened it became a newsstand. I knew Jerry Olson, the kid who sold papers there every afternoon after school. He was older than me, sixteen or maybe seventeen, but even so I was impressed that he could run a newsstand all by himself. It wasn't like having a paper route; any kid could ride a bike and throw papers on the same front porches every day. Being a newsboy was different, a newsboy played a role in the drama of city life. I had seen how the part was played in the movies; newspapers with black headlines rolled from presses and then newsboys ran through the streets waving the papers and shouting "Extra!" and the grown-ups in the movie bought them and were excited, or worried, or frightened.

So when Jerry asked me to run his stand for two weeks at the end of the summer, I wasn't sure I was up to the part. I began the last week in August. On the first Monday I stood on the corner, feeling exposed and ridiculous, like an actor who has walked onto the wrong stage, into the wrong play. A truck swept up to the curb and a man threw out two bundles. I cut the string and piled the papers on the stand. Now I would have to play my newsboy role.

I looked at the headlines:

HITLER LOOKS TO MUSSOLINI

AS MEDIATOR: BRITAIN IS FIRM

I began to shout: *"Hitler Looks to Mussolini!"* and people began to buy. Cars stopped and I thrust papers through their windows; pedestrians grabbed papers and walked away reading. I warmed to my role; Hitler and Mussolini weren't people, they were words in my newsboy part. I shouted them with fierce intensity: *"Hitler Looks to Mussolini!"* It was easy, after all; I could yell that line all day.

Tuesday was my birthday; I was fifteen. The headline that day was tense: war or peace, it was up to Hitler. On the front page trucks full of German soldiers drove toward Poland. I shouted *"War or Peace?"* and people crowded round the stand. On Wednesday the war of nerves continued, and that's what I yelled: *"War of Nerves!"* On Thursday the British were mobilizing, and on Friday the Germans were invading Poland, and Poles were calling on Britain and France for help. The tension was rising, you could feel it; something terrible was going to happen that would change everything; it was there in the headlines, in the words I shouted.

On Saturday the pressure seemed to ease: Britain and France delayed action, Hitler drafted a reply. So maybe the terrible change wouldn't happen after all. There was nothing worth shouting about that day; where was the drama in delaying and drafting? Those weren't words I could yell.

The stand was closed on Sundays—downtown was dead, the stores and offices were closed, nobody walked past Tenth and Third. When I opened it again on Monday and piled the papers on the top, the headlines were war news: a British ship had been sunk, the Poles were driving their enemies back. A subhead reported celebrations in Warsaw: Britain and France had declared war on Germany. While I was reading the Sunday funnies and shagging flies down at Chicago Field, the Second World War had begun. I had missed my chance to play the movie-newsboy part as it was written, to cry out to a terrified world (or at least to Third Avenue and Tenth Street): *"War Declared! War! War!"*

The change had happened. But not where I lived, not in my street, my neighborhood, my town. In September I went to school as usual, I went home, rode my bike, delivered groceries for the A&P, played football at Chicago Field, went to the Nokomis, hung around the White Palace. It was all the same.

Yet from that day, that first Monday in September when I had just turned fifteen, there was a difference. Now war was a part of what existed—not close to our lives but far off, a remote flickering drama like a movie seen from the back row. I read about it in the papers, I saw its images in newsreels—German tanks rolling across fields, Polish cavalry trotting and wheeling, frightened civilians crowding roads with their carts and animals and children—and heard about it on the radio when Big Ben's solemn strokes rang in our living room and Edward R. Murrow told us the bad news from London. It was like that moment in early fall in Minnesota when the wind swings around to the north and blows down from the Canadian prairies and you feel the coldness of it and know that winter will come—not today, not this week or even this month, but soon.

CHAPTER ELEVEN

What you noticed first at Mrs. Miller's was the ivy. It grew out of pots in the corners of the store, up the walls and across the ceiling and down the other side, luxuriantly, making the whole room leafy and green. That, and the broad-leafed plants in the windows where the cats—one marmalade, one calico—slept in the sun, made Mrs. Miller's seem more like an arbor or a clearing in the woods than the corner store it was. It smelled of milk, and cigarette smoke, and cats.

It's hard to say what kind of store Mrs. Miller ran. Some folks called it a luncheonette because it had a soda fountain along one wall, and a couple of round marble-topped tables in the middle with little chairs with looped-wire backs like carpet beaters; others said it was a grocerette (a term I never heard used of any other store) because of the cans and sacks and boxes of groceries stacked on shelves against the walls between the climbing ivy vines. We just called it Mrs. Miller's.

At lunchtime the store filled with kids from the high school across the street. They ate their lunches there because they didn't have a quarter to buy the hot meal that was served in the school cafeteria—at Mrs. Miller's you could buy a Pepsi for a nickel and eat the sandwiches you brought from home, she didn't mind; or because they hated the cafeteria food, the pork and beans, the shepherd's pie, or because if they ate at the school they'd be joining *them*—the principal, Old Jarvis, and his sour assistant Miss Thomas, and the teachers, and the kids who ate there because they did everything right, even eating lunch. Or they came simply because they were new kids in the school and didn't know anybody, and it seemed better to be alone in the crowd at Mrs. Miller's than alone at a table in the cafeteria.

Everyone who ate at Mrs. Miller's smoked. Smoking was forbidden in the school and on the school grounds; if you didn't smoke, you were one of the obedient ones, the kind of kid who ate lunch in the cafeteria. If you crossed the street and smoked, you were escaping the rules, playing at being a free grown-up; it was like driving a car, drinking, staying out late. It was what you did in high school if you were *against*.

Except me: I didn't smoke, because I didn't know how. I hadn't learned when the other kids did—maybe because I was younger—and now it was too late, if I tried I'd cough and turn red in the face and they'd all know. I watched how they did it. Girls held their cigarettes between their first and second fingers, and pointed them up in the air, casually, like Bette Davis in the movies. Guys held theirs between thumb and first two fingers, with the burning end toward the palm (a style that made sense if you were outside where the wind was blowing, but didn't seem necessary in a grocerette), or in the same fingers but pointed away, like a dart they were about to throw. A few held their cigarettes in the corner of their mouths, drooping, letting the smoke curl up, holding their eyes half-closed against it. From time to time they took long drags, and paused, and then let the smoke out slowly through their nostrils, or blew it in a jet into somebody's face, like George Raft. I knew that I could never do that, could never be so casual and sophisticated with my mouth full of smoke. So I stood in Mrs. Miller's at lunchtime, my eyes burning in the blue air, and ate my peanut-butter-and-banana sandwich, and tried to look like someone who could smoke if he wanted to, but didn't feel like it at the moment.

The guy with the straight black hair standing beside me in Mrs. Miller's is a corner-of-the-mouth smoker. He holds his cigarette there and looks around the room, his eyelids lowered against the smoke, and smiles (which can't be easy with a cigarette in your mouth), as though the other kids are some kind of a show, and he's the audience. A little guy with frog eyes on the other side of me asks me if I've got a cigarette, and when I say no he asks the black-haired guy, who silently pulls a pack of Lucky Strikes out of his shirt pocket and gives him one, and then, because I'm standing there between them, offers one to me. I say not right now.

Somehow the transaction has made the three of us acquaintances. Frog Eyes tells me his name is Hub—for Hubert (he makes a face at the name his folks have stuck him with). He's new at Central, he's been at St. Joe's until now because he's a Catholic. He's talkative and funny, and doesn't seem to mind being short and bulgy-eyed. Black Hair's name is Blake—no first name, just Blake. He's new, too: another Catholic, come over to the public high school because it's a better school than the Catholics have, and because it's free. I don't say anything; I like these guys, I don't want to tell them I'm different, I'm a Presbyterian. And anyway, I don't think I am one anymore, not in the way they're Catholics. My father won't like it if I tell him I'm making friends with Catholics. But of course I won't tell him. The less you tell your parents the better.

When the bell rings we walk back to school together. Blake goes on smoking as we climb the terraces—not up the walk, but across the lawn. You're not supposed to smoke on the school grounds, but who's going to catch him? And if they should, what can they do? Warn him? Scold him? Tell his father? He hasn't got a father—not at home anyway. He flips his butt toward a "Keep Off the Grass" sign with a fine contemptuous gesture. We enter through a stone archway under carved words: THE COMMONWEALTH REQUIRES THE EDUCATION OF THE PEOPLE AS A SAFEGUARD OF ORDER AND LIBERTY.

Inside, the school is a clamor of bright noise: light glares down from the ceiling on crowding heads, locker doors crash, feet shuffle; from the typing room comes a clatter of keys, from the chemistry lab a smell like rotten eggs, from the door of the greenhouse a whiff of damp earth, from the auto shop exhaust smoke and the sound of a hammer on metal; clatter of plates and cutlery and the leftover smell of lunch from the cafeteria; from biology, formaldehyde; from the gym, sweat. And above it all a steady inarticulate din, like the sound of a high-powered engine running, that is the compound voice of two thousand kids talking, laughing, quarreling, conducting their lives.

The crowd in the corridors begins to thin, kids drift into classrooms, the engine of energy stops and they become students of the subjects the Commonwealth requires: world history, geometry, English, German, U.S. history, botany, civics. Serious subjects, worth learning about. From their desks at the front of the room teachers fire facts like spitballs—lists and tables and irregular verbs and dates out of textbooks to be memorized. Some of those facts stay in my mind: the rules for the use of German prepositions (*an, auf, hinter, neben, in, über, unter, vor, und zwischen* take the dative—or is it the accusative?), the Pythagorean theorem, some amendments to the Constitution, the difference between a sepal and a petal, the name of the kid in *Silas Marner* (Eppie, little Eppie). Random scraps, like the stuff you find in the bottom of your desk drawer, the bits of string, the bent paper clips, the rusty keys that no longer open any lock. Or like pieces of old posters, torn and flapping on a wall.

Most of the teachers have the same fragmentariness; they aren't flesh-and-blood, they're only chalk-and-blackboard creatures. Only a few—the eccentric, the passionate, the cruel—

become more than chalk people, reveal themselves by their gestures and by their unguarded remarks to be whole human beings that a kid might love, or hate, and maybe even learn from.

Civics. At the front of the room O. K. Kuenster squats on a wastebasket, flapping his arms like wings and cackling: "Kut-kut-kuh-DA-kut!" He is demonstrating how a hen lays an egg. No one in the class understands what laying an egg has to do with civics. O. K. is a small, dapper man with a large head, an egg-shaped body, and tiny feet. His face is smooth and waxy and his dark hair, stuck down on the back of his skull, looks like a toupee but is probably his own. A wire runs from his left ear to a hearing aid fastened to his belt.

O. K. returns to his desk, apparently satisfied with the demonstration, and begins to question his students: How many railroads come into Minneapolis? How many gas stations are there in the city? What is the mayor's name? His speech is like singing, rising in moments of excitement to a high falsetto and full of extended vowels and rolling *r*'s and stretched-out polysyllabic words like *mu-nee-cee-PAL-ee-tee.* It's a tune none of us has ever heard before.

From the side of the room by the window a low humming noise begins, and slowly rises in volume. O. K. glances around suspiciously, turns up his hearing aid, and rushes toward the windows in small scurrying steps. The humming ceases there but begins on the other side of the room, by the blackboards. He turns and hurries toward the new sound, which stops as he approaches. Over by the window it begins again. O. K. turns his hearing aid down again and returns to his desk and opens the textbook. A low whisper of giggles sweeps across the room. O. K. goes on talking until the bell rings. He hears it, rises, and faces the students: "Place your hands on the rrrrectangle when you exit the rrrroom," he says. That means push the door open before you go out. We go.

German. Frau Drechsler is reciting a poem, making the grunting, guttural noises that the German language requires. At my desk I am doing something I shouldn't: whispering, passing a note, or simply looking like a kid who isn't listening. She goes on to the end of the poem, and then says: "Sam, come out into the hall." I follow her out, smirking at my friends as I go; there's a sort of glory in being singled out for bad behavior.

In the hall, Frau Drechsler stands looking sternly down at me through her pince-nez glasses. She is taller and broader than I am; she looks the way German sounds, heavy, humorless, threatening. "Sam," she begins, "I've had nice Jewish boys in my classes. Why can't you be nice?" I want to say, "No, you've got it wrong, I'm not Jewish, I'm Irish. Hynes is an Irish name." But I don't; I just stand there looking up at her and say nothing. She turns and goes back into the room and I follow her, not smirking now. She thinks I'm a Jew, like Bernice Rosen, somebody who keeps wine in the cellar and doesn't believe in Christmas. Well, if Frau Drechsler wants to make me a Jew, that's okay. It makes me different from her, anyway.

I was wrong, though, about her Germanness. Her name was Alice Fitzgerald Drechsler, she was as Irish as I was; it was her husband who was German. And her subject was really French. I suppose she was teaching German to my class because there was no one else to do it, and teaching it as methodically as any German, driving grammatical rules into our heads—*aus, auser, bei, mit . . .*—rules that sank down into the sludge at the bottom of my mind and stayed there.

She taught me more than that. Long after I'd left her class lines of poetry would float up from the sludge uninvited, lines she'd recited in her deep, solemn voice: *Ich weiss nicht, was soll es bedeuten, Dass ich so traurig bin,* and *Sah ein Knab' ein Röslein stehn, Röslein auf der Heiden.* Not whole poems, only a momentary breath of poetry and a little of the feeling, like the perfume of a pretty girl after she has passed by.

Public speaking. Miss Henry says she loves the arts. All of them. She loves painting and poetry and plays and the dance. She treats poetry as a form of drama, or sometimes ballet. When she recites a poem to us she floats around at the front of the classroom, her arms extended and waving, her silvery hair drifting round her head like a dandelion gone to seed. She wants us to recite in the same way, and some kids do; they gesture with their arms, and raise their voices, and stare at a spot on the ceiling as though Shelley's skylark was flying around up there. But most kids just mumble the words; they're embarrassed to be standing in front of everybody saying poetry out loud.

"And who will volunteer to recite a poem?" she asks the class. Nobody speaks, or looks up, in case Miss Henry should catch their eye. Finally Michaud says he will. I'm amazed; free spirits like Michaud don't volunteer. He walks to the front of the class, faces his audience, plants his feet firmly, and begins: "The Ra-a-a-a-ven, by Edgar Allan Po-o-o-o-oe." In the back of the room Hub and Blake snigger behind their hands; this is going to be good. "On-n-n-ce upon a midnight drea-ea-ea-ea-ry, While I pon-n-n-n-dered weak and wea-ea-ea-ea-eary." Miss Henry waits for the rising pitch, the gestures, the drama. None of that happens. Michaud stands calm as a statue on a monument, his gaze fixed on the back wall, slowly and distinctly saying the poem his way. The muffled giggling has stopped; the whole class is listening! When he has drawled the final line— "Shall be lifted—Never-er-er-er-er-mo-o-o-o-re"—the class bursts into applause, not for the poem but for Michaud. The poem he has recited isn't Miss Henry's "Raven"; it isn't even Poe's "Raven"; it's Michaud's "Raven," the slowest and steadiest poem in the English language. As he walks back to his seat

Michaud glances down at Hub and Blake: "Do you mi-i-i-ind?" he says.

I like poetry, but I don't like the performing part. I like the mystery in poems, the way the form seems to keep the poet from quite saying everything he has to say, or saying it really clearly, so there's room for a reader to finish it in his head, to imagine the place and make up the action. One poem I especially like begins: "We'll go no more a-rowing by the light of the moon." I can see that romantic scene in my head, the dark lake, the setting moon making a path of light on the water, the boat, the lover rowing (but not too hard, not sweating or anything), his girlfriend sitting on the seat at the back of the boat, trailing the fingers of one hand in the water. Miss Henry tells me the word isn't *a-rowing,* it's *a-roving.* She's ruined the poem.

There's another poem I like, but I don't talk to Miss Henry about it. It begins, in my version, "Jenny kissed me where I sat." I know that can't be right, but I don't look it up and correct it, because it's funny and sort of dirty the way I remember. And Jenny *might.*

Economics. Mrs. Pink's economics class stages a wedding every semester. The girls get very excited about it: they quarrel about who will be the bride, and what she should wear, and who should be her bridesmaids. The boys are embarrassed, they slump down in their seats when Mrs. Pink chooses the groom; but on the wedding day they turn up wearing ties, and one of them is the preacher and wears a suit. Mrs. Pink says your wedding day is the most important day of your life. But what does it have to do with economics? I ask my father, and he says, "That's the day when the bills start coming in," and Nellie snorts and says they do it for practice, so they'll get it right when the time comes. She's thinking of her two unmarried daughters.

American history. Mr. Hawker prowls the aisles of his classroom while he talks about the Declaration of Independence. In his thin face his eyes are dark shadows, like the eyeholes in a skull. From time to time he pauses beside some boy's desk to ask him a question, and as he speaks his hand falls on the boy's shoulder and grips, fingertips just below the collarbone. He waits for an answer, and the grip tightens . . . and tightens . . . and tightens, until the answer comes. My turn. The hand drops, and grips. I mustn't squirm or cry out. I blurt an answer. It must be the correct one; Hawker moves on, the hand falls on Blake's shoulder, and grips. Blake jerks away and yells: "Hey, that hurt!" Hawker smiles his skull smile.

I want to be a writer. No, that's wrong; I'm fifteen, and halfway through high school, and I *am* a writer, in the same way that Buck is an athlete and Keys Johnson is a musician. Writing is something I can do, might be able to do, want to do, do—I don't know. It isn't something I inherited, so far as I can tell: nobody in my family has ever been a writer. Though maybe my mother wanted to be one, maybe if she had lived . . .

There were two ways of being a writer at Central—two directions, and two teachers to lead you. One was my English teacher, Abigail O'Leary. Miss O'Leary had a stern, denying look about her, what I imagined the Puritan women who came over on the *Mayflower* looked like: gray hair clawed back in a tight bun, thin, bony face, steel-rimmed spectacles, eyes that could freeze or burn, and a mouth set in a permanent pursed-lipped expression of distaste for the imperfect world in which she found herself. Among the school's teachers she was the defiant outsider, a Roman Catholic and a political radical. Some kids whispered she was a Communist.

Miss O'Leary held herself aloof from the common life of the school. When she walked down the hall, picking her way fastidiously, avoiding contact with anyone, I thought of Mrs.

Hegg crossing the barnyard in her Sunday churchgoing clothes, trying to keep herself clean in a dirty world by not touching *anything*. She despised the school, you could tell that; it wasn't worthy of her talents. In class she mocked the other teachers— their minds, their educations, their conservative politics, their cramped lives. They were beneath her, all of them. Beneath you, too, if you were her student, if she'd chosen you as a follower.

In her class I was introduced to modern poetry. Not the *most* modern—Minneapolis is a long way from New York and London—but poems by American poets who weren't dead yet, or only barely. We read about how the fog comes in on little cat feet, and how to swing on birches (I thought about the birch trees in the Heggs' woods, and wished I had known about birch swinging then), and a long poem about patterns that I didn't understand. We learned by heart a poem some woman poet wrote about trains, that ended: "There isn't a train I wouldn't take no matter where it's going," and at night when I lay in bed and heard the freight trains calling like loons across the flat town, I thought: "No matter where? Even Duluth? Even Fargo? Even *Wausau?* I bet she never went to Wausau." (My brother hated Wausau, and his job in the dime store there; it would be terrible, I thought, to take a train to Wausau.)

Miss O'Leary taught creative writing, and was adviser to the school's literary magazine, *The Quest*. Kids talked in the halls about her writing classes, how she yelled at you and then praised you, how she used anger and contempt against students who didn't agree with her, or didn't understand her passionate ideas. She could be very cruel to dissenters and kids she thought were dumb: "She's so *mean!*" girls said, and sometimes they cried. Boys looked sullenly at their shoes and said nothing.

Some kids loved her. My friend Nelson Peery did; he believed in her wisdom, and did what she said. She encouraged him to write about being a Negro, and he did. She also introduced him to her radical friends, and later on he became a Communist, and spent the rest of his life being one. But I didn't love her, and I didn't join the circle of her followers.

There was another kind of writing at Central. You could learn it from Mr. Mulligan. Mulligan taught journalism, and directed the writing and editing of the *News,* the student paper. He was a big, untidy man, all black and white, like a photograph in a newspaper: his black suit, which he wore every day, was white with chalk dust where he leaned against the blackboard; his hair was silver gray streaked with black; and his broad Irish face was white as paper, except for the eyebrows, which were black and thick as caterpillars.

Mulligan was the opposite of Miss O'Leary, as far as writing went. The kind of writing she taught was personal, passionate, and literary; in her classes you spent a lot of time talking about your feelings, and the right metaphors for them. Mulligan hated metaphors, and every other kind of decoration. To be a good journalist you had to learn to leave things out: adjectives, polysyllables, clichés, figurative language, *yourself.* What was left was good writing, plain as a pine board, clear as well water. Hemingway was a good writer because he'd been a good newspaperman first, that's what Mulligan said. I began to hang around the newsroom, and to write little pieces for the school paper.

Mulligan didn't treat his students the way Miss O'Leary treated hers. He didn't seem to have any particular affection for any of us newsroom kids, he couldn't even remember our names most of the time. He was an adult and we were just kids; we needed him, he didn't need us. But he cared about our writing. When it was bad, clumsy or trite, or just not accurate, he reacted impatiently, slashing his thick blue pencil across our copy, his caterpillar eyebrows twitching up and down, muttering to himself "No, no, no, oh *no!*" But though he could be harsh in his criticism, he didn't use anger or contempt to chasten his students the way Miss O'Leary did; he didn't take our failures personally. He didn't praise, either; in his company you learned to live without praise. He never lost his temper and he never laughed, though sometimes he smiled a small private smile, as though he knew jokes about the world that high-school students wouldn't get, because he had been there and they hadn't.

We could see that Mulligan was different from other teachers. Sometimes in the middle of a class the big body would slump forward, the half-shut eyes would close completely, and he'd fall asleep; but only for a moment, then he'd wake with a jerk and go on teaching as though nothing had happened. Kids said that was because he had been gassed in the war. That was how kids always explained odd behavior in their male teachers—absentmindedness, or a stammer, or a whistly way of breathing—it was always gas in the war. In Mulligan's case it could have been true; he had been a machine gunner in France, we knew that from an article in the *News*. The article didn't tell us anything else, about gas or wounds or killing Germans, all the exciting stuff about war that a kid is curious about, and Mulligan never spoke of it. He'd have thought the particulars of his war were none of our business, and anyway, we wouldn't understand. But the fact that he'd been to war made him different from the other teachers; it entitled him to care less.

After the war he'd worked as a reporter in town (on which newspaper? Nobody knew), but eventually he quit, or was fired, and turned to teaching journalism to high-school kids. He must have felt it as a sad descent, from the *Tribune* or the *Star-Journal,* or maybe the *Pioneer Press* over in St. Paul, to the *Central High News*. But he remained a newspaperman. He taught his students how to write a lead paragraph that said the important things—Who, Where, When, What—and what to put in a two-column headline, and where to place a picture on the front page. And he taught us to respect the facts, and to keep ourselves out of our stories.

Whenever he had a chance he took his students off high-school reporting and sent them to cover things that happened downtown in the world of real news. When my stepsister Eileen was on the *News* staff he sent her with another girl to interview Helen Hayes, who had just come to town to play Mary, Queen of Scots. They spent two nights hanging around the stage door before they finally sneaked in and saw the actress, and got the interview. They sat up all night writing it, and proudly handed it to Mulligan the next morning. He took it without a word, and returned it to them with the terse note: "I asked for an interview—not a novel." They rewrote it, and it won first prize in a state journalism contest.

The prizes in the contest would be awarded at a ceremony at the University. Winners from all over the state would be there. Eileen said she wasn't going, she didn't have a coat, not a proper dress-up one. Nellie said, "Wear your mackinaw, it's good and warm." But she wouldn't go, and the next morning pictures of all the other winners were in the paper, and Eileen cried all the way through breakfast. As soon as breakfast was over Nellie took her downtown and bought her a warm cloth coat (*warm* was important to Nellie). It cost $14.95, Eileen always remembered that.

Eileen's wasn't the only prize Mulligan's students won; most years the *News* got some kind of award. The year I was editor we got high honors in a state high-school press contest up in Hibbing. Hibbing was okay, but it was nothing compared to the national prizes Miss O'Leary's students won. Craig McCarthy, the smartest kid in our class, wrote an essay for her that she entered in a national contest, and it won third prize. But when it was published Craig said it wasn't the essay he wrote; Miss O'Leary had rewritten it. Mulligan would have smiled his little smile about that.

All that time I was learning other skills in other places. Stealing is a skill that's easy to learn, if you begin young and don't get caught. And if you don't call it stealing. Call it snitching, or hooking, or swiping. Or don't call it anything; then when you do it, it will only be a nameless act of freedom. My own career as a thief had begun badly in the Lake Street dime store, and I never entirely recovered my nerve—always I felt the weight of the store manager's big hand on my shoulder, and heard his deep man's voice asking me what that was in my pocket, and even heavier, the weight of my father's principles.

Two guys I knew in the neighborhood seemed to me to live lives that were freer than mine—lives of perfect anarchy, unburdened by anxieties or fear or guilt, unburdened even by parents. Moe and Snipe lived across the street from each other on Park Avenue, a few blocks south of my house. Their houses were identical small bungalows of the respectable kind that South Minneapolis is full of. Their circumstances were identical, too; neither had a father, at least not a visible one, or a brother or sister, both lived with a mother who worked and was away from home all day. Snipe's mother, whose name was Nan, was a Western Union operator; Hazel, Moe's mother, was a stenographer in the Northwest Bank.

Moe was the ugly one. A pad of flesh across his forehead above the eyes made him look like a boxer who has fought a lot of bouts but hasn't won many, and his ears stuck out (Snipe said he looked like a taxi with both doors open). His nose was big and hooked ("I wish I had your nose full of nickels," Snipe said), and his long jaw thrust forward belligerently. With a few more years of wear that face would be tough looking enough for a bodyguard part in a gangster movie, the guy who glares at the hero and says: "Big Looie says I got to bump you off."

And yet the girls voted him the cutest boy in our class. *Cutest:* I didn't understand what they meant by that. Not *handsomest,* not like Sonny Dahl, who looked like a lover in the movies, but something else that girls saw but I didn't. Maybe it was the way he flirted with them and teased then and made jokes. Yet he never dated any of them, that was puzzling.

Moe was a complete kid-anarchist: to him stealing wasn't a crime, it wasn't even really stealing; it was a game of skill, his wits against the owners and protectors of things—the store-keepers, the clerks at their counters, the cops. He didn't seem to think of things as belonging to somebody, everything was just there in the world, lying around waiting to be picked up by any guy who had the nerve. I knew there were people like this, I had read about them in books—Blackbeard the Pirate and Robin Hood and Raffles the gentleman crook. I thought Moe might grow up to be like one of them. Or maybe John Dillinger.

Snipe was smoother than Moe, and handsomer; with his long, slicked-back hair and his wise-guy smile, he looked like a confidence man, a guy who would sell the Foshay Tower to some yokel from Nebraska, or the barker at a carnival freak show with a two-headed man in it. He seemed to have learned more about the world than the rest of us had, about the human heart and its defections, about greed and stupidity and how you might exploit those qualities in other people. I thought he might become a politician someday.

When I went home with Moe or Snipe after school there was never anyone around. Their houses were swept-and-dusted looking, more even than our house was, and very quiet, with the spooky total silence that rooms in a museum have where old furniture stands around with nobody looking at it. We never did anything in those silent unoccupied houses that a mother in a starched apron wouldn't have allowed; we didn't drink their mothers' whiskey, or bring girls in, or break anything, we didn't even raise our voices. It was as though we were restrained by the silent unmoving air, by the watching furniture, by the emptiness, as though we were in a vacuum where misbehavior was impossible because it would meet no resistance.

If I visited Snipe's house he would bustle into the kitchen and make toasted cheese sandwiches by his own recipe, of which he was very proud. There was no written recipe, of course, but if he'd written it down it would have gone like this:

SNIPE'S TOASTED CHEESE SANDWICH

2 slices Wonder Bread
4 slices Velveeta Processed Cheese
butter

Butter the two slices of Wonder Bread (it *must* be Wonder Bread) heavily on both sides. Put them under the oven grill until brown on one side. Put slices of cheese on the toasted side of one piece. Return to oven until cheese is melted. Cover melted-cheese piece with other piece of toast, toasted side down. Toast both outside sides. Serve.

That probably sounds pretty much like anybody's toasted cheese sandwich, but Snipe's really was different. It was the extravagant amount of butter he put on both sides of both slices, so that it soaked right through the bread, and the toasting of all four sides of the bread, that made Snipe's sandwiches both crisp and oozing, so that the toast crunched as you ate, and the hot butter ran down your chin. The whole process, the preparation and the eating, was very domestic, like a tea party. I was surprised that Snipe, being so free in his life, should have such homemaker's instincts.

Most Saturdays Moe, Snipe, and I—and maybe a few other restless kids—hitchhiked down to the Loop. Saturday was shopping day, the stores and sidewalks were crowded with people with their arms full of packages. My father said these were hard times, nobody had any money, and in our house that seemed to be true; but on Nicollet Avenue I could feel money all around me—money to spend, things bought with money. The people there were dressed in money. They talked animatedly to each other; they smiled; they showed their purchases. Spending had made them happy.

Dayton's department store is the biggest store in town, the most luxurious, the most confident of its rich importance. We drift with the crowd, through the revolving doors into the vast bright hubbub. Glass cases stretch across the floor: perfumes (even the air is sensual here), jewelry, clothes—expensive objects on display for as far as I can see, like a museum. More than a museum, a cathedral of possible possessions; all the desirable things in the world, spread out for money to buy. Or for a kid without money to steal, if he has the nerve.

Snipe stoops and picks up a flimsy piece of paper from the cluttered floor—the carbon copy of a charge slip that some shopper has carelessly tossed aside. He studies the name and address on the slip. "Watch this," he says. He crosses the store to the men's department, picks out a bright-striped shirt, and gives the clerk the name and address he has memorized. I lurk at the opposite counter, waiting for bells to ring and whistles to blow. The clerk writes the address in his book and hands Snipe the shirt in a Dayton's bag. Snipe strolls away, very slowly, pausing to look at ties. I jitter nearby, not wanting to be quite with him when the cops come.

"That's all there is to it," Snipe says. "Try it." He picks up another charge-slip carbon and hands it to me. Snipe and Moe watch me: this is a test. I take the elevator to the book department and walk slowly among the shelves and tables looking for books that are serious—I want to impress myself—and yet are the kind of books an innocent kid would buy. I choose the Modern Library *Nietzsche* (I've heard of him, he's serious, he's German) and *The Theater Guild Anthology*. The clerk accepts my phony name, and I walk out with the books.

Now I am an outlaw; but I am also a book collector. I have stolen my way into that state of mind where you believe that the books you own become part of you and make you different. I learn from Nietzsche that forgetfulness is a blessing; I read in the theater anthology a play in which an Arab says, over and over, "No foundation, all the way down the line." I quote both sentences, and think I have gained something, that those ideas are *my* ideas.

For lunch we go to Walgreen's on Tenth and Nicollet. Walgreen's is one of those drugstores that has a lunch counter at the front by the door and an eating space with booths at the back. There are more of us now; Blake has joined us, and a skinny guy with big round glasses named Otto. I'm reluctant to go in with the others; I only have a quarter in my pocket, how can I buy a lunch? Moe says don't worry, and leads us to a booth in a far dark corner, and we all order hot beef sandwiches with mashed potatoes.

When the checks come Moe explains the scheme. After you've eaten you get up, put your check in your pocket, and head through the crowd toward the cash register by the door. But you don't go all the way; instead you slide onto a stool at the counter and order a small Coke. Then you go to the register and pay the Coke check. It's easy, Moe says, and he demonstrates, moving through the steps calmly, indifferently, as though it were a dance he had often danced, or some ordinary daily act like brushing your teeth. There are no rules and no authorities that apply to him; in Walgreen's drugstore he is entirely free.

I follow him through the same moves, but not so calmly, and Blake and Otto and Snipe follow me, and we're out on Nicollet Avenue again.

"That was stealing!" Otto exclaims.

"Fuck 'em," Moe says. "Walgreen's has plenty of money." Snipe smiles his conspirator's smile. He knows that the schemes he and Moe invent will always work, that they'll never get caught, that nothing they do will have consequences.

CHAPTER TWELVE

C ars were a kind of knowledge. Any kid could walk down any street and name the parked cars, one by one: '35 V-8, '31 Model A, '40 Chevy, '38 Plymouth, Dodge, Graham, Olds, Pontiac, Buick, Hudson, Rio, even the rare, odd-looking ones like the Pierce-Arrow, which had headlights that grew out of its fenders like the eyes on a lizard. When somebody came into Mrs. Miller's and said there was a Chrysler Airflow parked down the block, we all went out to stare at it and argue about the design: Was it the most streamlined car ever built? Did the swoop of the roofline really make it go faster? Would you want to own one? Or was it too funny looking?

The best car in Minneapolis was the Cord, we all agreed on that. There was only one, and it never came to our neighborhood: Why should it? But if you went swimming at Lake Calhoun you might see it sliding along Calhoun Boulevard on its way to the Minikahda Club, quiet as a cat, making only the low, satisfied murmur a cat makes when it's happy. You'd stand and watch it out of sight, admiring the color—it was bright yellow—and the way the top folded back, and the silver exhaust pipes curving out of the long hood. Just to have seen it was something special, like seeing the King of England, or John D. Rockefeller.

Some guys had cars of their own. Ackerberg had one. That was because he was older than the rest of us, already out of school and working at some job—racking balls at the Idle Hour

Pool Hall or maybe something in a factory—not a job that paid Good Money as Nellie understood the term, but enough to buy an old Chevy, if your standards were low enough. Ackerberg's car looked like the wrecks you see abandoned in vacant lots, dented all over and so dirty you couldn't tell what color it was; the seats were covered with Indian blankets, and the door on the passenger's side didn't work, and had to be wired shut. I didn't like to ride in Ackerberg's car; it sounded like it wouldn't get there, wherever *there* was.

Otto had a better car, a long black 1930 Buick—the sort of car bootleggers drive in the movies, and mourners ride in in funeral processions. He didn't own it; it belonged to his father. But his father only used it on Sundays. The rest of the week Otto had it for himself.

Otto's parents were Swedes; they talked Swedish to each other at home, and they cooked Swedish food, all that stuff you get in smorgasbords. At Christmas they made Otto eat lutefisk, a dried fish Swedes fancy that looks like the soles of old shoes and smells like dirty socks when you cook it. Old Man Leonardson was a Lutheran minister; every Sunday he preached on the radio in Swedish. That's why he bought the Buick, so he could arrive at the radio station in dignified style, with him in the back and Otto driving.

One thing about the Buick Old Man Leonardson didn't know; when you pushed the horn button it played "Sweet Adeline." Otto never pushed the button on Sundays, but other days you could hear him arriving at school, or waiting outside your house on a Saturday night. My father hated the sound of that horn. He could hear the bootleggers in it.

Cars were important. "You have to have wheels," Snipe said bitterly. "You can't do anything without a car." He was sore because his mother had a '39 Graham and wouldn't let him drive it. She trusted him with her house all day because she had to;

but she didn't have to lend him her car, not while buses and streetcars ran. My father felt the same way; a kid could do anything my father could imagine, any innocent kid-thing, on his feet, or his bike, or in a streetcar.

But you needed a car for the things he couldn't imagine: to take a girl to the Marigold Ballroom and then park with her and neck; to drive out to Spring Park Casino at Lake Minnetonka; just to drive around with the guys.

If you had a car you could wander after dark. You could drive along Skid Row on Washington Avenue, with the Long Island tracks on one side and tall, sooty tenements on the other, and look up at the red lights in the windows and speculate on what went on inside.

"Whorehouses," Moe said, "all those rooms with red lights have whores in them. Five bucks they charge."

Snipe said the lights were exit signs to fire escapes.

If you had a car you could fill it with guys and park over by Powderhorn in the empty darkness of eleven o'clock and listen on the car radio to "Lights Out," a weekly program of horror stories full of dreadful sounds—the creak of a coffin lid closing on a living person, the beating of an enormous chicken heart, the rising hum of a swarm of giant bees coming to sting the whole world—and be scared and yet not scared, because you were sitting in Murtha's mother's car on Tenth Avenue South and Thirty-fourth Street and what could harm you there?

If you had a car you all could drive out to Cedar Lake after supper on a warm spring evening in early May and dare each other to take the first swim of the year. There'd be no one around, you could undress on the beach and run naked across the sand into the water, taking high prancing steps, deeper and deeper and finally plunging, the cold grabbing your body like a fist when you went under, so tightly you couldn't cry out, or even breathe. And turn and run back into the warmer air, your pecker shrunk up almost out of sight, and jump and slap your body to get warm. "Jeez, it's cold this year!"

If you had a car you could edge closer to the liberties and sins of the grown-up world. You could drink (drinking and cars went together if you were a high-school kid). Moe knew a liquor store over on Cedar Avenue that would sell you a half-gallon bottle of muscatel for a buck and not bother about your age. You could drive south out of town to where the houses end and the land shifts uncertainly into country, cornfields and junk-yards side by side, and stop by the edge of the road and drink the sweet wine, passing the jug from hand to hand, wondering if what you felt was what being drunk was like.

And talk about sex. We sit at the side of a road somewhere in the country night. The radio is playing a classical piece, urgent and pulsing. "That's Ravel's *Bolero*," Hub says, "it's the rhythm of fucking." I listen: BUMP-*tiddly-iddly-iddly*-BUMP-*tiddly-iddly-iddly*-BUMP. Is that how you do it? I don't think I could move any part of my body to that beat for very long. But maybe it doesn't take very long.

Girls didn't go on those nighttime drives, except for a few—the restless, risk-taking ones like Jo-Jo Riley. Jo-Jo was richer than us; she lived in a big house out on Minnehaha Parkway with her father. No mother, no sisters or brothers. No father, either, most of the time; Mr. Riley had invented an instant fudge mix, and he was usually away, traveling the state selling his invention to grocery stores. Jo-Jo seemed to live entirely alone in her big house, like a princess in a fairy tale.

Sometimes when we had nothing else to do we went out to Jo-Jo's house to hang around and drink her father's liquor and eat his fudge. Every table in the house had a plate of fudge on it. But it wasn't fun to go there; it was a shadowy, silent house, only one room was ever lit, and there was nobody there except Jo-Jo. What had happened to her mother? Had she run away? Or died? Moe said she was locked in the attic, like the crazy wife in that novel.

Jo-Jo told us about a haunted house on Lake of the Isles Boulevard. A rich man and his wife lived there until one morning at breakfast they had such a fight that they both got up from the table and walked out in different directions and left *everything* behind them—the food on the table, the copy of the *Tribune* beside the husband's plate, the furniture, the clothes in the closets, everything.

But they made up, didn't they? some girl asked, wanting the story to have a happy ending. No, they didn't, Jo-Jo said. Because she *died!* and now she haunts the house, and her husband can't bear to live there.

The way I heard it, Ackerberg said, he *killed* her. Chased her down the driveway and hit her with a poker. He's in jail for life up at Stillwater, but her ghost comes to the house looking for him, to get even.

How come the ghost doesn't know he's in Stillwater?

The house is still the way it was the morning they had the fight, Jo-Jo said—the breakfast, the paper, the furniture and clothes, all covered with dust and cobwebs. You can sneak in through a basement window, she knew kids who had; only you have to watch out for the neighbors, they keep an eye on the place, they'll call the cops.

Ackerberg drove. Along Lake of the Isles Boulevard the rich people's houses stood back from the road, confident and secure on their wide lawns. Light streamed from their windows, and people moved about inside as though there were parties going on. Only one house was entirely dark, windows like blind eyes, lawn all a blackness. Not just a house with its lights out, an extinguished house.

Ackerberg parked around the corner and we walked back, stealthily; we didn't belong here. The Boulevard was shadowy and empty. We walked up the drive of the dead house and paused for a minute, listening. Nothing. Jo-Jo pushed a cellar window open and one by one we slid through it. I thought of the house I'd gotten into when I was a little kid, the pissing-up-the-walls house. It seemed a long time ago. What if I got caught again? My father would think I was a habitual housebreaker. I dropped into the darkness, feeling the thrill you always feel when you're doing something you know is wrong and it's too late to turn back.

At first I could see only shadow things in the darkness: shadow sofa, shadow dining-room table set with shadow dishes, shadow pictures on the walls; the other kids were shadow silhouettes against the windows; our feet made shadow footprints on the dusty floor. Dust furred the surfaces of things. There were many rooms: one just for books, one for eating breakfast, a porch for sitting in the sun, a vast kitchen. A rich person's house, emptied of light and life.

"Let's go upstairs," Jo-Jo whispered—though there was no need to whisper, no one was there. I didn't want to—it seemed a worse crime to walk into somebody's bedroom, bedrooms were private—but I didn't say so. The beds in the dark bedrooms were made, and clothes hung in the closets, waiting for people who would never wear them. We stood in the big front bedroom, not knowing what to do now. A car passed slowly on the Boulevard, its headlights sweeping across the room, and we seemed spotlit there, like robbers in a movie when they're caught in the act. We turned, all together, and ran down the stairs, making noise now, and climbed out through the cellar window and scuttled down the driveway and around the corner to the car.

As we drove away I listened for sirens and watched for the lights of squad cars; surely the cops were on their way to arrest us, we'd just got away in time. None of us had stolen anything, or done any damage; we hadn't gone there to be thieves or vandals, we'd gone because of the ghost, and the story. But the cops wouldn't understand that, housebreaking was a crime. Now that it was over, I was scared, the way you always are, *after*. Only Jo-Jo seemed exhilarated by what we had done.

If you don't have a car you have to bum rides. It's a Sunday morning in March: still cold, the sun sloping from the south, but a smell of moist earth in the air—the kind of March day that gives you hope, in Minnesota. Somebody at school has planned a picnic at Lake Harriet. We meet outside Mrs. Miller's and climb into the cars that have turned up; I get into the front seat of a car driven by a guy I don't know named Larry. We drive through the pale morning along Thirty-sixth Street, around Lake Calhoun (the ice is still on the lake but it's gray and porous looking, you couldn't skate on it), and up the hill toward Lake Harriet. On the north side of the hill it's still winter, dirty snow covers the slope; but as we come over the top we drive into early spring, snow melting, damp patches of earth steaming in the morning sun.

Larry is driving fast, the tires squeal on the curves; he doesn't know his passengers, and he's showing us what a hot driver he is. We speed down the slope, past picnic tables under the bare trees where kids are unpacking baskets, and into the parking lot. The lot is wide and empty, except for three girls who have been down to look at the lake and are walking back to the picnic. I know one of them, her name is Rosemary Murphy (the guys call her the Float, for some jokey reason we've all forgotten). I like her, I think maybe I'll ask her for a date, later on. Larry heads toward them, not slowing down, swinging the wheel right and then left so that the car swerves back and forth. The girls look up, frightened, seeing the speeding car; they jump to the left, back toward the lake, and Larry swerves away from them, toward the picnic ground. We'll just miss them. And then the Float, terrified and uncertain, jumps back to the right, straight in front of where I sit in the passenger's seat, I can see her face rushing toward me, her mouth open. I can't hear what she cries out.

At that point the morning becomes a silent slow-motion movie: the car moves toward the girl, she moves toward the car, we meet, her body bends forward over the hood and her face smashes down on it, but it makes no sound, I hear nothing, not even the car's engine, or the brakes grabbing, or the other guys in the car, or Larry at the wheel, and she falls to the side and I see her body rolling beside me like a tumbleweed, her face not a face anymore but a mask of blood. Then we are past her.

Kids come running, their eyes wide, their mouths opening and closing; but I don't hear them. A police car comes, its lights flashing, then an ambulance, men in white coats crowd around the body on the pavement. Is she dead? No. But she doesn't move. Then she is carried away. I can't talk to anybody. I have never seen someone my own age so injured, so broken.

I went to see her in the hospital sometimes after school, or after supper if Nellie would let me, hitchhiking down Park Avenue through the spring twilight, and then summer, and fall, and winter, and she was still there. She lay on the hospital bed with her leg in a long plaster cast pointed at the ceiling and her face wrapped in bandages, and talked and cracked jokes and laughed. How could she lie there, hurting and laughing, for a whole year? I couldn't do that.

When she came back to school in the spring, she was different from the other girls. At first she was on crutches, and her ankles were wrapped in bandages above her saddle shoes, and scars on her face showed red against the pale skin. But it was more than that; the accident had changed her. You could see the difference when she sat on the high-school lawn with her girl-

friends. It wasn't just that she wore a coat and a hat, though it was warm spring, or that her legs were still bandaged, or even that she sat a little apart at the edge of the circle. It was the smile. She knew something the other girls didn't know yet.

I wrote an editorial in the *News* to welcome her back, and put an admiring headline on it.

Courage of Rosemary Murphy Should Provide All Students with Inspiration

But I didn't ask her for a date.

Mouse Olson says there's a movie downtown on Hennepin Avenue that has a naked woman in it. No kidding, completely bare-ass. It's called *Ecstasy*. They only show it at night, and you have to be eighteen to get in. But we might as well try.

We hitchhike downtown in the early spring dark, Mouse

and Snipe and Hub and me, and walk down Hennepin, looking over our shoulders and all around, furtive as burglars—past the Pantages, past Bridgeman's ice-cream parlor, past the Lumber Exchange, nearly all the way to Skid Row before we find the narrow entrance to the movie house. We push our money through the ticket window, and the woman inside looks at us— fifteen, sixteen years old—and sighs, and gives us our tickets.

Inside, the theater is dark and stale smelling; not so dark, though, that I can't see that the audience is all men and boys, not talking to each other, most of them sitting alone, just hunched there, unmoving and silent. The film begins and we watch, not understanding the story because the characters all talk German, waiting for The Scene. And finally it comes; in the fluttering half-light on the screen a pale figure scuttles across the far side of a field and is gone. That's it. Most of the men in the audience get up and leave, but we wait for the end because it would be embarrassing to walk out now, the woman in the ticket booth would see us and know what we came for.

Mouse is pissed off. "They cheat you," he says bitterly when we're in the street again. And it is a disappointment, to come for a look at a woman naked all over and bigger than life, and see only a flash of something that might just as well have been a white rabbit. But maybe that's what sex is really like—something brief and sudden that happens in the dark, something you can't make out clearly but that nevertheless arouses you because you know that nakedness is there, in the darkness.

Snipe and Moe know a girl they call La Motta. She seems to have no first name, only La Motta. She lives with her father somewhere way out on Chicago Avenue, far from our neighborhood. I imagine a homemade shack, walls made of tarpaper and old tin signs and roof of corrugated iron; it stands apart in a field, I think, maybe on the edge of a dump. Inside the girl sits alone. Her father is at work, she has no mother, no sisters or brothers. She doesn't go to school. She just sits here and waits for Snipe and Moe to arrive; then she does whatever they want her to—takes off her clothes, lies on her back, I don't know. When they're through they leave. And she sits again, waiting.

I have never seen La Motta, none of us has, but I can see her in my mind: dark (because of her Italian-sounding name), with a thick body and heavy, pendulous breasts. The expression on her face is sullen and angry; whatever she does with Snipe and Moe doesn't make her smile, or express any pleasure. She isn't doing it because she likes it. I don't understand why she is doing it. Snipe and Moe don't know either. But they don't care.

The expression I gave to my imagined La Motta was borrowed from a photograph a fat kid in the next block showed me. I didn't like the fat kid, he was oily looking, and told stories that were dirty without being funny. He lived with his two brothers and a sister, and some guys said the sister did things with her brothers. I only went to his house once. No adults were there that day, only the three boys and the sister, who hung round us sullenly and didn't say much. That was when the fat kid showed me the photograph: a whore, he said, a whore he knew. He took the picture himself. The naked girl in the picture was young—my age, I thought—but yet not young, and not so much a girl as an animal in a cage. She was doing what the fat kid wanted, exposing her sad body to the stare of his camera, but you could see that she hated doing it, hated him, hated everything: she glared up from the dirty sheets of her bed with a fierce despair in her eyes.

As I looked I realized—though this didn't seem possible—that I knew this girl; she was in my fifth-grade class in Bancroft School when we were ten years old. I even remembered her name, it was Alma. What could have happened in the years since then to turn that Alma, who was just like all the rest of us, into this lost, snarling creature?

The fat kid put the photograph back in his wallet. Pretty good, huh?

The Marigold was a flat one-story building on the edge of the Loop. It might have been a warehouse or a garage, except for the marquee with its row of lightbulbs 'round the edge and MARIGOLD BALLROOM painted on the sides. My father didn't call it a ballroom; to him it was a dance hall, which made it sound like a place of temptation and sin (our maid Gladys had gone to dance halls on her Thursday nights off, and look what happened to her). He didn't like me going there. I wanted to go. We compromised; I wouldn't go dancing on Sundays.

What you saw first when you entered the Marigold was yourself, reflected in a long mirror facing the door. I see myself there, dressed in some borrowed finery, Murtha's best sweater or Otto's camel-hair sport coat, holding the arm of my date, who wears a fuzzy angora sweater, a tweed skirt, and penny loafers (you can't slow-dance in saddle shoes). Beyond the mirror, beyond the bouncer in his tight tuxedo, the ballroom—broad, low-ceilinged, windowless, without furniture except for a row of booths on one side, without decoration, just the polished floor stretching to the walls, reflecting the lights from the ceiling. It will be shadowy and romantic when the music starts and couples move across the floor; now it is simply a waiting emptiness.

The men in the band come onto the stand; their bright blue dinner jackets are cut long and loose, like zoot suits. They sit behind music stands decorated with the initials of the band's leader: G/O—Glad Olinger—and begin to arrange their music, tune up, settle their instruments on stands. The girl singer appears and sits demurely on a straight chair by the piano, her hands in her lap. Her strapless evening gown shows the tops of her breasts, round and white and soft looking, like marshmallows. Glad Olinger comes last, waving and smiling to the waiting dancers. He announces the first number, raises his baton, and the music starts—a Glenn Miller arrangement, or maybe Tommy Dorsey or Benny Goodman. The dancers move to the beat. Guys who have come without dates move onto the floor and cut in on dancing couples, and the displaced partners go off and cut in on somebody else. The evening has begun.

The tunes we dance to are the classics of the European musical tradition, though we don't know that: "Till the End of Time" is Chopin, and so is "I Found You in the Rain"; "The Moon Is Low" and "Full Moon and Empty Arms" are Rachmaninoff; "The Lamp Is Low" is Ravel; "Tonight We Love" and "The Story of a Starry Night" and "Moon Love" and "June on the Isle of May" are all Tchaikovsky; "You'd Be So Nice to Come Home To" is Saint-Saëns; "My Reverie" is Debussy; "The Valley of the Moon" is Dvořák; "Midnight Masquerade" is Ibáñez. We dance, and my date sings in my ear: "Can this be moon love, nothing but moon love?" and "Our dream of love was not in vain, for I found you in the rain." All my life the trite words will return; in concert halls when the musicians in their boiled shirts fiddle and blow and the great conductor bobs on his podium, I will hear those words behind the music, and be back in the Marigold.

Between dances we drift toward the booths and order Cokes, and everybody else smokes. I learn how you light a girl's cigarette. She holds it to her lips between two extended fingers, languidly, and you light a match and raise it toward the cigarette, but don't quite reach it, and she cups the fingers of her other hand lightly under yours and guides the match to the cigarette between her lips, and lights it, inhaling slowly and lingeringly and looking up at you through the smoke from under half-closed eyelids. An intimate gesture, a kind of public love scene we've learned from the movies. Almost as good as Paul Henreid with his two cigarettes at once.

Midnight: the band plays "Good Night, Sweetheart" very slowly. The lights of the ballroom sink toward darkness; the Marigold's evening is coming to an end. It is a guy's last chance to hold his girl close, and feel from her body promises of what may happen later in the back seat of someone's car. The band stops playing, the lights go quickly up again, and the mood is broken, all the magic and romance extinguished in the glare of ordinary light. Everyone moves, chattering, to the door, to the parked cars outside. They will drive all the way across the South Side to Edina, to the one late-night restaurant that they must all go to, be seen in. There they will all eat exactly the same late-night meal—breaded veal cutlets—and smoke, and talk about what happened at the dance.

And then drive back, two or three couples in each car because there aren't enough kids who can get their parents' car to drive separately, but also because numbers impose limits on passionate actions, and so protect both the girls and their dates from the scary mysteries of below-the-waist. Maybe they'll do what kissing they can manage on the drive home; or maybe, if all the couples in the car are on serious necking terms, they'll park beside Lake Harriet and half sit, half sprawl in the darkness, saying nothing (how can you speak of love when two other kids are wordlessly kissing at the other end of the seat?). Little waves may break along the beach, maybe the moon is up and trails its light across the midnight water; but the couples in the car aren't aware of the outside world, or of anything inside except their own bodies and their breathing. Then one of the girls asks, "What time is it?" and it's late, and they sit up, still excited, but sleepy, too, it's past their bedtime, the girls comb their hair and put on fresh lipstick and carefully wipe the old lipstick from their dates' faces, and they drive home, talking now, the urgent part of the evening, the love-sex part, over for tonight.

I'm editor of the *News;* I can put what I want into it. I write a two-column headline:

Irene Johnson Elected Commercial Club Prexy

Irene Johnson only appears in the first sentence of the article, the rest is about other student clubs; and the Commercial Club isn't even an interesting club, it's just for girls who take typing and shorthand and want to be secretaries. But I haven't put Irene Johnson's name into the headline because she's important in the school. The headline is a love letter, though I don't know if she will understand that.

She isn't called Irene at school; she has decided that Irene is the wrong name for her. Perhaps it sounds too much like the sort of name her parents, who rent out rooms in their house down on Stevens and Sixteenth, would think of—a boarding-house name. She tells the other kids to call her Nicky. That doesn't surprise me: all the popular girls have names they weren't born with: they're called Stub and Midge and Christy and Sammy and Bunny. The plain ones accept the names they were given: Grace, Donna, Mabel, Hazel, Edna.

Nicky is different from other girls. When she walks through the crowded halls she is solitary and untouchable—like Joan of Arc, I think, or a queen, and her gray eyes look at the rest of us, at me, across a distance that is more than space. For a long time I can't cross that distance to speak to her, and then I can, but not about anything that matters. Finally, in a desperate blurt of words, I ask her for a date. She smiles her serene smile and pauses, and when she speaks her voice is low, barely audible in the clamor of passing classes. "Yes," she says quietly. Just that: "Yes." I am in love.

Love is everywhere in our kid lives. We see it from the back row of the Orpheum on Saturday nights, in huge screen-filling close-ups. Paul Henreid lights his two cigarettes at once and hands one to Bette Davis, and she takes it, and looks up at him, bulgy-eyed, through the smoke. Ingrid Bergman watches from a window as Leslie Howard walks down some steps and gets into a boat. He is leaving her; it's over, he's married. Her eyes, each a foot wide, are full of tears. Joan Fontaine yearns toward Laurence Olivier in a big house; but he is in love with his dead wife. Bette Davis loves George Brent, and goes blind in a garden, and dies. Movies give our beginner's emotions possible shapes: they tell us that love has plots and scenes and stories, that it isn't just feelings. Love is meeting, quarreling, misunderstanding, reconciling; most of all it is renouncing, separating forever, the afterlife of the broken heart. Even while a boy and a girl are happy in love they are anticipating the Final Scene that is coming, writing their lines in their heads and visualizing the poignant stagy gestures with which they will embrace or refuse embraces, give and receive heart wounds, and at last turn tearfully away. Like Bette Davis. Like Ingrid Bergman. Like poor Paul Henreid. We make our love scenarios out of school-kid stuff—going steady, giving Hi-Y pins, breaking up and getting the pin back, writing emotional notes in class and getting emotional replies while in front of the class the teacher talks on about subordinate clauses—but the plots and the gestures and the overwrought language aren't ours, they come from the movies. The halls of Central are full of last reels.

Love is at the Marigold, too, when the band plays a slow ro-

mantic ballad, and the lights go down, and boys feel girls' breasts
pressed against their chests, and girls put their heads on boys'
shoulders, and they dance almost without moving, while the
band's crooner sings, "I'm getting sentimental over you," and
the girl vocalist sings, "Time on my hands, and you in my arms,"
and the shadowy room seems pulsing with warm emotion. Love
is slow dancing; slow dancing is love.

I want to be like that with Nicky Johnson. I take her to
Marigold, and she dances close enough that I can feel the con-
tours of her body, and yet she remains somehow distant; I kiss
her in the back seat of Otto's big Buick, and she receives my kiss
politely, as though it were a postcard; I give her my Hi-Y pin
and she agrees—reluctantly, I think—to wear it. She invites me
to visit her at home, and I hitchhike down to Sixteenth Street
and ring the boardinghouse bell.

She opens the door at once, as though she had been standing behind it waiting, and takes me very solemnly into the living room to meet her parents, a worn-looking couple who sit in
worn chairs and don't say much. The house smells of cooking
and stale air. Then she leads me up the stairs, past the closed
doors of the boarders, into the attic, where she has made a room
for herself under the rafters.

Her room is neater, brighter, more attractive than the rest of
the house. A flowered spread covers the narrow bed, and repro-
ductions of paintings hang on the walls; I recognize Van Gogh's
sunflowers by the window. The low sloping ceiling makes it
seem romantic, a room where a poet or a painter might live in a
movie. It isn't really a bedroom, it's a stage setting for a different
life that would be better than this one, if it were real.

She carefully closes the door, and sits on a straight chair,
stiffly erect with her hands in her lap, like Whistler's mother in
the painting. I sit on a stool, uncomfortably, facing her. I am
alone with her, in her room with the door closed; but I know

this won't be like my daydreams of such a meeting. We won't lie together on the bed, my hands won't touch her body. She talks, in her low, husky voice, about nothing in particular, yet expressing somehow her dream of what it will be like when she lives a life different from this, in a house more beautiful than a boardinghouse, full of beautiful things, and how she will know everything then, about music and art and manners, and will have . . . But no, that's wrong, she isn't thinking about possessions, or wealth, or class; it's a more shadowy vision she sees, of a kind of *being* that will be better, beyond imagining, than a boarding-house on Clinton Avenue offers. She wants life the way I want love, without knowing what it is she wants. I go back down the stairs after a while, unkissed (or barely), defeated by the need she has that I don't understand, and certainly can't satisfy.

And so we quarrel, and the pin comes back with a sad, formal note that is like a judge's verdict. I'm unhappy, but I don't appeal the sentence: What good would that do? Instead, I mope. One spring evening I hitchhike back down to Clinton Avenue. It's April, misty and damp. I stand in the black empty street and look up at Nicky's high window. Her light is on, she's up there, dreaming her dream, like Rapunzel alone in her tower. I know that however much I yearn, whatever apologies I offer for whatever it was that caused the quarrel, I will never climb to that high room again, and she will never come down to me. Standing there in the dark street, I feel wounded and sad, like a soldier after a lost battle; I'm sure I will carry the scars of this defeat always.

But you can't stand in the middle of Clinton Avenue all night. After a while I walk back to Portland Avenue and hitch-hike home.

CHAPTER THIRTEEN

B lizzards aren't anything special in Minnesota. I was used to
waking in the morning to see my bedroom window
blinded by driven snow, used to walking to school leaning into
the stinging wind, my face wrapped in a scarf, eyes closed to
slits, lashes crusted with rime. Where the sidewalks were, between the piles of last week's shoveling, new snow and sleet
drifted and the shoveler's weren't out yet, knowing it wouldn't
do any good until the wind dropped; I walked in the street in
the tire tracks some car with chains had made. When a car crept
toward me, headlights dim and haloed in the streaming snow,
not lighting anything, I jumped aside into a drift to let it pass,
and went on walking. Blizzards were just winter weather.

Armistice Day 1940 was different. Long after, folks talked
about it: "Where were you in the Armistice Day Blizzard?" And
everybody remembered, just as they would remember where
they were on Pearl Harbor Day.

It began as the kind of day kids hate: no school, because it was
a holiday, but rainy and dark outside, nothing for kids to do on
a day like that. I walked up the alley in the rain to see if Michaud
was at the White Palace's pinball machine, but the diner was
closed because it was Armistice Day, so I walked back home and
just hung around, getting in the way and annoying Nellie.

By noon the rain had become sleet and the wind was rising
and rattling the windows. As the temperature dropped the sleet
became snow, and day faded into night. I couldn't see the houses

across the street. Car traffic slowed and then stopped; nobody drove down Columbus Avenue and the early tire tracks filled with snow. By midafternoon the blown snow was piled to the windowsills. Up at the corner, on Thirty-eighth Street, the buses had stopped running. My father phoned from his gas station to say that he was closing up and putting chains on his tires to drive home. That drive, which usually took him twenty minutes, took two hours; he drove all the way at ten miles an hour with his headlights on, but the lights lit nothing but the flying snow, and he had to steer by instinct. It was the worst storm he'd ever seen. Don't bother to shovel the sidewalk, he said, we're snowed in. Snowed in! Like Scott at the South Pole! And Admiral Byrd! That was heroic, being snowed in.

The storm blew all night. Next morning Nellie woke me, cheerful as always, to tell me there'd be no school today; she'd heard it on "Dayton's Musical Chimes." The snow had stopped, she said, but the drifts were even higher—up to the eaves of the bungalows across the street. The radio said that on the farms animals had frozen—sheep, cows, horses, all dead. And thousands of Thanksgiving turkeys. Terrible for the farmers, Nellie said.

After breakfast I dressed ("Wrap up good, it's six below!") and went out into the world the storm had made. The snow lay still and of a perfect whiteness and the sky was clear, brighter than blue, colder than ice. There were none of the usual winter sounds, no crows cawing in the high branches, no sparrows in the bushes, no distant traffic, no human voices. Only the snow and the light and the silence.

I walked down the middle of my street, stumbling and falling in the waist-deep drifts. At Chicago Field the wind had carved the snow in a long unbroken curve from the warming-house roof to the ground, one perfect, frozen gesture. The houses along Park Avenue hunched under deep roofs of snow.

Smoke from their chimneys rose straight in the calm air. No one was out but me.

I was headed for Pat Champion's house over on the other side of the field. It was the sort of place you'd go to on a day like this; you could hang around there, her mother, Beulah, wouldn't mind, she'd make coffee, and we'd talk. You could talk to Pat, you didn't have to be always flirting and showing off.

We sat together on the sunporch in the morning brightness and listened to news of the storm on the radio. Along the Mississippi duck hunters had been found frozen to death in their boats; near Mankato a mother and her daughter had died in their stalled car; trains had crashed head-on. In the city thousands of buses and cars were stalled and buried in drifts. Streetcars couldn't run: at the Bottleneck on Lowry Hill they slid backwards downhill. Fire trucks couldn't reach fires. Power lines were broken and telephone lines were down. Plateglass windows in downtown stores were shattered by the wind and lay on the snow in fragments, like shards of ice.

Hearing those radio stories was like reading war news in the paper; terrible things had happened, but somewhere else, nothing to do with us, sitting warm and dry in the sunlight, drinking coffee. Something vast and powerful had swept through like a great army, leaving death and destruction behind, and had moved indifferently on.

The next day the schools didn't open. Kids dragged their toboggans to Chicago Field and made slides on the hills, and shoveled the snow off the hockey rink and played a game that went on all day. But for grown-ups it was a working day; people skied to work downtown, or walked on snowshoes, but they went. My father drove down to his station and began shoveling. It was just winter again.

Everybody had a blizzard story, their own or someone else's.

A farmer's privy blew away and he never did find it; a mailman's sack of letters was buried somewhere under the snow on Portland Avenue where he'd left it to struggle home; the cut where Excelsior Boulevard passes through the Minikahda Golf Course was full of abandoned cars under fifteen feet of snow; the trash barrel at my father's station had blown three blocks down the street and wrapped itself around a lamppost.

And there were stories of all the dead: a family in a car on a country road, father, mother, and three children found under a tall drift, sitting there in their seats, upright, blue-white, dead for days; hunters, frozen on prairies in the appalling snow or drowned in freezing rivers, turned into ice-persons. One story in particular held me, of a solitary duck hunter on the Mississippi. The morning of the storm he had paddled his skiff to an island in the river and built his duck blind there. When the storm broke and the wind and waves rose, he tried to row back to shore, and had almost made it when his boat capsized. He waded through the shallows—how cold the water must have been, how fierce the wind, how blinding the snow in his face— and reached up to an overhanging willow branch to pull himself out of the water. And died there, his hand gripping the branch. I imagined him at the river's edge, flesh turned to ice, arm still raised in a stiff heroic gesture, like a statue on a war memorial or an ice sculpture at the Winter Carnival, waiting for spring.

A lot of the guys I knew lived with only one parent. Moe and Snipe had no visible fathers; Blake lived with his mother and a bunch of kids; Mouse had no mother; Murtha lived with his grandparents, and his mother when she wasn't in Seattle; Jim Brugger lived with his mother and sister. In those hard times men lost their jobs, or their courage, or their health, or their will to endure, and just gave up—died, took to drink, or ran away—

went west, as Americans always had; women died, or took the children and ran, or ran without them. I never knew what had happened to my friends' missing parents—you didn't ask a guy where his father was, he might be crazy, or in jail, or dead.

To be one-parented (or no-parented, like the fat kid) was, I saw, a kind of freedom. Without two adults in your house setting the rules and living them in their own lives, you could just float, weightless in the world, doing what you liked, or nothing. But it was also a kind of loneliness. Not the ordinary loneliness most kids know, the feeling that other kids know how to be happy and popular and you don't. Not that kind but the other, lonelier kind—the loneliness of empty houses, of love gone absent, of not being the child of two people (even if they're mean) that you can see and touch.

Mouse was the loneliest. He lived alone with his father in a little house, just three or four rooms, on Portland Avenue. It was a sad, echoing sort of house, like an unoccupied tourist cabin on some back-country road, furnished with a minimum of plain, worn furniture, the kind of stuff the Salvation Army might give you. No growing plants, not even mother-in-law's tongue, no books, no pictures on the walls; no sign that a woman had ever lived there, not one decoration that a woman might have made because she thought it would be pretty, a sampler or a pillow cover or an antimacassar. A house without any hope that ordinary family living might go on there, some day.

Mouse's father worked on the railroad, and was away a lot. When he was on a run Mouse cared for himself, kept house after a fashion, even went to school. His nickname wasn't a mocking joke, it was simply descriptive: he looked like a mouse, small, thin and nervous, with big ears and long front teeth, and startled hair. And lived like a mouse—furtively, almost invisibly. At school he scarcely seemed to be there; he went to classes but he didn't say anything, he didn't join clubs or play sports (what sports would a mouse play?), or write, or sing, or play in the band. He didn't go out on dates (who'd date a mouse?). He was just there. Other kids liked him; he was kind and generous, and could be very funny, and he gave affection to his friends without expecting any back. Those are virtues sad people have, if they're *good* sad people.

Murtha was the quiet one. He was one of those guys who have neither a first name nor a nickname among his friends. That is, he had a name—it was Donald—but nobody used it, or even called him Don, and nobody seemed to see anything about him that would inspire a nickname. Because he was quiet he tended to fade into the background of things. He was the one who stood at the edge of a group, content to be the listener who contributes nothing to the scene except his silent presence.

Yet you'd notice him in a group: you'd see that his eyes were a deep surprising blue, and his lashes long and black (though his hair was blond), and that his mouth was full and red. Grown-ups thought he was handsome, even maybe beautiful: "Those eyes!" Nellie would exclaim. "What a girl wouldn't give to have eyes like that!" But beauty isn't an advantage to a boy. Maybe the opposite. Girls didn't seem attracted to the silent immobility that went with the eyes, and Murtha was a lonely kid, the kind of person you went to the movies with on a Thursday night when nobody else was around.

Murtha lived with his mother, when she was in town. But family life didn't seem to suit her, not in long stretches, and after a while she'd pack up and move to Seattle and live there. Then Murtha would live with his grandparents. Murtha's grandfather was a little old man—shorter than me by a head—with the biggest ears I ever saw on a human being. Ackerberg said if only he could wiggle them he could fly. They were that big, Ackerberg said, because Murtha's grandfather was so old; your ears and nose go on growing as long as you live. Murtha said your hair and fingernails grow even after you're dead; if someone digs you up months after you've been buried, they'll find fingernails as long as your arm. We were silent for a minute, thinking of the old man in his grave, all nose and ears and fingernails.

In his youth Grandpa Murtha had been a bugler in the army; he'd charged up San Juan Hill with Teddy Roosevelt, he said, bugling away. He still had his bugle, and he played it for us sometimes, though he could only hit the low notes now. In the spring he made dandelion wine, which he kept in a wooden keg in the cellar. When the old man was out of the house, Murtha and I would steal down the cellar stairs and tap the keg. The wine was yellowish, not like white wine made from grapes, more like the dog-piss stains you see on winter snow. It had a sweet, vaguely chemical taste. We couldn't steal a lot—Grandpa Murtha was a suspicious old man, he'd notice if the level in the keg fell much—not enough to make us drunk, though we wanted it to, but enough to feel different, because we'd been drinking wine, *stolen* wine.

Keys Johnson was the kind of boy mothers like; why don't you spend more time with that Johnson boy, they asked, he seems so nice. And he was nice: smiling and round-cheeked, with a dimple in his chin and black, slicked-down hair; a neat boy, the kind who wears a necktie to school: a gentle, soft-spoken boy who never swore, or even raised his voice. Not like the rest of us, he never played ball, never had a girl, never tried drinking; all he ever does, the guys said, is play the piano. It was a kind of accusation, as though playing the piano too much might be a Solitary Vice, like jerking off; but not really, because we saw, without understanding, that he couldn't help it; that's what Keys was, he was a piano player.

He played the piano all the time. At school he accompanied singers and dancers at assemblies. He played for a girl who sang "I Concentrate on You" out of tune and out of rhythm the whole way through, and kept with her and made her sound better than she was; he was the accompanist for a girl tap dancer when her bra fell off, and he never looked up or missed a beat. Once, when a program had collapsed in confusion and there was no one to perform, he strolled smiling onto the stage without any music and played a Lizst Hungarian Rhapsody until a singer appeared, and then he accompanied her through Victor Herbert favorites.

Keys would turn up at my door after supper, alone and uninvited, and if the folks weren't home, or were invisible in their room, he'd sit at the piano in the front hall and play jazz for a while. He knew how all the great jazz pianists played: he could do right-hand runs like Tatum, and Father Hines's striding bass, he could even play Count Basie's silences. And blues. He liked to play blues, chorus after chorus, slow and brooding, like sad talk. And I, listening there in the hall (though he didn't seem aware I was there), learned from him, a little—about what jazz was, and why it was a right and necessary music for a guy like Keys.

Being gifted as he was, Keys was lonely, we all knew that. When we gathered at Mrs. Miller's he'd be there, a little apart, over by the window where the cats slept; but he was also somewhere else, somewhere beyond our ordinary lives. He'd always be different from us. We could imagine ourselves in the adult world, working at desks in downtown offices, having houses and wives and kids some day. But what would Keys do?

What he did was go on playing the piano. After the war when I got back to Minneapolis, I inquired about him. Up in Fargo, somebody said, playing in a bar. Then he was in Sioux Falls, and after that Bismarck, or Des Moines, always playing bar piano somewhere in the Territory. Along the way he married a nightclub singer, but nobody had met her. And then he died, in Omaha; but that was a lot later. The Float went to his funeral, not because she was his special friend but because she was in

Omaha and was the sort of person who would go to a funeral just in case nobody else showed up. But other people did come, she said, and after the funeral there was a wake, and the widow sang "I'll Be Glad When You're Dead, You Rascal You." The Float didn't know exactly what that said about their personal life.

Spring comes late to Minnesota, but it comes. In early May the trees are in leaf and the air is warm, and the grass on the high-school lawn is turning from winter brown to green. Those of us who are seniors respond to the season like colts in a pasture; we escape from our classrooms onto the green terraces. Spring is freedom; soon we'll be through with school, forever.

Someone has driven a Ford convertible onto the school grounds at the north end where the terraces flatten out. The prettiest girls instantly gather around it, as though they have the right to be near a convertible with its top down, because they're pretty. They flow over it, sitting on the back of the seat, leaning on the open doors, lying along the fenders. Their hair shines like silk, and swings when they turn their heads, their eyes are bright and clear, and they smile the smiles of girls who know they're better looking than other girls.

From where I am lying on the grass with some of my friends, I watch the girls covering the car like climbing roses, and I see something that I hadn't understood before—that it's no good pursuing any of these pretty girls, they're beyond reach. They already belong, in the future somewhere, to the sort of guys who will own convertibles like this one, guys who don't go to Central but to Washburn (where kids who are richer than us go), or if they're even richer than that to some snotty school, maybe in another city, even in the East, guys who will grow up to run Minneapolis, become businessmen rich enough to buy houses on Lake of the Isles or out at Minnetonka and play golf at the Minikahda Club. The most beautiful and remote of these girls might go farther than that, to Paris, or Rome, or even beyond, marry a French millionaire or an Arab sheikh, or *not* marry him, and forget they came from Minneapolis, and never be heard from again.

Blue Green is one of the guys lying on the grass. He has brought a little flask of medical alcohol from the pharmacy school at the University, where he is a first-year student, and we each pour a little into our bottles of Orange Crush, and drink it while we look at the girls on the convertible, and talk about sex. Because Blue is a year or two older than us, and a college boy, he speaks with authority. He says girls' bodies are different from ours, and we all nod wisely; even I know that much. For instance, Blue says, there's a little spot at the base of a girl's spine, right where the crack of her butt begins, a little flat place. If you can just touch that spot, on her bare skin, she'll do whatever you want. We believe him. We take for granted that you have to make a girl crazy, somehow, before she will go all the way: get her drunk, play her Ravel's *Bolero,* touch the base of her spine, something to derange her; experience has taught us that sane girls won't go even halfway. I think of that secret, magical spot on a girl's body, down there beneath the twin-set sweaters, beneath the blouse, the slip, the garter belt, the underpants—as far from sight or touch as the gold in Fort Knox—and I know that if that's where I have to get, I who can't even get inside a blouse, I'll never experience whatever it is that comes next. Blue doesn't actually say he's been there himself, but he smiles as though he has. After all, he's in college and we're still in high school, even if we are seniors.

Late in the spring, later than the first shot of Blue Green's alcohol, later than the girls on the convertible, the class yearbook appears, and turns our school lives into history. There we all are, the administrators, the teachers, and the students, all the clubs and the teams and the games won and lost, the school plays, the prizes—past tense now, the things we did then, when we were high school kids. There's Old Jarvis the principal and his assistant Miss Thomas, like an old couple who've had too many unruly children, and are looking back, now that it's over: Jarvis with his long thin face, tired eyes, and mouth that sags at the corners, and Miss Thomas, grim-faced, massively bosomed, immovable, a brick wall, solid as the school building itself. Beside their photographs are their last words to us. Miss Thomas is confidently stern: "Face life squarely and think your problems through clearly"—that's all there is to it. Jarvis is less confident that life's problems can be handled so briskly: "We have tried to help you to learn how to learn and live. We are conscious of failures . . ." For them there will be next year, and the year after that; there will be more failures, and Jarvis will be conscious of them and Miss Thomas won't.

The teachers who taught me are there, posed at desks or standing in front of blackboards. Some of them have written on the board words that give them their school identities. O. K. Kuenster is giving a civics exam; on the board behind him are two lists, one of terms—NAVY, INTERIOR, U.S. MARSHAL, FRANKING PRIVILEGE, and one of definitions: HE AWARDS CONTRACTS FOR . . . HE RECOMMENDS POST . . . Frau Drechsler is teaching French; she has written the words of "Au clair de la lune." But the expression on her face is German: you *will* learn this!

Others have written no words. Miss Henry, the art lover, stands holding an ancient-looking lamp and smiling at it, as though it contains a jinni that will appear when, in a moment, she rubs it. Joe Markley the football coach slumps at his desk in the boys' locker room; his in-basket is full of boxing gloves. Hawker, the cruel man, sprawls back in his desk chair and gestures over his shoulder at a meaningless diagram on the board behind him. He doesn't look at the board. His skull eyes stare coldly at nothing. Mulligan the good journalist is at his desk in the newsroom. He holds a pencil poised above a copy of the *Central High News*. He is smiling; he's found an editing error.

After the teachers the seniors, each with a photograph and beside it a list of the achievements that made them a person in the school, not nothing. There is Nicky, prim in her sweater and white Peter Pan collar: President Commercial Club; and Keys, smiling sadly: Class Cabinet and Hi-Y; and Buck: football and swimming. But, I think, that's not who they really are, that's just school. Only Moe and Mouse seem truly self-identified. Moe's entry reads simply FRANK BULLARD and nothing more; he's been true to his guiding principle: don't join them and they can't touch you. Mouse is just JEROME OLSON, without any named achievements, but for a reason different from Moe's; Mouse is a kid who's too lonely, too far from other kids' lives, to come in.

I carry my yearbook around school and people write in it; that's what you do when you're a senior. Friends, acquaintances, kids whose names I never learned write notes—"Do you remember?" "Don't forget"—that are farewells. We have come to the end of our lives as children.

I stop at Miss O'Leary's room and she opens the book, not to her photograph, because of course she won't allow her face to appear in the same book with her despised colleagues, but to the page where the staff of her magazine, *The Quest,* sit stiffly in a group picture (Nelson Peery is there, looking belligerent and proud among all the white faces), and writes: "Good luck to a student it was a privelage to 'try' to teach—Abigail O'Leary." The Mulligan-trained editor in me notes that she has misspelled "privilege." Then down the hall to the newsroom, to the teacher I admire most. Mulligan opens the book to the page with his picture on it and writes "J. E. Mulligan." Either he thinks inscriptions are for children or he's already forgotten my name.

I get my last report card. It's not very good—I've failed Mrs.

Pink's economics class, the one with the mock marriage in it. At the bottom of the card are two spaces to be filled in by my homeroom teacher, Mr. Lander, a stern-faced man who teaches machine shop. One space is labeled: "Personality: Assets." Lander has written the same judgment that he has entered there every semester for the past three years: "nonconformist." I'm pleased that he regards this as an asset. The other space is "Needs help with." Here Lander has tried small variations over the years: first "conceit," the next year "egotism," and in my last year "egoism." I take these to be synonyms, more or less, that clarify what Lander means by "nonconformist": to him I have been a three-year pain in the ass. I wonder if he speaks for all the school's grown-ups.

Seniors in their caps and gowns march one at a time across the auditorium stage. The school orchestra plays selections from *Pinafore*. Old Jarvis hands out diplomas. Parents clap. The graduating students smile and wave. They seem glad to be done with schooling; for most of them their diploma is a passport to a grown-up world—Nellie's world of jobs and Good Money, where you work hard, save, work your way up. They can live away from home now, stay out late, buy a car. Eventually they will marry—probably someone who is walking near them in this black procession—and rent a house on the South Side like the one their folks live in, and have children. Their stories have already been written; they only have to live them.

But at this Commencement a different story has become possible. The subject Craig McCarthy chooses for his Valedictory Address is Military Training Camps, and the girl who is Salutatorian talks about Women in Defense—as though what is really commencing, on this June evening in 1941, isn't the rest of our ordinary lives, but a long diversion from them. The war our country is not yet in has begun to enter our lives, furtively, like fog stealing into a house through the cracks of the windows and under the doors, dimming the lights and thickening the air. Eighteen-year-old boys in this class will have to register for the draft.

I leave the school by the main entrance, under the confident carved words that by now I know by heart: THE COMMON-WEALTH REQUIRES THE EDUCATION OF THE PEOPLE AS A SAFEGUARD OF ORDER AND LIBERTY. The long June evening is sinking into darkness now. Down at the corner Mrs. Miller's lights are still on; she is selling one last loaf of Wonder Bread before she locks the door. Across Fourth Avenue I can see the window where I first saw a girl's naked body: dark now. And beyond the first row of houses the roofs and lights of the flat retiring city. Out there is the world where people work all their lives. And beyond it, the world where men fight.

CHAPTER FOURTEEN

Sometimes, that summer of '41, it seemed that nothing had changed in our world, or ever would: the band would always play "Moonlight Serenade," guys would date girls, the slow dancing and the backseat kissing would be the same, forever.

On summer evenings we drove out to the Spring Park Casino on Lake Minnetonka—twenty miles west on Route 7 to Excelsior, then north on a two-lane road between bays of the lake, the last light in the west making the bay on the left sky-colored, and over a bridge into an open space with low buildings around it that was all the village of Spring Park had for a center.

By then the light was gone from the sky except for a pale blue-greenness at the zenith, and the water of the bay had turned dark and silky; masthead lights on moored boats tilted, and along the shore toward the point the lights of the big summer houses were coming on. After the heat of the day the air was cool, and a breeze blew from the water. On the far side of the open space colored lights along a roofline marked where the casino was, and you could hear the music. Everything you saw and felt, there in the summer twilight, said: "You'll be happy here."

That summer Spring Park was a garden of girls. They came out from town in bunches, bouquets of girls, and rented cottages with an older sister or a pliable aunt for chaperon, and waited to be asked to go dancing. Or they came as mother's helpers in the big houses along the bay, and had their evenings free. I knew a mother's helper, a small, dark, pretty girl whose name was Marie du Pre. She must be French, I thought, with a name like that, and that seemed a romantic thing to be. I was almost in love with her for her Frenchness.

I knew Marie liked me, she had written in my yearbook: "I hope the summer will hold a great future for us." I called for her at the house where she worked and we walked along the curve of the beach toward the casino. The colored lights shimmered toward us on the water, and the music of the band drifted across, soft with promises. I could hear the girl vocalist singing: "Those green eyes with their soft light . . ." I held Marie's hand, and she pressed her shoulder against mine. I knew she would let me kiss her, and would kiss me back, and dance very close when the band played a slow romantic song. The summer *would* hold a great future for us. A whole summer seemed a wonderful long time.

That summer my two stepsisters left town: Rose Marie married an Iowa farmer and went to live on his farm and Eileen got a government job in Washington. Now the house was an empty, silent place; nobody argued over supper, or talked about strikes and murders, nobody brought laundry home to be washed and sat at the kitchen table talking while the washing machine walked around the cellar, nobody came to Sunday dinner.

When we talked at meals, it was about me. I was a high-school graduate without a job. Nellie thought that was unnatural.

Get a job, she said. You ought to have a job.

I said my teachers thought I should go to college. I should study journalism and be a writer on the *Star-Journal*.

My father said yes, that's what I should do, my mother would have wanted that.

Nellie said all right, go to college. Only not now, not this

year. I was only sixteen. Wait a year. Work. Get a good job and
save your money. Then go. Work would be good for me, she
said. Everybody should know what it's like to have a full-time job.

That's how I became a banker.

Dick Anderson, the head messenger at the First National Bank
on Marquette and Fifth, sat at a desk in the corner of Account-
ing. He explained my job. All day long I would go in and out of
downtown office buildings, up and down elevators, along downtown streets, wearing a leather wallet full of canceled checks,
which I would deliver to businesses.

The offices were all alike, just people working; they were no
fun. But the streets outside were a show for me to stop and stare
at, like the circus or the midway at the State Fair: two cars col-
liding, a fire in a store (fire engines blocking the street and cars
honking and hoses snaking everywhere and people gawking and
firemen yelling), a thief stealing a woman's purse and the
woman screaming, an epileptic having a fit on the sidewalk by
Dayton's ("Call a doctor!" "Put a pencil in his mouth!"). Once
it was a freak show in a store over on Hennepin: the World's
Thinnest Man and the World's Fattest Lady, a man with the skin
of an alligator, a nearly naked person whose body was hairy on
one side and hairless on the other ("That there's a morphodite,"
a man behind me explained to his kid), Jack Johnson the prize-
fighter, Al Capone's bulletproof car, a dead whale in a tank,
while the checks in the wallet waited to be delivered.

On hot sunny days I walked up Marquette to Tenth Street to
the Foshay Tower and rode the elevator to the top, not because I
had checks to deliver there, it wasn't even on my route, but because it was the tallest building in town, the tallest in the whole
Northwest. It stood on its own block, a square three-story base

like a clenched fist with the tower thrusting upward from the center like an extended middle finger. Thirty-two stories high!

An observation deck ran round the outside of the tower on the thirty-first floor. From there I could see the whole of the city where I had lived my life as a kid: the streets running off in converging parallel lines like a lesson in perspective drawing, the houses low and hidden under a canopy of trees. I could see the ballpark, and Central High, and the Sears building, and the bright string of the lakes, and closer in the dome of the basilica and the square tower of St. Mark's, and on the other side, beyond the downtown buildings, the tall grain elevators by the river, all calm and quiet in the summer sun. A flat, reasonable city. My town.

Up there in the wind and light I could see beyond the town into the Territory—across the flatlands south to the Minnesota River Valley, north to the upriver country towns, west beyond Minnetonka, east over the bright scrawl of the river to St. Paul and the blue heat haze beyond. *Beyond,* that was what drew me to the Tower's deck; up there you could see how wide the world was, how the flat land faded into distance and slid over the round edge of the horizon, into elsewhere.

Sometimes I shared the deck with other people, country families who had come to town just to stand at the top of the tallest building and look out. Their reasons were different from mine; what they looked for were familiar places. They pointed out the landmarks of their lives with astonishment and a kind of relief, as though to have seen them from the Foshay Tower proved they were really there: "There's the church steeple in Eden Prairie!" "I can see Coon Rapids!" And then looked straight down to the street, farther below their feet than anything in their lives had ever been before, farther than the barnyard from the haymow or the water trough from the top of the windmill, and were scared by that deep space, and stepped back.

My father told me the story of the Tower, how Mr. Foshay

built it as an obelisk like the Washington Monument, tall and tapering with a four-sided point at the top, to be a tribute to the founder of our country, and how when he finished it in August 1929 (so I was exactly five years older than the Tower was), John Philip Sousa wrote a march for the dedication ceremony, and the Secretary of War came and made a speech. And how three months later Foshay lost all his money in the stock-market crash and had to sell the building.

I said that was a sad story, losing his fine new tower.

Served him right, my father said. He was a crook. They arrested him and tried him in court and sent him to prison. He'd cheated his investors.

There was another story about the Tower that my father didn't tell me. I heard it from the guard on the observation deck. A woman who was on the trial jury tried hard to get Foshay acquitted, and afterwards it turned out she had worked for him, and lied to the court about it. She was tried for perjury and convicted. But before she could be locked up in jail, she and her husband and their two children all got in their car and put a hose from the exhaust pipe through the window and started the engine. And sat there together and died. My father didn't tell me that story, for the same reason he didn't tell me the end of the Pig Woman's story; he couldn't tell what he couldn't imagine, parents killing their own children.

Fall came. The wind off Minnetonka blew cold, and the lake was flat and gray. The flocks of girls left the little cottages, and Spring Park turned off its garland of colored lights and closed until spring. Marie came home and went back to Central (she was a senior now), and found a new boyfriend, and a new great future. I didn't mind; it had only been let's pretend. But I felt that something more than summer had ended.

War seemed a long way off, that fall; the fighting was in places like China and Africa, and above the English Channel. Still, it reached us on Columbus Avenue. In October Bill joined the Army Air Corps. Nellie was stunned; why would you quit a good job and enlist, when your country wasn't even at war, and there was nobody to fight? Bill said there would be, soon enough. He wanted to go now. I understood that feeling; if there was going to be a war you'd want to get in it right away. Waiting around selling groceries when you could be flying would be like holding your breath forever.

Nellie didn't say much after Bill left. She just got a little red-and-white banner with a blue star in the middle and hung it in the front window. That meant we had given a son to the service. I didn't understand the giving, exactly; surely he had done the giving, not us.

Some nights that fall we drove, in Otto's car or Ackerberg's, down highways south of town to roadhouses, German and Polish and Scandinavian, where polka bands played Old Country music and bartenders weren't particular about how old their customers were, beer-smelling taverns where you could buy a drink and sit at the bar listening to the *thump-thump* of the music and watching the sweating dancers, or talk to the bartender, or just sit there and read the mottoes that hung on the wall above the rows of bottles:

IF YOU'RE SO SMART, WHY AIN'T YOU RICH?
VY IZ ZER ZO MANY MORE HORZEZ AZZEZ ZAN ZERE IZ HORZEZ?
TOO SOON OLD, TOO LATE SHMART.

Drinkers' mottoes: the philosophy of losers. If you had brought a date you could go out on the dance floor and try to dance the polka and the schottische—one-two-three-hop, one-two-three-hop, one-hop, two-hop, three-hop, four-hop, counting it out, round and round the hot smoky room until the lights and the thumping music and the beer spun in your head, and drive home half-drunk, singing.

We drank beer, mostly, because it was cheap, and because it seemed a friendly drink—"Tree-point-two," the old-timers in the polka bars said, "it vill neffer hurt you"—but sometimes we drank shots of cheap blended whiskey, just to show each other that we weren't high-school kids anymore. I didn't like whiskey; it puckered my mouth and scalded my gullet going down, and when it hit the bottom my stomach clenched in angry protest and tried to send it back up. But I drank it, and struggled to keep it down, because I was with the guys, and because drinking whiskey was way outside the rules.

I learned that fall how it feels to be really drunk, how time leaks from the clock, how gravity pulls you sideways and the floor tilts, how your voice becomes someone else's; I learned how it feels to vomit what you've drunk, how the sourness burns again coming up and leaves you shivering and sweating, and your stomach goes on clenching though there's nothing in it now; how when at last you lie down in your bed, the room turns over like the rolling earth and you have to put one foot on the floor to stop the turning; and how you wake in the morning tasting your own foul breath and wonder what you did, how you got home, and whether your folks noticed.

Mostly they didn't seem to. One night Blake drove Otto home, very drunk, in the Buick with the "Sweet Adeline" horn, and put him to bed, and stayed the night. The next morning this dialogue occurred:

Mrs. Leonardson: Poor Otto. He wass so sick this morning.

Blake: He must have eaten a bad hamburger last night.

Mrs. Leonardson: Yahh, the butchers, they are not careful.

Guys who had drunk too much to go home and chance meeting their parents went, or were delivered, to Mouse's house, where there were no parents. Mouse would take you in, put you to bed, clean up after you if you puked, and in the morning feed you with his own remedy for a hangover, which he called Graveyard Stew.

MOUSE'S GRAVEYARD STEW

2 slices white bread, toasted
milk
butter

Heat milk in a saucepan. Butter toast and place it in the bottom of a shallow bowl. Pour heated milk over it. When butter has melted into the milk, eat. But cautiously; you never know how a stomach will respond to food, even food as bland as this, after a rough night.

A night in November. Snipe phones at suppertime. He's met three girls who have an apartment down by Loring Park. You, me, and Moe, he says, how about it? I tell him I have the flu, I didn't go to work that day, I'm sick. They're nurses, he says. *Nurses,* underlining the word. They know the score. I'm sick, I say. They're waiting, he says.

We ride the streetcar downtown and walk across the park in the early dark, past couples on benches who don't look up as we pass. It's a damp night; the snow that fell during the day has melted, and a misty vapor rises from the wet ground and hangs in the air. On the far side of the park the lights of apartment buildings shine through the mist in luminous rows, welcoming, promising knowledge.

The girls have no faces. One is probably taller than the others, another is the fat one, but such details don't register, don't matter; they're just girls, nurses. Their apartment has three rooms: a bedroom, a small living room with a sofa, and a sunporch with a daybed. We pair off—without choosing, it seems to me, just divide up into pairs like the animals entering Noah's Ark—and withdraw, each pair to a room. My nurse leads me into the sunporch and closes the glass door and the curtains. We lie down on the daybed and fall to necking, as though we were in the back seat of a parked car with two other couples, kissing and touching and squeezing together, the customary sex experience of the young and fully clothed. There is no other sound from beyond the glass door. Hours seem to pass, but very slowly. I sense that things aren't going as they should; I don't know what the next step is. Moe and Snipe know, they've had La Motta to instruct them, but I'm a beginner. Around midnight a brisk voice from the other side of the door says: "Hey, we've got to go to work in the morning." The party is over.

We walk back through the park. The couples are gone, the paths are empty, the lights in the high buildings have gone out. Nobody is awake but us. We catch the uptown streetcar and stand on the muddy back platform, and Snipe and Moe smoke and talk about their nurses. I don't say anything; I feel funny, floating and misty-headed. Then I am in a heap on the platform floor, looking at the mud and spit and cigarette butts close to my face, and Snipe and Moe are grinning down at me.

"You passed out," Moe says.

"It's the flu. I have the flu."

"Naw, it isn't that. It's lover's nuts. Too much necking, not enough screwing."

So sex, if you do it wrong, can make you faint dead away. So much to learn.

Late November. The first heavy snowstorm has blown through and moved on east, leaving the earth white and the night sky clear. We're in a car—Moe, Snipe, Murtha, Mouse, Blake, and I—driving up the Minnesota River valley toward Shakopee. There's a beer joint there, behind the town ballpark, called Nettie's. In summer it's full of grown-ups from the ball games, and Nettie won't let kids inside the door; but in winter it's empty, and then she'll sell a drink to anyone who's tall enough to reach up and put a quarter on the bar.

Just another night with the guys. Except that this time I'm driving. My father's car. It's a Nash—blue, four doors; nothing special, not the sort of car kids stop and stare at, just what the ads call a family car. But it's the first new car my father has ever owned. Last year, when it was still brand-new and smelled of the assembly line, he would let me drive it around the block with him sitting beside me watching, but he wouldn't let me have it on my own. I didn't blame him; if I owned a car I wouldn't lend it to me. But tonight he changed his mind. I can see the neon sign up ahead: NETTIE'S in pale cold letters that shine on the snow.

We hang around the bar, drinking and talking, until Nettie gets tired of us and closes up and turns off her neon sign. It's after midnight; time has passed oddly in the bar, slowly at first (it's only nine-thirty, it's been nine-thirty for hours), and then very fast (it's midnight, I'll be late getting home, my father will be sore). Coming out of the bar, I feel the winter air sharp and cold in my lungs like ice water in the throat, and my brain is shocked to a cold consciousness that is almost like being sober. I can drive all right. I'll be fine.

The moon is full above us; it drifts in the sky, now on my left hand now on my right. The car floats between the moon and the snow and I float, too, along the empty road. In the backseat Moe recites one of his long dirty poems, "Paul Revere's Ride" or "Kefusalem the Harlot of Jerusalem"; the forbidden words fill the car, but I don't really hear them. I am drunk and serene. On a night like this, Snipe says, you could almost drive without headlights. I turn the lights off, and drive by moonlight. The farms we pass are patches of darkness, the groves are bare and black; everything else lies white and frozen in the moon's cold light. One car rushes toward me and at the last minute I turn my lights on and it passes with a snarl of its horn. I don't mind the angry driver; I turn the lights off again and white peaceful night returns. I will drive forever between the snow and the moon.

Back in town I turn the lights on and drive cautiously. I don't want to be stopped. What would my father say if yet another cop came to the door? I drop Murtha off and drive south down Park. As I approach Thirty-ninth Street Mouse wakes suddenly in the backseat and yells: "Turn here! This is my corner!" I turn hard right. Brakes squeal: there's a car on my right side close to my fender. He swings his wheel over, jumps the curb, crosses the corner, and bumps down into the cross street just in time to hit me as I turn. Not hard: just a firm, reproachful thump. We all get out and look at the damage. To his car, none; to the Nash a bend in the running board. We soberly exchange names and addresses and drive off.

The alley behind my house is empty and quiet in the moonlight. The house is dark. I put the car in the garage and slip into the back hall to my bedroom. There in the darkness, lit only by the moonlight through the window, my father sits on my bed. I can smell the stale smoke of many cigarettes in the cold air; he has been there a long time. He looks up at me standing in the dark doorway: "I just wanted to be sure you got home all right, son," he says. Then he gets up and goes back to bed. The next day he has the running board straightened. He doesn't say anything about the damage.

Dick Anderson, the head messenger, tells me I won't be delivering checks on foot anymore. He doesn't say I'm too slow, or spend too much time at the top of the Foshay Tower, he just says from now on I'll be on the state-capitol run. Every morning I'll carry a briefcase full of checks over to the capitol building in St. Paul and bring a briefcase-full back. It means a long streetcar ride, Dick says, an hour at least each way; and another waiting around in the capitol. Pretty boring, he says.

It isn't. I read all the way on the streetcar. I read sitting on a bench in the capitol corridor. I read coming back. Books I've bought in a secondhand bookstore down on Marquette, a dark cave of a place that smells of mildew and dust, with books in leaning shelves up the walls, and piled on tables, on the windowsills, on the floor, everywhere. Not new books, not clean books with shiny dust jackets, tired books with broken spines and names written on the flyleaves and notes scribbled in the margins: *used* books. I like books like that, that people have handled and worn in the process of getting out what is in them. When I buy one of those books I take my place in a long line of readers, neither the first nor the last.

In that moldy store I bought the first book about war I ever read: Hemingway's *For Whom the Bell Tolls.* The cover was ringed with coffee stains, and on the front flyleaf was written in pencil: "69c." I read it on the streetcar to the capitol, pausing as we crossed the river to look down on Bohemian Flats to see whether the houses were flooded yet, and how the ice was

forming along the riverbanks, and out across the flat-roofed factories of the Midway when the tracks rose onto an elevated
stretch, not thinking about the scene but about war according to
Hemingway, how you should behave in war: determinedly,
against the odds, Hemingway said; skillfully (I learned from him
how hard it is to blow up a bridge); silently, if you had to suffer;
stoically and sacrificially when your end came, like Robert Jordan, lying wounded in the forest, waiting to kill one more fas-
cist before he died. It was a novel about the Spanish Civil War
that had just ended, but I wasn't reading back into history, there
on the Como-Harriet streetcar; I was reading forward. It would
be great to be in a war, Hemingway told me; you might even be
Robert Jordan, waiting alone under the pines.

Winter settled in, more snow fell, and was covered by more
snow. On a cold Sunday afternoon I walked across the Chicago
Field skating rink to Pat's house. Moe was already there,
sprawled on the chaise on the sunporch, half-asleep in the
winter sun. Pat lay on the floor reading the funnies, Beulah
was making coffee in the kitchen. We talked about nothing in
particular—a dance, somebody going steady or breaking up, a
movie—until Beulah appeared in the doorway. The look on
her face stopped our conversation. "They've bombed Pearl
Harbor!"

That afternoon was like the day after the Armistice Day
Blizzard. We sat on the sunporch listening to the radio while the
light faded slowly and the western sky turned lemon-yellow the
way it does on a bright winter day in Minnesota, and the an-
nouncers repeated the story of the disaster, the dawn attack, the
sunken ships, the dead sailors. When I went home the snow was
blue with twilight.

Next day when I got home from the bank, I found my father sitting in his big chair in the living room, not listening to the news or reading the paper, just sitting there. He looked up when I entered.

"Chuck's enlisted. In the Air Corps, like Bill."

I wasn't surprised, it was what Chuck would do, go straight to the recruiting office on the first day of the war and join up. He was patriotic, like my father. And there was the other motive, I understood that, too; up in Duluth now, in another dime store that was just like the one in Wausau, with a future that could only hold more lonely towns, more rooms in other people's houses, more dime stores, the war must seem to him the opposite of the life he was stuck with—a promise of foreign places, danger, a chance to do a man's work with other men. And dignity, he must want that, too: to be in a uniform that folks respected, part of a unit, a squadron (wonderful word, *squadron*), and not a guy answering women's complaints about the rayon stockings.

Nellie hung another blue-star banner in the window.

In a few days Chuck came home to say good-bye and to leave a suitcase full of the stuff of his civilian life. After he left I looked through it. There wasn't much, a few books, some clothes. Some of his things surprised me. Among his clothes was a white dinner jacket with all the accessories—a ready-tied dark blue bow tie, a cummerbund, pants with a shiny strips down the seam, and a bright blue boutonniere made of feathers. Where had he worn that getup in Duluth?

And a pair of light gray spats.

Spats?

Yes, spats—pearl-gray, like the ones old Mr. Andrews the floorwalker wore. They were more mysterious to me even than the white dinner jacket. If my brother wore spats, then I didn't understand him as well as I thought I did. Nellie put the clothes in a trunk in the attic, and closed the lid on my brother's dime-store career.

A week or so after Chuck enlisted my father tried, too. He didn't tell me, I don't suppose he even told Nellie what he was going to do; he just walked into a recruiting office and offered himself to the Army. He was fifty-three years old, over six feet tall, well built and strong; and of all of us he most wanted to be in the war. Men in our family had always been soldiers when their country needed them. My father told me about them, proudly: Thomas Hynes and his brother Andrew had been officers in the Virginia Militia during the Revolution, and fought the British and the Indians in Kentucky; William Rose Hynes was in the War of 1812. My father could remember from his childhood the uncles who had served with the Indiana Volunteers in the Civil War—old men when he knew them, they sat on their front porches in Rolling Prairie and talked about Shiloh and Chickamauga. One of them had been in the Confederate prison at Andersonville, Georgia, and though he survived he never worked again, just sat on the porch quietly watching whatever passed, a buggy or a wagon or a yellow dog, not saying anything. What he had to eat at Andersonville had ruined his stomach. Another uncle died at Vicksburg; he was only nineteen. Two years older than me.

So of course my father wanted to fight for his country: it was his right, like his right to vote, that's what the Constitution said, he had the right to bear arms. He'd been twenty-nine when the United States entered the other world war, and he was fired up to go. But my mother was sick, he had to stay and take care of her, he couldn't volunteer. He waited until he was drafted, and by then it was 1918. He was put in a private's uniform and sent to Camp Monmouth in New Jersey, and while he waited there the war ended.

What I knew about his war came from two pictures in the family album. One is a posed studio portrait. He stands very straight, with a determined look on his face, conscious of the importance of the occasion and of the uniform he is wearing. In the other he is lounging in the doorway of a tent with another soldier, and he's smiling, or almost. There aren't many pictures of my father

smiling, but he'd have been happy there in the Army with other men, waiting to go to battle; it was where a patriotic man ought to be. Though he'd have hated the coarse easygoing part of army life, the smutty talk and the drinking.

Now there was another war to be fought, so it was natural that he should go to the recruiting office and try to enlist. The recruiting sergeant was polite, he said he appreciated my father's eagerness to serve and he was sure he'd make a fine soldier, with his experience. But the Army wasn't accepting men with false teeth. He couldn't enlist—not in the Army, not in the Navy, not in any service. My father came home hurt and angry: what kind of an army would reject a man as healthy as he was, and as willing? What difference did false teeth make, anyway? Did they expect soldiers to *bite* the Japs to death? My father was proud of Chuck for enlisting, doing what men of our family always did, but he must also have envied him. To be young and go to war! A man who could do that was fortunate. He never would. Two world wars had left him out.

He had another motive for enlisting that he didn't tell me. Slowly, over the last year or so, my father had gone broke. Not bankrupt, *broke:* in the world we lived in, losing all the money you had was almost a physical catastrophe, like a fractured leg or a broken back. Only worse, because it was shameful. Going broke was as bad as getting divorced, or having a drunk in the family. My father didn't say anything, not where I could hear it; he just stopped dressing in his Sam's Cities Service clothes in the morning and going to work. The army must have seemed a solution to this crisis; but the Army wouldn't have him.

Murtha came by one night in early spring, after supper. He seemed excited; he waved a copy of the *Star-Journal* opened to the want ads.

"Listen to this," he said, and he read from the paper: " 'Drive my car to Seattle. You pay gas.' You want to go?"

"What'll we do there?"

"Get jobs. There's lots of good jobs in Seattle. We'll work

for Boeing, making B-17s! Earn good money, and save it, and go to the U in the fall."

"But where will we live?"

"With my mother. She lives in Seattle now."

I wasn't sure Mrs. Murtha would be keen on having us in her house; she'd spent her life running away from her children and the complications of family life. But I liked the idea of building those bombers; better than delivering checks, that was for sure.

I said I'd go.

In Seattle the war seemed close at hand. Warships lay at anchor in the harbor, warplanes roared overhead, the streets were full of sailors and rumors: a Jap submarine had been seen in Puget Sound, a Jap plane had just bombed San Francisco, or maybe it was San Diego, the Japs were planning an invasion. We heard the rumors and were excited by them; just being there near the Pacific Ocean, where the fighting was, made existence seem somehow more urgent. A Japanese floatplane was launched from a submarine off the coast of Oregon—this was reality, though it sounded like rumor—and dropped a bomb that set fire to a forest, and we all sucked in our breaths: here comes war, here comes danger, falling bombs and people dying in the streets and buildings exploding and burning, all the images of urban civilian war we had seen in newsreels of the war in Europe.

I couldn't get a job at Boeing; you had to be eighteen. I went to work for the U.S. Army Engineers—delivering mail. It was an empty, lonely life. I didn't know anybody in the Engineers office, or in all of Seattle, for that matter. I didn't have a girl. I didn't know where anything was in the city, or how to get there. I just walked down the hill from Murtha's mother's apartment every morning, into fog that lay in the streets by the bay like water in a bathtub, and walked back up every evening. On the wall of the Engineers office where I worked someone had hung a sign: DON'T WORRY, IT WON'T LAST. NOTHING DOES. I took comfort in that sign, at first; I wouldn't have to deliver mail forever, or spend the rest of my life in Seattle fog, the summer would end. But gradually it came over me that the second sentence of the sign was more inclusive than I liked. *Nothing* does.

Seattle is a city built on seven hills, like Rome; we lived at the top of First Hill. On the night of the city's first blackout I left the apartment in the early dark and walked to the top of the hill, where there was a wide space without buildings or trees. An overcast night, neither moon nor stars; only the lights of the city made the darkness visible. Then the sirens began to keen, some near, some far-off, and the lights on the seven hills went out, neighborhood by neighborhood; out beyond Lake Washington where the university was, south toward Tacoma, along the Sound, places disappeared, fell out of light into darkness like falling angels.

Now the night was entirely dark and featureless, cloud and earth one black emptiness. Then searchlights began to poke and sweep the sky, making moons on the cloud cover that shifted and slid, searching for an enemy. Who is not here, I told myself, of course the enemy's not here, how could he be? But still the searching beams probed and paused and slid along the clouds. War must be like this, at night, on a battlefield: a darkness that is strange and empty and yet full of enemies. And of imaginable fear.

A gray Saturday morning. The rain that fell in the night has stopped, but clouds still hang low over the downtown rooftops, and puddles stand on the sidewalks. I sit on a bus that is slowly crossing Government Square, in the heart of the city. The bus stops at a light in front of City Hall. Along the sidewalk beside us a long line of people with suitcases. I can see they are all Japanese—old men and women, younger couples, children. They stand with their heads bowed, looking at the pavement, motionless, waiting. Then slowly they begin to move, and climb aboard buses. They're being sent to detention camps out in the Washington desert; they'll have to stay there until the war is over, because they're enemy aliens. The light changes, my bus moves on. I look back over my shoulder. The patient line of my country's enemies shuffles obediently forward through the puddles to the waiting buses, to their desert prisons.

The end of August: this is the time when we take the money we've earned and go back and go to college. Mrs. Murtha is relieved; having kids in her house has made her nervous. We're relieved, too. But there is no saved money to take back, only enough to buy us two coach tickets on the train. For two days we sit on dusty plush seats and watch the West unroll like a movie of our journey out run backwards. At night we try to sleep, but can't, and look out into the darkness at nothing, and the night air blows in through open windows, hot and full of soot from the engine, and so we ride eastward, homeward.

On the last day we run out of money entirely, and live on water from the tap at the end of the coach. And arrive the next morning at the Great Northern Station, like two Prodigal Sons, empty-handed, hungry and dirty. Seattle has been a failure. But I don't regret it; I've lived without my family, I've felt war flow around me, I've been in a blackout. And I've crossed half a continent, gone farther west than anyone in my family ever went before, and come back safely. And in a few days I'll be eighteen.

We walk out of the station into the August morning: air motionless, sun hanging red in the summer haze, street smelling of hot tar, cars and trucks and streetcars making a honking rumbling clattering clamor. It's all familiar. I'm home.

But it's different. Soldiers and sailors are everywhere, sleeping on benches in the depot or just sitting there waiting, strutting along downtown sidewalks, drinking in bars. They weren't there when I left. There are new rules for ordinary living: blackout instructions, rationing. Rationing doesn't make much difference to life in our house that I can see, we've always been rationed; but the folks don't like it. My father can't get a new tire for the Nash, and Nellie complains that she can't buy butter at the store, she has to take margarine and color it yellow herself. Imagine! In Minnesota, the land of lakes and dairy cows, eating margarine on your bread!

Most people don't complain, though; it's the war, they say, don't you know there's a war on?

Back on Columbus Avenue we knew there was a war on: Bill was gone, and so was Chuck, and there were those two blue stars in the window. A few days after I returned from Seattle Bill came home on leave. The Army hadn't let him be a pilot (I thought maybe he was too old—he was twenty-six); they'd made him a bombardier instead. And an officer. On the last day of his visit he stood in the front yard beside his mother, and my father took their picture. In the photograph Bill stands at stiff attention, uncomfortable looking in his new second lieutenant's uniform. He's not wearing wings above

the pocket of his blouse; he must not have finished his training yet. Nellie presses close against her son's side with her arm around his waist (you can see her fingertips poking out under his arm), as though she might protect him from war's dangers if she just held on tight enough.

She couldn't, though. Two years later, on the way back from a bombing mission in the Philippines, his plane will crash into a mountaintop. The whole crew will be killed.

CHAPTER FIFTEEN

Nobody called it the University of Minnesota; it was simply "the U," the only university there was. Nobody I knew left the state to go to college. Only a few even left the city; why would you, when the U was right there on the bluffs across the river, a streetcar ride away? And you had a right to go there; if you had graduated from a high school in the state, the U had to take you in. It was your university.

The night before classes began that September my father came into my room carrying a small pile of books. "Here," he said, "you should have these. They were your mother's." He thrust the pile toward me and hurried away.

I spread the books out on my desk: *The Poems of Elizabeth Barrett Browning* in worn red leather with gilt edges, price five cents, a penciled note on the flyleaf said; Alfred Lord Tennyson, *Complete Poems* in green leather (the fuzzy kind that looks like suede and extends limply over the edges of the pages), the covers loose (but maybe not when she bought the book, maybe she'd loosened them with reading); Robert Burns's *Poems,* a small book the size of my hand with a colored picture of flowers in an oval frame on the cover (a pretty little book, she must have thought); and another in the same series. *The Lady of the Lake* by Sir Walter Scott, the oval picture this time of a lady in a big hat, the flyleaf inscribed "To Mabel, from Florence, Xmas 1903" and another inscription erased, so there had been two owners before my mother. I was the fourth.

My mother's books gave me a faint whiff of her reality, the turn-of-the-century poetry lover shopping in the secondhand bookstores on the south side of Chicago where she went to Normal College, not having much money, excited when she found Mrs. Browning for only a nickel (and in red leather!). She left no marks in the books, didn't write her name on the fly-leaves or underline favorite lines or make comments in the margins, as though she knew they weren't hers to keep for very long, but only to pass on. Perhaps my liking for battered books came from her. My mother and I were the same, then.

My father gave me another book that night—a bankbook in my name with a balance of four hundred dollars, money my mother had saved for my education, he said, her legacy to me. It must have been a struggle for her to save such a sum, poor as they were; a quarter at a time from her grocery money, probably, the way she had bought my father's silver watch chain. My father had carried that legacy with him through all our hard-time journeying—to Julesberg, through the Great Plains blizzard, to Philadelphia, to Moline, to Minneapolis—banking it when we paused in our wanderings, and never touched it, not even at Fairhope, down to his last five bucks and eight hundred miles to drive to where the work was. It seemed a lot of money to him, and to me, too; a hundred dollars would pay a whole year's tuition at the University, I could go all the way through on my mother's four hundred, I'd only have to earn enough along the way to buy books and lunches and maybe a few clothes. I sat at my desk and thought about my mother, dead thirteen years now. She had been determined, back then when I was five years old and she was dying, that I would read her books and spend her money to go to college, that I would be her, when she was dead.

———

Professor Burt teaches English history in Burton Hall, in an auditorium as big as a downtown movie house. He's a nervous little man, he paces back and forth across the stage as he lectures, tossing out dates, and the names of kings and battles, and the price of wool. Professor Burt wrote the book we use in the course, and sometimes he refers to it—not vainly, but with a quiet confidence that whatever we want to know about his subject, the best place to look is in Burt. It would be fine to write a book, I think, so you could say to your students, offhand, "You'll find this point discussed in chapter twenty-three of my book," and they'd all write it down. I don't know the subject of my unwritten book; but I can imagine how it would feel to have written it.

In a basement room in Folwell Hall Mr. Dearing roams between the narrow window and the radiator, talking about poetry. Trucks rumble by on University Avenue and students shout and shuffle in the corridor, but he doesn't hear the noise, he just goes on talking. Mr. Dearing is younger than Professor Burt, and taller, and not so bald; his black hair grows down his cheeks in sideburns like bunches of black wool. He hasn't written a book yet; kids say this is his first year of teaching.

My job, he says, is to teach you to read a poem.

We already know how to read.

Yes, he knows that. But not poems. Poems are harder to read than the funnies. You have to look at every word in a poem, because words can mean more than one thing; and you have to notice the syntax, sometimes it's tangled up; and listen to the tone, and figure out who's speaking, and to whom. Interrogate the poem, Mr. Dearing says; ask it questions.

I open my book and stare at the words on the pages, and think of questions to ask them:

Who is Lucy? Is she really dead? How do you know?

Fleas are disgusting, so how can there be a flea in a love poem?

Why is Buffalo Bill defunct, and not just dead?

Why are the women talking about Michelangelo?

Where is Dover Beach? Does it matter?

How are faces in a crowd like petals on a wet branch? Is this a riddle?

Yes, it is. All poems are riddles, and reading them is a sort of word game. You don't have to know anything to play it, you just have to be good at finding meanings. The person with the cleverest, most complicated meaning wins.

When we come to a poem Mr. Dearing doesn't like, he reads it aloud: "I arise from dreams of thee"—he sighs—"in the first sweet sleep of night, when the winds are breathing low, and the stars are shining bright," and we know he's mocking Shelley's dreaminess. He reads Housman's "Loveliest of Trees," making the words sound too simple, too easy. I determine never to like Shelley and Housman. I write down in my notebook the words Mr. Dearing uses: *romantic* (bad), *sentimental* (worse), *ironic* (good), *paradoxical* (even better). When he mentions a writer I haven't heard of, I write the strange name in the margin of my notes; at the top of one page I write: "Proost."

I take a course in trigonometry, and learn to do logarithms and use sine and cosine tables. Math is another kind of game, using numbers and sometimes letters, but with exact and necessary answers, not like poetry. When I tell my father I can do fancy math, he says it's in the family; his grandfather, old Thomas Woodruff Hynes, was professor of mathematics at Hanover College, down in south Indiana when he was young. But only on weekdays, on Sundays he was a circuit-riding preacher. Maybe I'll be a mathematician. Not a preacher, though.

Autumn faded toward winter, and the campus wasn't strange anymore. I was easy there, among the students and the professors and the books; college was games I could play. But it was too late: in the fall of 1942 war was the only game worth playing. War yelled at you from newsstands and displayed itself in newsreels: in the Orpheum on Saturday night before the Joan Crawford movie you watched bombs tumbling from the open bellies of planes, armies marching, battleships firing, cities burning. That fall the war seemed poised, neither side winning or losing: the Germans were at Stalingrad but couldn't take the city; the British were holding the Germans in North Africa near a town called El Alamein; American troops in the Pacific were fighting hand to hand on Guadalcanal.

On the campus war was a presence as palpable as smoke. I sat in the Varsity Café at lunchtime and argued with my friends about the options war offered us. Adventurous guys said join the Army Air Corps. Be a pilot, fly fighters, wear a uniform with wings! Or fly for the Navy, from a carrier out in the Pacific. How about submarines? somebody asked; but could you stand being underwater all the time? Tanks would be good, like wearing armor. Or a navy fighting ship, a destroyer or a battleship, you'd see the world.

Cautious guys said don't be dumb, you don't have to go at all. Join the ASTP, the Army Specialized Training Program, you only have to go to basic training in some army camp, then they send you back to college to study—engineering, mostly, the Army needs lots of engineers. You wear a uniform to class, so old ladies won't ask you why you're not in the service. And when the war's over and the dumb guys come back with their medals and their wounds and their dumb war stories, you'll already have your degree, and you'll get the best jobs.

What a terrible thing to do to yourself, I thought, stay in school in a uniform that doesn't mean anything, walking from Engineering to the Union to get your mail, eating hot roast-beef sandwiches in the Varsity, doing *homework,* for Christ's sake!

While beyond oceans guys you know are fighting real battles. Imagine being young while a war is going on and not wanting to be in it!

In October my stepsister Eileen married her boyfriend, Johnny. Two weeks later she was alone; he'd shipped out of San Francisco on a battleship. Her brother, Bill, couldn't come to her wedding; he was a bombardier with wings now, waiting with his squadron in California to fly to the war. Chuck was in Texas learning to be an airplane mechanic. The web of family was stretching thinner and thinner, hardly a family at all now, only a remembered one.

University life went on as it always had. I went to classes, wrote papers, took exams. I dated a girl who was a Pi Phi, and went to her sorority ball and got drunk. The campus was as full of students as ever, they streamed along the paths and lay in couples in the fallen leaves on the Knoll, and crowded around the mailboxes in the Union. But it all felt empty; the guys I liked best weren't there anymore, they'd gone to the war.

In my other life, in the beer joints and up at the corner, it was the same; one by one my friends were joining up and leaving town: Moe was in the Air Corps learning to be a navigator; Sonny Dahl and Ackerberg were in Air-Corps pilot training; Murtha was in the Army, Michaud was a sailor somewhere; Buck was already a Marine fighter pilot. And I was here at home, eighteen years old and still a civilian. A college boy!

So going to war or not going wasn't a choice I had to make; the world around me had already made it for me. Of course I would go—not for patriotic reasons, nothing to do with my country or its enemies, or democracy, or humanity—none of that recruiting-poster stuff. I'd go because *not* to go was impossible.

The only question was, into what service? That decision, too, had already been made, though I didn't know exactly when, or how. But I knew now, suddenly and certainly, that I would be a pilot, if I could. Flying would be like that snowy night when I drove along the Minnesota River valley with my lights off, when nothing could touch me and everything was all right.

Not the Army Air Corps, though; everybody joined the Air Corps. I'd be a Navy flier, maybe a Marine, if I was good enough.

At the Navy Recruiting Office on Fifth Street I told the yeoman I wanted to go to flight school. It seemed an extraordinary thing for a kid like me to be doing—a totally adult, self-determined act, like getting married, or robbing a bank. Surely the yeoman would see how astonishing it was. "You'll need your father's permission," he said, and gave me some papers, and turned back to his work as though today was just a day like any other.

My father was sitting in the living room when I got home, holding the evening paper but not reading it, just looking beyond it at nothing. He often sat like that in the evening, too tired even for the headlines. I held the enlistment forms out to him.

"I want to join the Navy. And be a pilot."

He took the papers and held them in his two hands for a while, looking down at them as though they contained worse news even than the evening newspaper, and sighed. Then he signed his name.

Back at the Recruiting Office, I stood in a naked line for a physical examination: bend over, spread your cheeks, cough, line up the sticks, read the chart, stand on one foot, have you ever fainted . . . been dizzy . . . coughed blood? Passed. I asked the yeoman what I should do now. Wait, he said. Go home and wait. The Navy will tell you when it wants you.

Blake knew a guy named Bobby from South High—"You know him," he said, "skinny little runt, used to date Dotty Hand"—who broke into a draft-board office and stole a box of blank draft cards. He'll sell you one for five bucks, Blake said. You just fill in the blanks, add three years to your age, and you can buy a drink anywhere. Snipe, the wise counselor, said get a fake driver's license while you're at it; if you're going to forge one paper, forge two. That way, one will prove the other one.

I found Bobby and bought the draft card. That part was easy. But I was nervous when I walked into City Hall; this was where the police department and juvenile court were, and I was here to break the law. If they caught me they'd throw me in jail, or at least tell my father, and maybe the Navy. The dim marble lobby was silent and empty, nobody came and nobody went. Only the *Father of Waters* was there, a naked old marble man with a beard, lounging on a marble slab in the middle of emptiness, as though waiting for something to happen—like me getting arrested. But when I found the driver's-license room the clerk wasn't suspicious, or even interested in me; he just took my fifty cents and handed me a card. I filled it in, advancing my age, and walked away. Now I was twenty-one—a man, old enough to have already been drafted (why wasn't I in uniform?), to have a job and a wife, maybe even a kid. I was whoever I wanted to be, while I waited to be somebody.

On Saturday afternoons after that I put on my suit and went downtown to meet Blake at the Radisson Hotel on Seventh Street. The bar there was called the Viking Room; a model of a Viking ship hung above the bottles behind the bar (to make the

Norwegians happy, Blake said). The Viking Room was a grown-up drinking place, not like Nettie's or the Polack roadhouses out on the highway. Drinking was different here; men in business suits came in and ordered martinis and talked in low conspiratorial business voices, and once I saw a couple sipping champagne and eating caviar with hard-boiled eggs on top. When I walked into the Viking Room in my best clothes, I thought I might be taken for a young version of those murmuring businessmen, or the lover with the champagne. Or I might be a smooth con man, like the guy who stole all the money from the Youth Center on Portland Avenue and disappeared. Or Jimmy Valentine.

There was an element of danger about drinking in the Viking Room that gave excitement to the gray wintertime of waiting. I felt it in my gut like a shot of whiskey when I stood at the bar and the bartender asked, "You twenty-one?" and I handed him my cards. I wasn't Jimmy Valentine, and I wasn't twenty-one; I was an eighteen-year-old kid who had forged two official papers. The bartender knew that, anybody could see it; but nobody cared. He poured the drink and took my money.

Fats Waller is playing at the Happy Hour up on Nicollet. It's a scary place to go, Kid Cann owns it; he runs the rackets in town, he has people beaten up and killed, my father says he's the one who stuck the machine gun out of the car window and shot Marda Liggett's father. There'll be gangsters in his saloon, and a bouncer. But I go anyway, because Fats Waller's there.

The Happy Hour stands on a corner. The bar is at the front; farther back there's a small square room with a raised bandstand and some tables around. I walk in nervously, not through the front door—I don't think I can manage to walk the whole length of the bar looking twenty-one—but by the side entrance, into the room with the bandstand, and sit at a table and order a drink. The waitress looks at me doubtfully, asks for my draft card, and reads it, and shrugs. "Oh well," she seems to say, "if you get caught it's your tough luck," and she brings the drink.

Fats and his band come out of a back room and climb onto the stand. Fats moves ponderously, he's a big man. He lights a cigarette and squints out through the smoke at the crowded room, as though searching for someone. The men in the band sit unobtrusively; nobody has come to hear them. Then Fats nods his head, stomps his big foot to set the beat, and they're playing. Not real jazz, though, just some novelty piece. Fats sings the stupid lyrics, clowning and rolling his eyes, the trumpet player puts his tin mute on his head like a derby hat, and the other guys shout jokey lines. I feel sorry—for Fats, having to be a clown, and for me, sitting there scared at my table, listening to the wrong music.

When the number ends Fats sits for a moment, silent and motionless. Then he puts his big hands on the keys and begins to play. He's not thinking now about what the customers want to hear, he's playing a solo to himself: "Blue Turning Gray over You," or "Viper's Drag," or "Black and Blue"—one of his own tunes. His fat fingers are delicate and quick, right hand rolling high on the treble keys and back down, left hand walking lightly on the bass. It's all right, this is what I came for. They can arrest me now if they want to.

The guys who had left for the war came back on leave and hung around in their new uniforms and had their pictures taken: Sonny Dahl, rakish and romantic in his squashed Air Force hat and pink gabardine pants; Ackerberg, dressed the same but less dashing (though Nicky Johnson must have been impressed, since she married him—but that was later); and Mouse, in his sailor's dress blues and white gob's hat, skinny and frail, looking

like what he was, a mouse in a sailor suit; and Murtha, shy in the uniform of an Army private.

Michaud came from bootcamp in his Navy blues, and Brugger, back from infantry training somewhere in Missouri, and the three of us went together to Brady's Bar on Hennepin and Sixth and sat there all afternoon, drinking and talking about war and jazz and the bodies of girls. Whiskey made Michaud's drawl even slower: "This is the fir-r-r-st time I've ever been dru-u-u-nk," he said, articulating very carefully the way drunks do. "The ve-e-e-r-r-y fir-r-r-st t-i-i-i-m-me." We had another drink.

Moe came, an officer now. In the picture he lies on a chaise on somebody's porch. The yard outside is full of sun, but the porch is shadowy; his dark green Air Force shirt looks black, and his navigator's wings are a point of brightness on his dark breast pocket. Sprawled there, eyes closed, arms and legs spread any way, he looks like someone who has fallen from a great height

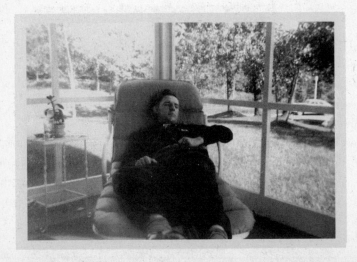

and has been left where he fell. The old Moe, the kid anarchist, the enemy of authority who did what he liked, is not visible; in that uniform with those wings he's someone else, someone with authority. He has passed tests, he has learned adult skills, he can guide a huge plane through cloud and darkness; in a little while he will go to where the war is, fly over Germany, drop bombs, be shot at. The space between him and me seems too wide to bridge, too full of the grown-up things he knows how to do, and I don't.

Brugger went back to Missouri to finish his training, stumbled over a live grenade, and blew himself to pieces.

The scattering of the family went on. Bill flew from the West Coast with his squadron, to somewhere in the Pacific. Johnny, my stepsister Eileen's husband, was in the South Pacific on his battleship; Jack, the quiet farmer my other stepsister married, was drafted and sent to an infantry battalion down south waiting to go to Europe.

Only Chuck was safe. He was in Guatemala. But the war was in the Pacific! The war was in Europe! The war was in North Africa! What was he doing in Guatemala? Defending the Panama Canal, he said in his letters, servicing the bombers that would bomb the Japs if they attacked the Canal. He sent home photographs of embassy parties in Guatemala City, banquet tables spread with china and crystal and flowers and wine, pretty girls in party dresses, and him in the middle in his sergeant's uniform, grinning at the camera like a guy who's just won the sweepstakes. But a little sheepish, too, because he's so far from the real war, the thunder and the blood of it, the fighting. Even though it's not his fault.

———

Friends dispersed, too, went back to their training-camp lives, shipped out, flew to the Pacific or to Europe. Moe was in England, flying missions over Germany. It seemed odd that he should be the first of the gang to reach the actual fighting. I didn't write to him, I didn't write to any of them; those other, uniformed lives seemed beyond reach, in a world so distant that mail wouldn't reach them.

In the fall Pat sent me a clipping from the *Tribune.* I was at Pensacola by then, learning to fly, and I could partly imagine what it must be like to die the way Moe died: how the high plane would break and fall, cease to be a plane and become simply falling wreckage, how it would strike the earth in a splash of flame, the detonation like an exploding bomb, the pieces of men and plane scattered over the ground. But only partly; I had seen planes crash, but I hadn't been to war, not yet.

Frank E. Bullard Missing in Action

Lt. Frank E. Bullard, 20, son of Mrs. Hazel V. Bullard, 4212 Park avenue, is reported missing in action in the European theater of war since Nov. 3, according to information received Saturday from the war department.

Navigator on a Flying Fortress, Bullard is a graduate of Central high school. He was awarded the Purple Heart Sept. 6.

He won his wings at Hondo, Texas.

Bullard

Blake's brother applied for a job with the FBI that winter—just some job at a desk, but the FBI investigated him and his family as though he was going to be a G-man, or a spy. The Blake family was at supper one evening when the doorbell rang. Blake's brother went to answer it. He came back to the table with what Blake described as a they-were-bound-to-catch-you-in-the-end look on his face, and whispered: "For you. FBI." Blake went to the door. Two men in snap-brim hats were standing there. "Give me your forged draft card," one of them said. "Now. Or you'll be in even worse trouble." Blake handed it over. Where did he get it? Blake couldn't remember. The two FBI men stared at him for a minute, as though memorizing his face, and went away and never came back. Blake stopped drinking in the Viking Room after that, but I didn't. My waiting time must be nearly up, and there were no rules. I walked invisible through city streets, already somewhere else.

Every school day I catch the streetcar at Chicago and Thirty-eighth. Most mornings a girl gets on at Thirty-seventh. She's a University student, like me; she carries an armload of books and her lunch in a brown paper bag. Not a strikingly pretty girl, but not ugly either; not noticeable, yet I notice her. The car rolls along toward the Loop, we roll along, not looking at each other, and transfer together to another streetcar and ride on, over the river to the U, and walk separately across the windy Mall until she turns off toward her building and I walk on toward mine. I never see her in classes, or on the campus paths; we are only connected by our streetcar journeys.

After a while she acknowledges me; she smiles when she climbs onto the car, and I smile back. Days pass, and one morning she speaks, something about the wind, or the first snow, and I say yes, it's cold waiting for the streetcar. And now we know each other, slightly; now, for half an hour some days, we sit beside each other with our books on our laps and talk. Her name is Theresa Ryan, but her friends call her Rosy, after the Millers' pitcher. I tell her I used to play Bounce Out with Rosy's kid. She says she lives on Elliott Avenue. Her folks both work. She's

a Catholic, but she doesn't have any brothers or sisters. I think
that's odd, but don't say so. She's studying business, she wants to
be an accountant. We haven't much to talk about: we didn't go to
the same high school, we don't know the same kids, we don't take
the same classes. But we talk. Winter comes on, she wears a heavy
coat and stadium boots with the zippers open and stamps her feet
as she waits for the streetcar. The streets are hard-packed snow
now, and snow is piled along the curbs. The heaters on the streetcars don't make the air warm, we can see our breaths as we talk.

Nothing else happens: We don't meet for lunch at the U, or
go to a lunchtime dance at the Union. I never ask her for a date,
never take her to a movie. We aren't headed in that direction;
that would be courtship, this is something else.

Rosy and I don't usually meet on the streetcar coming
home, but one day we do. As we approach her corner she stands
up, turns to me, and says: "Come on. There's nobody home."
We walk together along Thirty-seventh Street and turn into her
alley. It's hard to walk there, the ruts that cars have made in the
snow are frozen to ice, but we have to go this way, she says, so
the neighbors won't see us. And in by her back door.

Rosy lives on the ground floor of a duplex very like ours:
living room, dining room, kitchen, bathroom, two bedrooms;
the floor plan is the same, the furniture worn and plain like ours,
the half-light through the lace-curtained windows is the same.
Entering her house is like walking through a mirror into my
own life.

Inside the kitchen door she turns and kisses me once, hard,
more like a punch than a kiss, and turns again and enters her
bedroom. It's like mine: a meager single bed and a bureau, no
room for anything more. We kiss again, more gently this time,
and without speaking take off our clothes and climb into the
bed under the covers and embrace. The force that moves us is as
strong as sexual passion, but it isn't that; it's curiosity. We are des-

perate to know each other's body, but not personally; we want
to learn with our flesh what the other sex feels like, looks like,
smells like, tastes like; to know what you do, in bed with another person. There in the shadowy half-light we explore far
into that unknown country.

Not all the way though; Rosy is a Catholic and a virgin, and
she's afraid of getting pregnant. But not knowing *that,* the ulti-
mate sexual truth, the act at the end of it all, is not knowing *anything.* I say it will be all right; I'll buy a rubber. And I try. I go into
a corner drugstore—not the one on *my* corner, where the druggist knows me, but on another corner, and hang around at the
back of the store waiting for the pharmacist to come out of his
pill room and wait on me. His assistant, a hard-faced, middle-aged
woman, comes instead, and stares at me as though she knows
what I want and will certainly not sell me one. I buy some razor
blades. I try other drugstores, and lose my nerve, and try to explain to Rosy, who is impatient, now that she's decided. Finally I
stop on my way home at Seven Corners, the grimy intersection
at the end of skid row where we used to buy muscatel wine, and
a druggist there sells me a package of Sheiks without even looking at me. I put the rubbers in my wallet; they make a round
mark in the leather, and I know if Nellie sees it she will know
what I have there. I keep my wallet in my pocket day and night.

For the occasion, the act that will carry us into the adult
world, we move to her parents' room (it's just like the room
where my father and Nellie sleep). For a moment we stand
naked on opposite sides of the bed, silent, looking at each other
and at the enormity of what we're about to do, as though we are
each other's firing squad. Her body in the winter light is not
beautiful: a thin, girl's body, small arms hugging her breasts the
way girls do when they're cold, unsexual and unexuberant. We
climb into the double bed between her parents' rumpled sheets
and do what our curiosity requires of us. Afterward, it doesn't

seem that it was quite satisfactory, not to either of us; but what would satisfactory be? Neither of us knows. Something has happened, certainly, something august and grave, something that must have changed us both. But what was it?

Then I don't see her, waiting for the streetcar. Day after day I watch for her at the corner. She doesn't come. I try to phone her. Her mother answers the phone and says Rosy can't talk to me, and don't call again, and she hangs up. I know what has happened; somebody has seen us tramping up the alley and told Mrs. Ryan. I feel the way I felt when I stole from the dime store when I was ten; not guilty, but angry and resentful that I've been caught.

I'm walking across the Mall from the streetcar stop, hunched down into my clothes, my head bowed against driving snow when I meet Rosy in front of the library, sensing rather than seeing her coming toward me out of the storm. We stop by the library steps.

"It's been awful," she says. "Mrs. Johnson next door saw us, lots of times, before she told my mother."

(How many times did it take to convince the old lady with her nose to the glass that we weren't innocent?)

"My mother took me to the doctor to find out how bad we'd been."

(The *doctor*?)

"He said that technically I'm still a virgin."

(?)

"But Father Creehan says I'm not."

(If she's neither a virgin nor not a virgin, what am I?)

"I have to say hundreds of Hail Marys. And I can't see you anymore. Ever."

She turns and climbs the library steps and disappears inside. I walk on into the blizzard, past Northrup, past Westbrook, past the circle where the streetcar turns, and into Folwell, stomping the snow from my feet into the pool of dirty slush on the floor, and go to my class and try to think about algebra.

The waiting time goes on. It isn't real time, not the kind you live your ordinary life in, more like the minutes at the depot before the train you're going to take comes in, when there's nothing to do and nothing is interesting except the train, which isn't here yet, and the journey, which hasn't begun. Days pass, and I read the war news, and my head rings with the names of places I've never heard of where men are fighting and bombs are falling: Bizerte and the Kasserine Pass, Buna and Munda, Kharkov and Kursk, Rabaul, Messina, Wilhelmshaven. The whole wide world is at war. And I'm not.

By now I've gone through the money my mother left me for college. I've spent it on tuition and books and streetcar tokens and twenty-five-cent meals at the Varsity Café, but also on lunch with the Pi Phi at the Tent, and drinks in the Viking Room, and on my first overcoat (covert cloth, the color of dead grass), and on a pair of wing-tip cordovan shoes that shine like midnight mirrors and don't bend when I walk. Winter quarter of my freshman year isn't over yet, and I'm broke.

Nellie asks me how my money is holding out. I tell her it isn't. She gets that job-hunting look on her face, and finds me one, Sunday nights in a doughnut factory down on Park and Twenty-ninth. When I arrive for work, after Sunday supper, no one is there except the night watchman. The space I work in is echoing and shadowy, like a cathedral when there's no service going on. Along one side trucks are backed up against a loading dock, their rear doors open, waiting to be loaded with doughnuts and cakes and loaves of bread (because it isn't *only* a doughnut factory, that's just the way I think of it) to be delivered

Monday morning. There is no sound, nothing stirs. I move from truck to truck, quietly, counting the goods and loading the trucks, not whistling or humming, cherishing the silence, the solitude, the feeling of not being anywhere.

At midnight, when I leave, the streets are empty; no cars pass and I meet no late walkers on my way home down Park Avenue. The autumn leaves have fallen from the elms, I walk through corridors of branchy half darkness, with patches of light at the corners, where the streetlamps are. I have brought a box of doughnuts—powdered sugar, or maybe chocolate-covered—and I eat them slowly as I walk alone down the chilling night, thinking of nothing. Waiting.

There's a new Chief Yeoman at the Navy Recruiting Office desk when I walk in; it's Dick Anderson, who was Head Messenger at the bank back when I was daydreaming on the state-capitol run. I tell him I have to go to flight school. Right away. Now. I *have* to go. As the words blunder out, the desperation of my plight seems to increase. I have no money, that's part of it, but not the important part. It's the war! I'm afraid I'll miss it. And that (though I don't say this to Dick) would be like dying a virgin (if that's what I am).

Dick listens, not saying anything. Then he gets up and walks to a table in the corner of the room and ruffles down through a tall pile of filing folders. He pulls one out from the bottom of the pile and puts it on the top. Next week, he says; you'll get your orders next week. Don't tell anybody.

I walk out of the building, not back into Fifth Street but into empty space. It's like the feeling you have when you climb up the ladder of the diving tower at the lake and don't stop at the first level where you usually dive off, or even at the second where you might do a cannonball if you're feeling brave, but go on climbing all the way to the top and stand there high above the water and the people's bobbing heads, above the whole world, your toes hooked over the edge, looking down at the water far beneath, knowing you've gone too far but it's too late now, you can't climb back down, you have to throw yourself forward into that emptiness. And you jump.

The orders came just as Dick said they would, in a long white envelope marked "Department of the Navy: Official." I had never got an official letter before; standing there by the mailbox holding it in my hands, I felt my life take on a new seriousness, and I wanted to show it to someone. But nobody was home; by then *home* scarcely existed, only my father and Nellie and me in the duplex on Columbus Avenue. And now I was leaving. Then there'd be two.

. And soon not even two. After the Army rejected him my father had gone war-work hunting and found a job in a steel mill on the south side of Chicago. He'd leave in a few weeks. Why did he want to do that, I wondered—go back to where he'd lived with my mother, where his sons had been born, where he'd been young and happy? Why make a circle of your life that way?

Nellie would follow him as soon as she'd sold off the stuff in the attic and the jar of rusty nails. And then there'd be none. No house in Minneapolis that was ours, no place to go back to after the war was over. What we had had together, whatever that was, had burst apart like one of Nellie's Mason jars down in the fruit cellar.

While I was reading the orders, trying to understand the special language of the Navy—"You will proceed . . . rations will be chargeable . . ."—Nellie came in. I showed her my orders. She sighed and said: "Well, it's what you wanted, isn't it?" as though wanting war was a male mystery she couldn't comprehend. She didn't congratulate me.

We ate supper early the night I left, and then sat in the living room, waiting among the furnishings of our lives together: *Old Ironsides,* the silver pheasants, the Bountiful Crest. My suitcase waited by the front door. Familiar stuff, good-bye.

When it was time to leave my father rose from his chair, a little wearily, took up the suitcase (it seemed to weigh nothing in his hand), and went out the door into the March darkness. I turned to say good-bye to Nellie. I knew her mind was on Bill, flying with his crew somewhere out beyond the ocean, but she seemed sad for me, too, seeing me go. I felt sorry for her—for all her troubles and separations, for the emptiness of what was left. Was it possible I had come to love her? Like a mother, even? How could I know? Her presence had never had the tenderness of my fragmentary memories of my real mother, she had never hugged me or sung to me. But she had been as much a mother to me as she could be, and I had been her sort-of-son. In the morning she would put another blue star in the front window. I kissed her and followed my father down the front steps and into the Nash.

We drove toward the Loop, past the stations of my growing years: the streets I had walked along to school, Lake Street where Bernice Rosen lived, the apartment with John Dillinger's bullet hole in the wall, the Foshay Tower, the gas station where my father ran for his life, and along skid row, where my friends and I had once looked up at the red exit lights and imagined whores.

Washington Avenue was deserted, the air damp and chilly and smelling of coal smoke, like any March evening in my town. We parked by the Rock Island Depot and walked together, my father and I, through the empty station and onto the dark train platform. At the far end under a lamp a yeoman was reading names from a clipboard to a crooked line of young men in civilian clothes. We stopped partway along the platform, and I turned and hesitantly took my father's hand and shook it, thinking how odd it was to be doing that, how formal and adult. Then he let go, and I turned and went on toward the yeoman under the lamp, and joined the young men. When I looked back my father was far down the platform, moving rapidly away through spots of light and shadow toward the dark street.

ACKNOWLEDGMENTS

I am indebted to the following for their help in the preparation of this book: the *Minneapolis Star Tribune* photo library, for photographs of Laura Kruse and Bernice Rosen; International News Photos for the picture of the Teamsters' strike; the Minneapolis Police Department, for access to files of the Kruse and Rosen cases; Eileen McCormick and Rose Marie Brown for family photographs; Betty McIntosh for memories of West Thirty-fifth Street; William H. Hull for *All Hell Broke Loose,* his book about the Armistice Day Blizzard of 1940; Mrs. Esther Hegg of Litchfield, Minnesota, for her recollections of the Hegg farm; Dave Wood, formerly of the *Minneapolis Star Tribune;* and the old friends named in my dedication, for their patient sharing of memories.

FOR THE BEST IN PAPERBACKS, LOOK FOR THE

In every corner of the world, on every subject under the sun, Penguin represents quality and variety—the very best in publishing today.

For complete information about books available from Penguin—including Penguin Classics, Penguin Compass, and Puffins—and how to order them, write to us at the appropriate address below. Please note that for copyright reasons the selection of books varies from country to country.

In the United States: Please write to *Penguin Group (USA), P.O. Box 12289 Dept. B, Newark, New Jersey 07101-5289* or call 1-800-788-6262.

In the United Kingdom: Please write to *Dept. EP, Penguin Books Ltd, Bath Road, Harmondsworth, West Drayton, Middlesex UB7 0DA.*

In Canada: Please write to *Penguin Books Canada Ltd, 10 Alcorn Avenue, Suite 300, Toronto, Ontario M4V 3B2.*

In Australia: Please write to *Penguin Books Australia Ltd, P.O. Box 257, Ringwood, Victoria 3134.*

In New Zealand: Please write to *Penguin Books (NZ) Ltd, Private Bag 102902, North Shore Mail Centre, Auckland 10.*

In India: Please write to *Penguin Books India Pvt Ltd, 11 Panchsheel Shopping Centre, Panchsheel Park, New Delhi 110 017.*

In the Netherlands: Please write to *Penguin Books Netherlands bv, Postbus 3507, NL-1001 AH Amsterdam.*

In Germany: Please write to *Penguin Books Deutschland GmbH, Metzlerstrasse 26, 60594 Frankfurt am Main.*

In Spain: Please write to *Penguin Books S. A., Bravo Murillo 19, 1° B, 28015 Madrid.*

In Italy: Please write to *Penguin Italia s.r.l., Via Benedetto Croce 2, 20094 Corsico, Milano.*

In France: Please write to *Penguin France, Le Carré Wilson, 62 rue Benjamin Baillaud, 31500 Toulouse.*

In Japan: Please write to *Penguin Books Japan Ltd, Kaneko Building, 2-3-25 Koraku, Bunkyo-Ku, Tokyo 112.*

In South Africa: Please write to *Penguin Books South Africa (Pty) Ltd, Private Bag X14, Parkview, 2122 Johannesburg.*